Marsha Hunt was born in 1946 and grew up in Philadelphia. She studied at the University of California at Berkeley during the student riots of the sixties but soon left for Europe. In London she made her name in the hit musical HAIR, which both shocked and delighted audiences with its free use of nudity and its exuberant energy. Since then, she has had a varied career in rock, radio – hosting her own late-night chat show on Capital Radio – film, and the stage. She was a member of the National Theatre Company from 1982 to 1983. Marsha Hunt has lived in Los Angeles and Sydney and now spends her time in London and Paris.

REAL LIFE

MARSHA HUNT

HEADLINE

First published in Great Britain in 1986 by Chatto and Windus. First published in Great Britain in paperback in 1987 by HEADLINE BOOK PUBLISHING PLC.

ISBN 0 7472 3069 2

HEADLINE BOOK PUBLISHING PLC
Headline House
79 Great Titchfield Street
London W1P 7FN

Typesetting by The Word Factory, Lancashire
Printed & Bound by Wm, Collins, Glasgow.

FOR KARIS

ACKNOWLEDGEMENTS

Thanks to my family and friends for life support. To Ikey, Thelma and Edna, special thanks.

I am grateful to Andrew Motion for asking me to write this book and assuming that I could. I thank my agent, Laurence Evans, for enduring my absence while I did.

I wish to thank my caring editor, Ingrid von Essen, and my careful typists, Marjorie Taylor and Sonia Lane. My dedicated friends Steve Lovi and David Ruffell were always encouraging. Ben Churchill helped with fruitful discussions.

To my daughter, Karis Jagger, I am most indebted, because she allowed me to tell my story knowing that it would encroach on hers.

Finally, I thank my guides.

ILLUSTRATIONS

(*Between pages 128 and 129*)

CONTENTS

PROLOGUE

It was drizzling that afternoon in Paris when we slipped into the front row of the darkened Left Bank cinema. Mick Jagger arranged himself in the seat next to me so that his elbow was resting on my thigh. Our fourteen-year-old daughter, Karis, was sitting on his right.

Eddie Murphy's dark-brown face loomed large in Cinemascope as the title *Beverly Hills Cop* flashed onto the screen with French subtitles. The rock soundtrack pumped out at disco volume. Mick's profile caught the light reflected from the screen. He looked boyish in spite of the craggy lines and folds in his thin face, aged by two decades of fame, women, worry, decadence and ambition. His legs were stretched out in front of him, and I noticed that he hadn't bothered to change out of his running shoes, although he'd put on a tie. It was the sort of thing that made me like him.

He leaned over and whispered something to Karis. She swatted him. Anyone could see that we three had an enviable relationship. What didn't show was our long, raggedy struggle. It was a miracle that we were there together.

The stalls were crowded for an Easter Sunday. I was relieved that our seats were closest to the exit, and we could shoot off without Mick being stopped. The movie was fast and funny but whenever Eddie said 'fuck' it didn't register in the subtitles.

I wanted to concentrate on the film, but my mind was caught up replaying the events in my life that made this family outing possible in 1985. I think I know what I did wrong, but I don't know what I did right.

It had stopped raining by the time we emerged from the cinema. The air was damp and crept through my hair. On the rue Suger, we manoeuvred past languid strollers as we made our way to the Tour d'Argent, where Mick had booked a table for dinner. When he took my hand, his felt nearly warm and was as smooth as porcelain. In 1969 there always used to be a bit of grime under his third fingernail, which for some reason grew faster than the rest. Nowadays, he's manicured. I felt young holding hands and was thoroughly enjoying the walk. It seemed normal until a camera flashed at us from the direction of a parked car. None of us reacted. I prayed that we'd been photographed for somebody's private scrapbook. Nothing could be worse than landing in the newspapers with a picture and some concocted story just when the three of us were getting things into perspective.

Mick's girlfriend Jerry Hall had enough to worry about, too, with Mick on his own in Paris cutting an album with the Stones. She could do without a picture of Mick and me holding hands while we rollicked with our daughter on a Paris side street.

We turned at the river. I spotted Notre Dame just as the street lights came on. Mick apologized for the unexpected distance, but I wasn't sorry that we'd left his Mercedes near the cinema. Had I not been wearing high heels and a pencil-thin skirt, I wouldn't have noticed that we'd been walking for fifteen minutes.

A short, Mediterranean-looking hustler sidled up to Mick and asked if we wanted to score. I'm instinctively on guard when suspicious-looking men approach me on the street, especially if I'm with my daughter. I assume an aggressive air. In Europe my reaction may seem uncalled for, but I grew up in a big American city. We cold-shouldered the drug dealer, and I repositioned myself so that Mick was in a less vulnerable spot between Karis and me. It wasn't the move of a delicate female, but I've never learned how to be that.

There was a reverent atmosphere in the entry hall of the Tour d'Argent when a conservative-looking matron in glasses accepted our coats with a gracious smile. I felt she was welcoming us to her private home. A man in an impeccable pinstripe suit escorted us through a spacious anteroom, dominated by an enormous vase of fresh flowers, to a salon. Mick ordered pink champagne.

The tour guide that points out sights like the Louvre when you take a ferry cruise along the Seine describes the Tour d'Argent as one of the most celebrated and expensive restaurants in Paris. I would have been just as happy in a pizza parlour.

As a man with whitish hair was leaving, he introduced himself to Mick as the editor of the *Herald Tribune* and said he wished to pay his respects. I took the opportunity to slip off to the ladies' room to see how wild my hair looked after the walk in the damp air.

When I got back, Mick had a glass of champagne waiting for me. I don't drink and reminded him as I took the tiniest sip. In the dining room, when the tall young wine waiter in tails brought the red wine, I had to be counted out. The view of the Seine and the twinkle of Paris night lights outside the window suggested that we were several storeys up, but it wasn't possible to tell how many floors we had passed in the small private elevator.

With his forkful of beef poised at his mouth, Mick managed a smile as a middle-aged woman weighed down with gold jewellery hovered at our table for an autograph. She had no pen or paper. Others followed, interrupting his appetite and his train of thought.

I looked over at my daughter, who wore an air of patience. I remembered holding her when she was seconds old. I'd carried on for so long as a bachelor mother that it was hard to conceive that I had a male counterpart. To think that she was as much a part of him as she was mine was odd. I still detect the loneliness in Mick that first attracted me to him, but since then I've discovered that he can burn hot and suddenly cool to below zero.

I don't know how Jerry Hall can put up with all the fanfare that surrounds him. It can't be easy to play second fiddle to someone else's myth. I couldn't do it and wouldn't do it, although I loved him privately. He was just another part of my life that I took for granted. I lived other people's dreams.

I

MADE IN AMERICA

The atomic age dawned on 16 July 1945 at 5.30 am in the New Mexican desert with the success of a bomb with 20,000 times the power of TNT. I was probably conceived around that time, as it happens.

I guess you could say I got my start in an airplane factory called Brewster's, where my mother, Inez, and her sister, Thelma, worked at the time, just a commuter's distance from Philadelphia. Women were establishing themselves as an invaluable factor in the US workforce. Trained to read the blueprints, to rivet, to run the drill press or drill gun and build planes which were a main instrument of war, they would never again believe that their usefulness was restricted to home and child-rearing.

Franklin Delano Roosevelt had been dead one year and three days when I arrived, on 15 April 1946.

My genetic make-up was to prove a disability, because it automatically meant that the equality and freedom that were supposed to be endemic elements of the American culture were not going to be mine.

I am only referred to as American when I am out of the country. My skin colour is oak with a hint of maple. Of the various races I know I comprise – African, American Indian, German Jew and Irish – only the African was acknowledged, and I was labelled 'coloured'. This was changed to 'Negro' in more sophisticated circles. The less evolved would often call me 'nigger'. Over the years, I would encounter a slew of nicknames and variations on the theme of my complexion. Being colour-coded was a determining factor in who or what I could become.

Americans of slave descent are not purely African. Though we are a combination of races, this fact is avoided by all. The consequent dilemma is that entire aspects of our heritage, attitudes and behaviour are never attributed to our genetic make-up. This seems short-sighted on everyone's part, especially as Americans are so big on understanding human nature.

I am not merely what you see. I'm the total sum of my parts, and the dominant elements aren't necessarily the most visibly apparent ones. One morning in Paris, I realized that to come to terms with myself meant that I would have to come to terms with my ancestral past. It was 5 July 1985, the day after America's celebration of her independence.

While growing up in Philadelphia, the first capital of the United States, had enhanced my sense of the nation's history, I had never examined my own. As it was cautiously overlooked by everyone else, it had been easy for me to carry on as if it didn't exist.

I enthusiastically set out to trace my family tree. I took out a library book on genealogy. Tracing my family turned out to be impossible, since slave births and deaths were not recorded and marriage was not allowed. It's as if my great-grandparents just fell out of the sky.

While history is what is written about the past, I accept that it's drawn from deduction, supposition and conjecture, as well as some lies and deceptions motivated by politics, money and sex. No matter. It's good reading and great soap opera, so I'm sorry that there is no history of my ancestors to share with you.

My geographical and cultural heritage is largely American, and it's safe to say that my great-grandparents on both sides of the family were born there. I am not sure how my grandfather's mother came to be half German Jew or whether the man, Shouse of Danville, Kentucky, who fathered her behaved like a father. It won't change the fact that I am in part German Jew. My grandmother says that her grandmother was a Native American, but the rest of my ancestors must have come by sea.

Some were brought over against their will from Africa, and these ancestors weren't allowed to bring their culture or even their language with them or share in American culture at that time. They were captive labourers. I can't comprehend how these conditions must have stunted their emotional and intellectual growth, but that was probably the least of their worries.

A baby born to an African girl raped by an Englishman was half English as well as half African, but was considered a slave. Its development was restricted to the degradations of a slave's environment. Its Englishness would be overlooked and denied for the benefit of plantation economy. Nobody bothered to challenge this convenient deception, but wasn't the baby equally an enslaved Englishman? In this way, a new breed was born on American soil and forcibly chained to the American dream.

People see pictures of my father's family and ask me what race they are. When I hear myself say, 'They're Black,' it sounds ludicrous, because their skin is hardly brown. Since the sixties, the Black Power movement and radical chic, Black is what Americans of slave descent are called. Before that we were called Negroes, coloured, Nigras and niggers and Lord knows what else. As kids we used to say, 'Sticks and stones can break my bones but names can never hurt me,' but the naming of things is important. We rely on labels to identify and categorize everything around us.

The 26 million Americans that evolved out of the sexual abuse of the slave class never got a definitive name. Black is clearly inaccurate. Our appearances vary and represent the complete spectrum of facial features, skin colours, hair textures, eye colours and physical types. Even within a nuclear family unit there are those variations. As descendants of an enslaved people we developed socially and culturally in spite of our limited privileges. We were sustained by the promise that one day we might share in the freedom and equality that was talked about so much. One day it really should suffice to call us Americans.

On that 5 July in Paris, I decided that I wouldn't wait any longer for someone else to come up with a suitable name, and picked up the nearest dictionary. It happened to be a French/English one, a bit weather-beaten but still useful. I hoped to find a word that would describe my being of mixed descent and also suggest my African heredity.

When I stumbled upon the French word *mélange*, which means a mixture and also contains part of the word 'melanin', dark pigment found in the skin, it hit me like fireworks. Melange. I repeated it over and over out loud and in my head. I wrote it big and wrote it small and tried different endings until I heard myself saying 'Melangian' (pronounced mi-lan-jian with the accent on the middle syllable). It sounded right, but I wanted to get a second opinion, so I called a Melangian friend in New York to ask him if he liked it and made quite a screeching row when he did. Then I hung up the phone and put headphones on and turned up the music so loud that it nearly deafened me and danced by myself.

So let me start this again . . . I am Melangian. I was born of war. I am of the race which evolved out of slavery. We have a distinct cultural history, and in spite of all the shit, we've survived.

In the Melangian family women are particularly important because for a long time family units weren't lawfully permitted within the slave class. (If I said that during the first thirty years of the Victorian era, working-class people were not allowed to get married, you might get the picture and a sense of how recent it was.) I come from a long line of working women. They had no choice.

My grandmother, Edna Mae Graham, who helped raise me, was raised in Florida by her grandmother, Fannie Graham, who was born a slave. There's no photograph of Fannie, she probably never had one taken, but my grandmother described her as 'skinny and yella' with a crook in her nose like mine. From what I gather, she must have been a hellraiser. I wish I could remember more of what my grandmother told me about her.

Before Fannie died, her granddaughter, Edna Mae, a lean ambitious nineteen-year-old, had already hotfooted to Philadelphia, where she married a handsome friend of her family's, Henry Robinson. Within five years they had three children, Henry Jr, Inez and Thelma, all born before the Depression. Nobody is clear about Henry senior's line of work but, for some suspect reason, he had enough money to keep them living in certain style. Thelma, the youngest, still remembers the big house with the piano in the parlour. For a Melangian man in the 1920s that was no mean feat. Unfortunately, he took his money when he left during the Depression. Edna still managed. She had a beautician's licence and the family made do with the money she was paid for straightening women's hair.

I used to long to hear Edna's stories about her Southern childhood, but she rarely talked about it or her eleven brothers and sisters. Neither they nor her grandmother who raised her were enough to draw her back to Florida. She never went home again. She never talked about her home or her family except Fannie, and if you tried to pry, she'd shut you up pretty fast by saying that there was nothing to be gained from talking about that 'slaverytime shit'. She had a way with words and wasn't the kind of gentle little woman you could press into a discussion that she didn't want to have.

Once, though, she told about the time her father carried her on his shoulders to meet his regiment which fought in a war that she was never able to specify. (Considering she was born in 1896, I assume it was the small skirmish America had with Spain in 1898 over Cuba's independence.) I don't remember what made her break her silence, but throughout my own childhood it was the only mental image I had of hers. There are no photographs of her apart from one large portrait taken when she was nineteen. I never liked the picture in its oval frame. It made her look too much like George Washington and didn't show that her eyes were the colour of pale sienna set against her straw complexion, which was never marred by a pimple or a rash.

Edna's son Henry Jr finished high school and enlisted in July 1938 and by 21 October, he was assigned to a recruit training regiment at a naval training centre in Norfolk, Virginia. Edna's two teenage daughters, Inez and Thelma, were still at high school. Both girls were pretty and popular. After graduating, they joined in the war effort with jobs at Brewster's airplane plant. Henry was stationed at Pearl Harbor – his fleet just missed Japan's unexpected assault in December 1941. While he had to anticipate death like the rest of the fighting forces, Inez had created two new lives: my sister Pamela was born in 1942 and my brother Dennis in 1943. Edna was a devoted grandmother and Thelma a doting aunt, and a new generation fell under the command of the matriarch, which they maintained without male interference even after Inez's marriage to a brilliant medical student from Boston named Blair Theodore Hunt Jr.

Blair and his two brothers, Ernest and Wilson, had the opportunity to finish their interrupted educations when the war ended. Blair had been on a scholarship to Harvard, but there were still a lot of college years ahead before he would become a psychiatrist. Nobody was crazy enough to let my arrival in 1946 stop him from returning to Boston and Harvard. We weren't to see much of my father because of his medical studies. His appearances were rare but well received. Everybody was so busy surviving that I doubt they had much time to notice that I'd come and that he'd gone.

I had three mothers, with my grandmother Edna, my aunt Thelma and my mother, known as Ikey, sharing the load. It was taken for granted in our household that women were completely capable of everything from raising a family and bringing home a regular wage packet to self-defence. Edna's motto was: 'If you want something done, do it yourself.' To shovel a snow-banked sidewalk, stoke the furnace and provide was considered women's work. Edna had been raised in this tradition and it is likely that her grandmother was, too. I was very late to comprehend that elsewhere women were not ruling the roost, shovelling the shit and kicking ass.

What little I did hear about my ancestors was predominantly about the women, and it left me a lot of scope to elaborate on them in my imagination. They weren't prominent, but I did have them tucked in all the corners of my mind. Subsequently, it was these who spurred my determination and whom I idolized.

All my grandmother told me of her Indian great-grandmother, simply known as Grandma Mary, was that 'when an overseer came to mess with Mary in the kitchen, she rammed a knife in his gut'. It didn't enter my head that this may only have been a tale. Mary's courage was there for me to imitate and live up to. And when I heard that Fannie Graham 'wouldn't take no shit off nobody' and could do anything a man could do, Fannie became a role model and was always there for reference.

So the tradition I hoped to live up to as a child was as much established by these heroic foremothers as it was by my mother, her sister and my grandmother.

I can't see air, but I accept it's there. In the same way, I accept that I'm influenced by the unseen parade of women who have gone before me. Sometimes I wonder if I inherited them or if they inherited me.

There are things about me
Which I can't explain
There are longings in me
For which I make no claim

I feel a haunting
Which is infinite
For lives I can't remember
Yet can't forget

Soul upon soul
Stretching back in time
Stacked like a totem
Is my mother line

I am theirs
As they are mine
Within their trace
My life entwines

This mother load
Supports internally
Rooted deep in my heart
At the soul of me

I feel their pain
They laugh, now free
But in the mirror
There is only me

2

CULTURED PEARLS

To be coloured in 1946 was to be economically confined and socially isolated. Segregation laws did not exist everywhere, but the fact that they were upheld in many states reminded everybody who was boss.

Something positive still managed to grow over on the 'coloured' side of the tracks, where I spent my early childhood. A culture developed.

These social isolation bases in America where large numbers of Melangians reside are referred to as ghettos, a word that evokes only negative imagery. They weren't merely hellholes: they were cultural arenas. I'd like to call them reservations; as the dictionary says, 'reservation' can mean:

a limiting condition, or
an area of land reserved for occupation by a tribe, or
an area set aside as a secure breeding place.

In our section of the city, fear, poverty and restricted education were maintained by the promise that our patience and subservience would be rewarded by opportunities available to other Americans . . . maybe, eventually, somehow. While we were waiting, we made do with things as they were. Like some European working classes, in spite of poverty, we had a certain quality of life.

We had our own class system, language, religion and art forms. What we ate, how we dressed, and our manner of doing things were derived from the American culture which we imitated but could never have emulated.

America was a big beef-eating nation but on the reservation pork and chicken were favoured, because they were cheaper. No part of the pig was considered waste. This policy may have been a leftover from plantation days. Pig ears and feet, the lining of its stomach (called hog maws), the intestines (called chitlins), the hocks and the ribs were all gratefully received at the table. Chunks of pig fat called fat back were used to flavour the cooking. Most things were boiled or fried. Fried chicken was a mainstay (nobody had heard of Kentucky Fried). All kinds of beans were staples, along with rice and potatoes. Yams and sweet potatoes were favourites, although they weren't available throughout the year. Cabbage and greens such as collards, turnips, mustard and kale were boiled and then simmered, with a piece of fat back thrown in if times were good.

In 1985 on my grandmother's birthday, 27 March, I was home in London with my daughter Karis and spotted collard greens at my local greengrocer's. I don't rememer seeing this variety of green anywhere in England before. To commemorate my grandmother, I thought I'd cook some for Karis, who had never eaten them and only has a vague memory of Edna; I knew that the dreadful smell alone of the collards cooking would be nostalgic.

My grandmother would have cleaned them by soaking them first in her huge roasting pan that could hold our 30-pound Thanksgiving turkey. I plopped them into water in the kitchen sink. They were clogged with dirt and it took hours to get the damned things clean: I understood why my grandmother soaked them in such a big pot all day.

I decided to steam them rather than boil them to keep the vitamins in. I threw them in the Chinese bamboo steamers and slung a few strips of bacon in with them in place of fat back. The result was most unusual but I assumed they were cooked – they go a sort of mustard colour.

When I'd dished them out, Karis looked at them on her plate and then up at me. She didn't see me catching her sneak that last sly glance. She can be as English as they come: the accent, the manner, the attitude and even her sensibilities are so British that it just kills me. You'd hardly know she's mine sometimes.

She used her knife and fork to eat the collards, pressing them onto the back of her fork with her knife. I could hear some grit crunching on her braces when she tried to chew. I kept my eyes on my plate, so that I wouldn't have to interrupt this solemn commemoration with an apology that the collards were most likely undercooked.

When my grandmother did them, they melted in the mouth. It was often a pretty testy time at our place when collards got cooked, because my mother hated the smell. They do have an unfortunate odour when they've been simmering for hours.

Sunday on the reservation was a day for culinary extravagance when it could be afforded. Edna made biscuits with flour, milk and lard (like scones without the sugar and currants). There might even be some bread made from cornmeal, but this was usually her Friday-night treat, served with fried mackerel which had been dipped in a mixture of flour and cornmeal before it sizzled in the big iron skillet full of smoking lard.

Hominy grits were generally reserved for breakfast, although you ate them at any time if you were hungry enough. Hominy is kernels of maize. Grits – ground hominy – were boiled in salted water to a porridge consistency and topped with butter or margarine. We also ate something called scrapple at breakfast which was scraps of meat and meal ground together and fried. The occasional dinner of hot dogs and baked beans was apologized for but indicated that we were Americans to the heart.

The socially sophisticated Melangian, more integrated into American society, wouldn't eat like this today.

The American tradition of a free choice of worship found a zealous outlook on the reservation where store fronts, living rooms and any place big enough for a gathering of souls could serve as a place of worship. Faith kept people going and gave them hope. Evangelist, Holy Roller, Sanctified, Pentecostal, Seventh Day Adventist, Children of God, Jehovah's Witness and many other denominations had committed followers just like larger denominations such as Baptist, Methodist, Lutheran, Episcopalian and Catholic. I missed church culture on the reservation, because we were baptized Catholic with the intention of getting the advantage of a parochial school education. But the evidence and effect of the religious element in the community reached me on many levels.

Seeing a congregation socializing outside their church after a meeting was to see reservation fashion. All manner of hats were worn by men and women alike. The ladies' were usually adorned with a bit of netting, maybe artificial flowers or fruit like grapes or cherries, ribbons of silk or velvet. Maybe the lot. Hat, shoes, bag and outfit did not have to coordinate. Bright colours predominated.

When I was young, there was a Holy Roller church a few doors from our house. Holy Rollers are very devout and put great stock in their own translation of the Bible. The corner building wasn't a church by design, just the biggest house on the block owned and lived in by our landlady, Mrs White. Mrs White was ebony, and on meeting days she always wore a white dress and white hat indicating that she was an elder of the church, which was almost like being a minister. She was probably in her late sixties and she usually seemed disgruntled. I couldn't call her attractive. ('Yurgly' is how my grandmother described her. Edna could hardly sing out the word before she'd start rolling about laughing till the tears streamed from her eyes.) Mrs White had a scrunched-up face with not enough chin to offset her very big mouth. Her pea-sized eyes were hidden behind steel-rimmed glasses. She was heavy set and wore an upper and lower plate which she never had in her mouth if we dropped by unexpectedly to pay the rent.

Nothing was more exciting than to sneak over to Elder White's on a warm summer's night when we suspected there would be a meeting; it was usually a Thursday. A couple of us would creep along her side yard and right up to the window of her big front room where with a bit of luck we'd find the curtain cracked. If we were too early, we'd only get to see the twenty or so chairs of mixed description lined up in rows and waiting for a warm behind. There was often a partial drum kit and a saxophone near the piano which was next to the pulpit, a raised stage at one corner of the room furthest from the window looking onto our street. The pulpit was probably the carpentry work of one of the members, which doesn't imply that it was crude handiwork; every part of this place of worship was an extension of the members' lives. Some of the chairs were the same ones you might be offered to sit on if you came to the elder's for dinner.

Giving a testimony or bearing witness in the Holy Roller church was often a highly emotional and impassioned revelation that required a lot of energy. The testifier usually got so caught up with the spirit and in the spirit that not only would his or her testimony be sparked by jumping and shouting, but others might 'feel' the spirit of the testimony too. To 'jump and shout' was a religious experience which found its way into the blues, then into rhythm and blues, before it transcended into rock and roll.

'Feeling the spirit' and 'getting happy' must be experiences second to none, because perfectly healthy people would faint and have to be carried out in the midst of these revelations. Peeking through the crack in the curtains, we longed to see the sweaty heights of this excitement, but I usually got called home before the long meetings reached these emotional crescendos.

A good minister or preacher was not only versed in the Bible, he was able to stir his parishioners to a revelry that evoked their testimonies. 'Preachin'' was an art and a good preacher was a star in the community. While most religious services have some element of theatre about them, not many can claim the standard of performance exchanged between the minister and his congregation in some of the reservation churches. In addition, some of these churches boasted excellent choirs. A couple of the more renowned ones were broadcast on our local Sunday radio station. Long before I was considered old enough to plug the radio in, my brother and I used to sneak away to listen to these church services. We weren't allowed to, because my mother thought we were making fun of them, but it was just a way to get a dose of good music.

Music was a survival tonic, and free. To hear my grandmother singing 'Wade In The Water' was sometimes a sign that she was mad as hell about something, like being left alone to wash the dishes, but she made music just the same.

You could sing your way out of the reservation just as you could box your way out. While this was not the ideal of Melangians like my family, who had aspirations to become the doctors and lawyers of the community, musical talent was a passport to another America. And the church was as good a place as any to get your musical experience. Aretha Franklin, Marvin Gaye, Chaka Khan, Donna Summer, the Pointer Sisters, Al Green and Billy Preston are among the singers who started in the church.

The best reservation music to my ears was the a capella

singing of groups of boys on the street who would practise popular songs of the day and do their own special renditions, which they'd decorate with rhythmic little jabs of harmony thrown in here and there. These were casual groups of boys who happened to be socializing on the same street corner or sitting on the same stoop at the same time. Singing was an escape and a pastime, like playing a game of baseball in the middle of the street, especially for teenage boys who were too big to play marbles but not yet old enough to spend their time drinking in a beer garden, which was the grandiose name for a bar.

The boys who roamed the streets were usually pretty rough and rowdy, and while I thought it was divine to hear a few of them working out the harmonies for a song, they weren't a very savoury-looking bunch. They wore brimmed hats or peaked caps that were cocked to one side or perched some weird way or even worn back to front. The effect was not too becoming, but they were trying to look tough.

A lot of them had a special way of walking, too. I can't think what this particular habit grew out of. Most of them looked as if they had incorporated a simplified dance step with a stride which required a certain amount of rhythm and effort to look smooth. This was called 'bopping'. My grandmother hated it. She said they 'looked like overgrown simpletons loping up and down the street dragging one leg like a cripple'.

I didn't mind the crazy way they walked, but I did mind them taunting my mother or aunt with catcalls and whistles when we had to pass a bunch of them occupying nearly the whole street corner. We couldn't avoid them even by crossing over to the other side. If the catcalls and the whistles were only a temporary interruption to some song they were working out, it didn't stop me loving their music when they went back to making it. I loved to hear them singing in an alley that had an echo.

My family disapproved of the language that was spoken on the reservation, because it wasn't what the rest of the nation considered good English. To be fair, it was a dialect and should have been treated with a certain respect as Europeans treat their dialects. Instead, a lot of stigma was attached to it. How the children who had only ever heard and spoken this reservation dialect coped when they got to school is beyond me. *Fun with Dick and Jane*, which was the first primer, should have had a translation and a glossary.

Of all the versions of English I've learned to speak, Melangian is the most expressive and emotional. Maybe this is why it is the language of popular music today. Whether by Hall and Oates, the Stones or Michael McDonald, a lot of hits are written and recorded by non-Melangians in our dialect. It certainly says what it has to say and takes the most direct route. It has a flatness to its tone which is basically guttural and combines this with rhythm and a Southern American lilt.

When Charles Dickens wrote his American travelogue in 1846 after an extensive trip around the States, he said that the English that he heard spoken by women in the Southern states showed the influence of the mammies that raised them. So the Southern accent was affected by Melangian and vice versa. We picked up English how and when we could, as it was never formally taught us.

To hear it spoken, Melangian is like upper-class county English in that it's full of diphthongs and open vowel sounds. Consonants at the end of words are often dropped, as in the Scots accent, and when they are sounded, they're softened. This is probably why Melangian is so useful for modern singing. It lets the mouth hold open sounds for words like 'don't, 'last' and 'morning', to name but three.

Melangian was the language I relied upon to express myself on the reservation when my mother wasn't within hearing distance. We weren't allowed to speak it at home. I still enjoy using it when I get a chance. When an issue gets bogged down with unnecessary words, if I think in Melangian, I can keep a clearer picture of what's really going on. Of all the English dialects, Melangian is the one that best expresses joy and ebullience.

The class system on the reservation was more like a caste system, related to physical appearance. I guess it evolved out of the plantation politics, when how you looked may have determined whether you worked in the house or the field. Skin colour, hair texture and facial features affected your social status. Hair that grew wavy and long, light-coloured eyes and skin, afforded you more opportunity.

In the 1940s, educational opportunity was too limited for

Melangians to see education as an available route to a better life, although we had our own doctors, lawyers, teachers and professionals, most of whom were educated in small Melangian colleges in the South. There weren't many of these graduates. My father's chance to go to Harvard was not one to be taken lightly or interfered with. It compared with a boy from the Gorbals getting a scholarship to go to Christ Church College, Oxford. His academic achievements linked my family to the professional class even though we were struggling to eat, like everybody around us. Our mother worked especially hard to have us live up to our assumed identity and went to great pains to make sure that we spoke English as well as anyone else and that our education and ambitions weren't stinted in any way. For this she was often accused of acting white and treating us as if we were. On the reservation, no accusation was more damning. She turned a deaf ear.

It would be misleading to paint only a glowing picture of the reservation. If you saw a photograph of one without a caption, you might mistake it for a war zone. Young men prepared for combat, patrolling and armed and waiting; a rubbled landscape; an atmosphere of torment, confusion or resignation on the faces of both young and old, highlighted by a queer sense of abandonment.

The work that was available wasn't likely to improve your future status and crime seemed to pay.

3
THE FRONT LINE

Pearl Bailey's mother lived across the road from us, but 23rd Street was on the fringe of what was later to be known as the Crime Belt. I grew perversely proud of this distinction, but in reality I doubt it was much worse than any other section of North Philly. It was like boot camp, and I was happy there even though every passageway seemed like an obstacle course. Whether it was the hallway to the communal toilet, or the staircase, or the few feet of pavement that led to dinky local stores, you might encourage something dangerous.

I wasn't really allowed out much alone, so one of my favourite pastimes was to observe the world below by hanging my head a bit further than was allowed outside our third-floor window which overlooked the street.

Once, I happened to be looking out when I saw a thief riding off on my tricycle. It caught me off guard. 'That son of a bitch is stealing my bicycle!' is all I managed to squeal before my grandmother's big yellow hand had whipped me out of the window to drag me to the kitchen sink where my mouth was washed out with soap and water. Resisting this punishment was worse than the punishment itself. Thankfully a few tears came to evoke my grandmother's sympathy.

I could think bad words and no one would stop me, but whenever one would slip out before I could catch it and be overheard by my mother, aunt or grandmother, I'd get my mouth washed out. I cursed a lot although nobody knew it. I was only repeating what I heard, but since 'Do as I say and not as I do' was one of the house rules, cursing was considered to be very bad behaviour and what my grandmother termed 'streety'.

With the six of us living in two rooms, nerves got frayed, and among the adults a lot of swearing and shouting went on, although they pretended after the dust settled that nothing unladylike had been said. None of them swore in front of anybody outside the family other than the ice man, whom Edna cursed if his great big chunks of ice dripped across her clean kitchen floor before he could lodge it in the refrigerator or before she could put some newspaper down.

I spent a lot of time with my grandmother, because my mother and aunt were at work all day at the Signal Corps and my brother and sister were at school. Edna let me do things like go down to Max Bender's small food store and buy loose potato chips. Max scooped them from a big silver can into a brown paper bag. (They were cheaper if they were stale.) Max also sold margarine from a covered bowl. As part of your purchase, you'd get a little red capsule to stir into it to turn it yellow. Being allowed to stir was a reward for being good, and I tried to follow all the rules.

Once I'd started school, my mother told me to work hard, mind my own business and act like a lady, but I assumed 'take no shit' still applied. Easier said than done. As I was only five, combining those efforts required a political skill that I didn't have. My mother expected me to talk my way out of trouble, but on the front line, talk can get you into a lot of trouble.

To survive our tough little neighbourhood, you had to be alert at all times. Even though I was little, I was mentally prepared to react and defend myself. Just as you'd imagine a real war zone, even the youngest must learn to anticipate danger, to think and react at the same time, and to let fear serve as a natural alarm to warn you of danger, fuel you with the adrenalin that may be your only protection.

When I started kindergarten at St Elizabeth's Catholic School, I was worldly. I'd seen so many people in the streets with scars that I'd learned to distinguish how a wound had been inflicted: a jagged scar came from a knife cut and a smooth, thin, slightly raised scar came from a razor-blade slash. I was fully aware that people were getting beaten up, knifed, scalded and had lye thrown on them. Maybe what I heard was magnified in my mind and what I imagined was worse than what was going on for real.

A constant worry was that there seemed to be a vigilante street-level policy about what behaviour was bad and deserved punishment. Vanity was punishable and it wasn't unusual to hear that somebody could be threatened with a beating for 'thinking they were cute'. Appearing to ally yourself in any way to the other Americans, the white ones, was also taken as a serious offence and referred to as 'acting white' or 'thinking you were white'. Trying to be too dignified or too genteel could be construed as part of this offence. Between my mother's rules for my behaviour and the undeclared street laws, I sensed there was some discrepancy.

For me, the news of what was happening in Korea where my uncle Henry was at war hardly matched up to the gossip about frequent scuffles outside the beer garden where never a flower grew.

Growing up in this environment was not a tragic scenario for my childhood. I knew nothing else in those days before television and therefore couldn't make comparisons. I was very content, and feel that I had a wonderful childhood.

I was never hungry even though there was no cupboard always stacked with food. Max Bender's was open till six o'clock. My brother and sister and I were cherished by our three 'mothers', who bought us dolls and games for Christmas. There was always a cake on a birthday and the fairy godmother left a quarter when a tooth fell out. We were kept warm in winter even if it meant somebody had to throw their coat over us in our cots to supplement the available blankets. I can honestly say that I never wanted for anything and my heart had enough. My mother would play us a game of jacks or read me a story and if my brother and sister got their homework done, the three of us could always argue over a game of old maid or something.

You couldn't call us spoiled, but I'd say we had everything, though it may have seemed to others like little. That everything included roaches in our apartment didn't bother me a bit, and I even liked the mice and felt we saw too little of them. The hoo-ha that went on if a mouse was caught scuttling across the kitchen floor was an entertainment not to be believed. My mother and aunt would always jump on the kitchen table screeching and hollering the place down while my brother tried to swat the poor bitty thing with a broom before it would get away under the stove, which it always did.

The only misery in my life was a picture of my uncle Henry in his uniform. This photograph of him posed with a rifle was propped up in front of the only big mirror we owned, which was attached to the dressing table in the bedroom. I needed to use this mirror when I practised singing 'If I Were a King (I'd be but a slave to you)' or any song that I would make up. To see, I had to stand on the four-legged leather-seated stool that fitted neatly within this dresser, which was part of a mahogany bedroom suite left over from Edna's better days. Unfortunately, my uncle's picture scared me so much that I'd have to turn it face down on the lace doily, which was draped across the glass top, so I wouldn't have to look at it while I was looking at myself. There was nothing scary about this picture except the rifle. It was more that my brother Dennis regularly used it to torment me or to make me do something I didn't want to do. He always threatened that if I didn't, Henry would come in the night and shoot me. This made me scream and cry until help came, which never took much time since we had only two rooms.

Otherwise, Dennis and Pamala were extremely well-behaved and no doubt deserved the praise they got on their perfect report cards from school. My brother was so reliable at arithmetic that Max Bender used to pay Dennis, at the age of eight, to tally people's bills if the store got crowded.

Dennis and Pam (or Bubby and Dixie Peach, as they were nicknamed and known) were both shy, gentle children, so I can't say how it happened that I was the wild Indian that my mother always accused me of being. Following their example, I got pleasure out of being well-behaved and exhibiting perfect manners. When I finally got old enough to sit outside on the top step alone, I would charm the passers-by that I knew with 'How do you do' and 'How are you feeling?' and invariably go upstairs rewarded for these salutations with a fist full of nickels.

While I could understand that to be good meant to keep your voice down, to share and be helpful, I was never to be convinced that it also meant to be polite or passive in the face of aggression. Anyhow, Grandma Mary and Fannie Graham would have expected otherwise, and so would Edna.

Ikey was gradually becoming the head of the household, being our mother and the elder of the working sisters. Being Edna's child, Ikey was wilful or what Edna called 'headstrong'. Edna said she had 'a head like Connie's old ram'. I never did know what this referred to. Some of Edna's expressions didn't make sense but I liked them all.

To have a young mother who was smart and very pretty gave me something else to worry about, because I knew that men liked to make passes at her in the street and that she sported an attitude which people on the block called superior. As far as Ikey was concerned, she was a doctor's wife and the reservation was just a stopover. To her mind we were merely broke, which had nothing to do with being poor, and to my dismay she dressed us to prove as much.

Dennis and Pam got to wear a uniform to school, but I had to attend nursery in oxblood brogues, high argyle socks, a silly tam and a tailored coat because Ikey considered them in good taste. As the mother superior who ran the school said, we were not like the other children. Mrs Hunt's children did not swear and fight and cause trouble like some of the other 'coloured' children until . . .

Thump went my balled-up fist when it whammed up against the side of the boy's ugly head. I didn't even know his name, because I'd been so busy in the playground minding my own business that a lot of faces went unnoticed. His nose started to bleed into the dribble of snot already drying above his lip. Usually I cried at the sight of blood even if it was somebody else's, but I was too mad for tears. That he had the nerve to kiss me when I was off my guard was a liberty that I wasn't going to let go unpunished. So I hauled back ready to wallop him once again, but he was saved by the bell which halted my second blow. The cardinal sin of my self-defence was that I had broken a rule: no fighting in the playground. Normally, I was grateful for this regulation, because it nearly made our school yard a neutral zone in the neighbourhood. It was the only safe space where kids and air and peace mixed, unlike the sidewalk, which was designated off limits for me most of the time because of the vagrants and the bad kids. I was ashamed that I had defiled my only piece of paradise and that I wasn't living up to Pam and Dennis's flawless reputation, which was my mother's greatest glory.

My assailant cried so loud that the first nun to the rescue mistook him for the innocent injured party. The indignity of being considered the offender was worse than the punishment inflicted on me by this woman draped in black. Her polished black high-tops looked like army boots peeking out from beneath her heavy hem. I had to hold out my open palms while she cracked them with her wooden ruler.

My kindergarten class only lasted half a day. When the air-raid siren blared at noon, my grandmother was always waiting for me at the gate. She was mad that afternoon when she heard why my eyes were puffy from crying. She ground her teeth when she got mad and I could hear her doing this while she carried me home. I was too big to be carried, really, but I got a ride right up to Max Bender's where Edna got us a penny Mary Jane as she always did so that we could share it after my lunch. A Mary Jane was two little individually wrapped toffees bound by a red cellophane band which I liked to look through and which my grandmother always let me have. The fact that I got my red cellophane band that afternoon indicated that my grandmother was not annoyed with me. She said that I should've beaten the hell out of the son of a bitch that was kissing me and said she should have wrapped that rosary around the nun's neck. Afterwards she added that she wasn't scared of a son of a bitch living and wasn't scared to die. As we were living so near the notoriously dangerous Columbia Avenue, it was just as well.

It was another war cry to help her carry on. No doubt she'd seen enough injustices in her time so that even the featherweight significance of my little scrape jostled her memory and gave her a renewed excuse to convey her exasperation. But none of this stopped Edna singing 'If I Knew You Were Coming I'd've Baked A Cake'.

She sat next to her big double bed where I took my afternoon naps and stroked my temple, careful not to scratch me with her long fingernails, till I'd fallen asleep. To this day I don't know why the stolen kiss upset me so much. Edna said that anybody with the common sense they were born with could see that 'it was wrong to let that boy think that he could "kiss on you" and get away with it'. Her conclusion was that Sister must have lost her mind.

In spite of all my grandmother's comforting, Sister's reaction to the incident confused me temporarily. Did I have a right to defend myself when I felt it was necessary? Being taunted by a couple of bullies put me back on the right track soon enough. I guess you could say self-defence came naturally.

But the stolen-kiss episode was a turning point for me. I'd obviously lost my halo at St Elizabeth's after that. I endured the ruler punishment for the second time when a priest who'd come into my classroom claimed that I switched down the aisle when I was returning to my seat. 'Switching' was a term used for swinging your bum from side to side when you walked – the swagger of a sassy woman. The priest gave me a chance to walk down the aisle again, and when he said that I was still doing it, I was recalled to the front and punished in front of the whole class. The whack of the ruler on my outstretched palms wasn't nearly as torturous as the teasing I got for it in the playground.

Not long after this humiliation, Mother Superior found me with my hands in the sink when she checked the girls' lavatory on one of her rounds. Although I tried to explain that I was only washing my hands as my mother insisted that I must, Mother Superior hit me for playing in water when I was supposed to be using the toilet.

Like a criminal with a record, suddenly I became a suspect on other counts: guilty until proven innocent, which is how kids were usually treated on the reservation. Need I say that these false accusations by the holy purveyors of Catholicism made me suspicious of them and their teaching? They already looked pretty ominous in all that black and what with the stories circulating in the playground that the nuns shaved their heads (which I had earlier been willing to discount), I became a most reluctant Catholic. I enjoyed reciting a couple of the prayers, the 'Hail Mary' and the 'Hail Holy Queen', and continued to think that the picture of Mary and the statues of her with her baby were very nice, but I stopped believing in the priests and nuns, because they couldn't be trusted. This was one child that the Catholic faith managed to lose by the age of five.

One of the saving graces of being so young was that no emotional injuries seemed to absorb me for very long. Unfortunately they probably burrowed themselves into the deep dark crevices of my brain.

The streets imposed a greater fear than the church. My instinct to defend myself came back fortified. 'Take no shit' is a policy that dies hard. I couldn't stop being Goody Two-Shoes, though, because I enjoyed the role too much. And I can't say that I was ever tempted to get up to more devilment at this stage than to use one of my grandmother's elastic garters as a slingshot. It never crossed my mind to talk back to my elders, engrave PUSSY or FUCK on a school lavatory door, spit, or even take advantage of somebody smaller than me, although these were among the shenanigans that went on around me. I posed fearlessly in the face of threats and attacks but still tried to act like a lady most of the time for my mother's benefit, if not for my own.

My mother made sure that all her children could read and write before we went to school. This was handy, because there were other important things to take in during out last year on 23rd Street: the sights and sounds of people struggling to stay on top of life while there was too little of everything from hope to money and living space. I won't say that fear and frustration bring out the best in people or make them the nicest neighbours, but there was a lot to be learned from them.

The social isolation of the reservation was broken by an electrical device introducing the world outside, the other America where my mother and aunt worked each day. This device instantly became my best friend. Like my grandmother, it was always available. Television turned our sparse kitchen into an entertainment centre.

My family always laughed a lot anyway, and television gave us one thing after another to hoot about and something like a home fire to gather around in the evening. Whenever someone clicked the big right-hand knob that turned it on, we'd end up laughing. Everybody on it was white and really quite nice. They were always smiling when they told you about Bayer aspirins or Bromo Seltzer. People talked, sang and danced, and always wore lovely outfits and costumes.

I had enjoyed occasional visits from friends of Edna's: Miss Ossie and Miss Deet, Miss Ophelia and Miss Myrtle, whose gold front tooth gleamed when she flashed me a smile. I was usually allowed to sit and listen to them chewing the fat at the white enamelled kitchen table. Miss Ophelia was my favourite, with her steel-grey hair pulled back severely in a chignon like Edna's. But these visitors, who turned our kitchen into a parlour, couldn't compete with television. Shirley Temple and Bill Robinson dancing a duet, Tom Mix or Hoot Gibson in a shoot-out, Gene Autry – the Singing cowboy – Kukla, Fran and Ollie, which was my favourite puppet show, and the cat-and-mouse cartoons changed life in our kitchen.

Outside, the streets remained the same.

4
INFANT DIPLOMACY

Finally closing the door on those two rooms was not a sentimental experience for any of the family, but some of my sweetest early childhood memories will always be locked there, like the sight of my father in a soft lamplight as he showed me how to draw a ship with sails. That evening wasn't diminished by our four barren walls. Once I looked out of our window and saw the Oscar Mayer man in his delivery van which was shaped like a hot dog. It pulled up outside Max Bender's and parked there long enough for me to run down and get a close look at it with all the other children. For that moment, 23rd Street might have been a fantasy island. And I can still picture the store at the bad end of the street with a jukebox that played 'The Glory Of Love' for one nickel. For the pleasure it brought it could have been a corner of the ballroom in *High Society*. Still, the idea of us living in a house by ourselves made goodbye easy.

When we moved to Germantown in 1951, we only took the new television and my grandmother's bedroom suite. My mother had hoped that she was leaving everything else behind – the cussing and swearing, the thugs on the street corners. She was even letting us off the harsh discipline of Catholic School.

Germantown is a district of Philadelphia that was originally settled 300 years ago by thirteen Quaker and Mennonite families from Krefeld, Germany. In those days it was 5700 acres of land to the northeast of Philadelphia. It was divided by an Indian trail which remains its main thoroughfare, Germantown Avenue. Who knows what happened to the amiable Indians? Like fallen leaves, they disappeared without mention or trace.

The Krefelders and their leader, Francis Daniel Pastorious, an aristocrat and scholar, were part of William

Penn's 'holy experiment'. These Krefelders made the first public protest against slavery in 1688 when they declared that all human beings had the right to live as free men. At the time, this was considered too radical to be readily accepted by the Quakers.

For generations the community remained German. Both the Bible and a newspaper were printed there in German. The district didn't begin to attract the English until 1750, when William Allen, the chief justice of Pennsylvania, built his country seat there, Mount Airy. As more English followed him, English architecture merged with German into a specific style called Anglo-German. The district was considered a German township until about 1830, when the English became dominant, setting up their own press and linking Germantown to Philadelphia by train. For the next hundred or so years, right up to the Second World War, Germantown was one of the more fashionable districts of Philadelphia.

By the time my family moved in, there were too many Melangians in the district for it to be considered fashionable any more. It wasn't unusual in the summer months to hear the watermelon man hawking his wares in the street, selling watermelons for 25 cents or five cantaloupes for a dollar from his open-back pick-up truck. But some of the early historic residences and the Market Square with its Civil War monument were still standing, maintained by the Germantown Historical Society. They made impressions on me as permanent as 23rd Street. Germantown still had a decidedly German and English feeling about it. I didn't know to what extent at the time.

Our small seven-room terraced house with a front and back garden made an immense difference to our lives.

To help my grandmother plant our first garden was to discover with great pride that she knew the names of the flowers and trees and how to tend the earth and things that grew from it. Marigolds and dahlias, hollyhocks and morning glories sprouted, and I checked their growth each day with awe and anticipation. She planted some seeds for me that would grow into cobs of corn for popping, so the packet said. I can't remember if they did. She even bought the almanac to study planting times, but I discovered to my horror that her interest in what the moon and stars were doing was mostly astrological.

With her garden and her new sewing machine, Edna was nearly too busy for bad talk.

Our neighbours two doors away kept full-grown chickens in their back yard. Fluffy, our new cat, was often foolhardy enough to slip into their yard in the hope of a kill. He invariably returned pecked and injured, but he wouldn't learn. Once he arrived home so much the worse for one of these chicken attacks that he succumbed to letting me bandage him and put him in my doll carriage to cart him about for an entire weekend.

I didn't realize it at the time, but recently when I looked at a street map of Philadelphia, I noticed that North Philly couldn't have been more than a twenty-minute trolley ride away from us, yet I don't remember any one of us making the effort to go back.

There were a few odd characters in the neighbourhood, like Jet, the local hobo. He had a layer of grey whiskers covering his dark-brown skin, and his dishevelled clothes were various tones of grey, ill-fitting and dirty. He always wore a jacket and a brimmed hat as a formality, even in the hottest weather. He looked a mess. Some afternoons I'd see him shuffle along the street dragging his feet (the way Edna told us not to walk). His mangy-looking, nameless old dog was never far behind. They always moved at a deadly slow pace down the middle of the street, not on the sidewalk. He had a reputation for being regularly drunk, but I was afraid to get close enough to smell liquor on him. I used to run up to the porch and stand near the front door if I saw him coming up the street, more afraid of catching his dog's mange than I was of Jet.

For me, the new thrill was to be allowed to play regularly with other children on the block. On 23rd Street, my mother had to be so particular about our playmates that we nearly only had each other. With Pam and Dennis at school all day, Edna was my best friend, even though I could tell when they came home that Pam was her favourite. I like to believe that it was because Pam was the first grandchild, but I suspected that it was also because Pam was beautiful with jet-black wavy hair and slanted chestnut-brown eyes. She was quiet and read most of the time, but I could never tell whether her passion for books was her own or her way of satisfying my mother's ambition for us to excel at school.

Despite being Melangian, Ikey was the perfect Jewish

mother. She didn't feed us matzos but she was clannish, ambitious, competitive, guilt-provoking, adored her children and believed that a Ph.D. was the be-all and end-all of life.

I didn't find this too hard to live with and was under less pressure than Pam to succeed, as she was the eldest. The four years' difference in our ages meant that we never managed to be at the same school at the same time after St Elizabeth's. She'd always graduated or moved on before I started a school, leaving a dazzling record behind her. When trouble started for her at school in Germantown, I wasn't around to give her either help or moral support. The streets were littered with enough ammunition for me to have helped her stave off an attack even if I was too little to be of much use otherwise. I am ashamed to say that I considered sticks and stones and bricks fair play if the odds were stacked against me. It was my mother who taught us this line of defence in spite of all her talk about being dignified and ladylike.

In the early fifties, Germantown wasn't generally rough like North Philly but it had its bad elements, who decided to make my sister their object of torment and agitation because she was pretty. At ten she wasn't expected to defend herself against a gang of rowdy girls and had to be escorted back and forth to school until finally the police were called in.

I'd like to think that we Melangians have stopped persecuting our own for looking too African or not African enough. Appearance even had the potential to divide family loyalties.

It pains me to think of how often Pam suffered for being too pretty and too brainy. Her years on the reservation and certainly in Germantown were harsher than mine and, no doubt, if she gave you her version of our family's life, it would be quite a different picture. Pam neither bothered anybody nor had that early lust for the mirror or physical praise which would have given her airs to make other girls dislike her. Maybe the fact that she got the answers right all the time provoked them. I couldn't think why else they wanted to hurt her.

I don't know if anybody realized how much her victimization troubled me, but I kept my worry to myself and daydreamed that I was Wonder Woman and Supergirl rolled into one, on hand to swoop down from the tallest building to destroy all the ruffians when they taunted her. Of course, I also needed to plan what to do if they attacked me.

At six, I was not at all pretty. I doubt that every time my mother looked at me, she wanted to send me back, but I was not the least bit exceptional-looking. I had a big space between my two front teeth, and eyes so dark that they merely reflected the light bulb when I was asked to hold them up to the light to have their colour checked. My hair was so unfortunately thick that my mother had to divide it into three sections which she then braided. The braid on top was wound into a bun and pinned down to keep it from dangling in my face. The hairpins usually felt as if they were sticking right into my brain, and I yearned for thin hair and only two braids, although this was not the sort of vanity that I would have been allowed to express.

Soon after we moved in, two of my new friends and I were playing at dressing up on a rainy afternoon. They were wearing high heels; I only put on some rouge and pinned my two loose braids up with the one on top so that it looked like an upsweep. As soon as the rain stopped, we paraded ourselves to the corner store to buy some penny candy. The air was scented with that delicious city smell of wet tarmac blending with the sweet smell of wet grass after a summer shower. We passed an old man sitting on a low porch, rocking slowly, his hat pulled down so that his face hardly showed. A woman was standing at the screen door and I heard him say to her how nice we looked and add that the one with the braids on top of her head looked just like Doris Day.

I wasn't allowed to acknowledge strange men, so I kept walking and acted as though I hadn't heard him. Doris Day. One of the other girls repeated what he'd said when we were out of earshot. Trying to be nonchalant, I cocked my head to the side and looked straight ahead of me. Doris Day. I would have preferred it if he'd said Jane Russell, but Doris Day would do. I wasn't sure I'd look so much like her without the rouge.

Nobody could have conceived that my face would sneak its way onto a magazine cover. Anyhow, at that time Melangian girls didn't appear on any covers but *Ebony* and *Jet*, the Melangian magazines. If I'd heard my mother say it once, I'd heard her repeat a thousand times that 'looks will get you nowhere'. This seemed to contradict what little of life I'd observed, but maybe it was her way of making me feel less inadequate and it supported her conviction that college was our only hope of a good career. One thing was obvious, if being pretty attracted troublemakers, it was a quality hardly worth having and dangerous to flaunt if you did (as well as cheap, which was Edna's final verdict on the subject). 'Pretty is as pretty does,' she stated.

I was about to lose Edna's daily dose of homilies because as soon as I attended school for a full day, she got a job working for an Italian family who operated the local bakery. She probably got the job to help pay for the new fittings and furniture in every room. I knew better than to ask how we afforded it all, because it would have been considered none of my business and rude to enquire.

John Wister Elementary School was a three-storey brick building on Bringhurst Street not far from Germantown Avenue. It was a hundred years old and a big fuss was made over its wooden floors because they were the originals. John Wister was one of the early German settlers, and I was a very lucky girl, the principal told my mother before she carted me off to Miss Courtney's class, to start first grade at a school that was so steeped in history. I was given my very own desk which had a sunken ink well, although we could only write in pencil. The desks were in rows with each attached to the bench in front and held together and supported by elaborate ironmongery. The writing surface was the hinged lid of an oblong wooden box so that you could lift it up and put your things inside. I was seated near Miss Courtney in the front of the room and though I dared not turn round to stare, I could have sworn that all the other children were white. Thank God I'd been watching a lot of television and knew how to act.

Television carted me off to places I had never dreamed existed. It took for granted that I was ready to share experiences quite foreign to my own. Mainly, it exposed those other Americans to me, the ones who didn't live on the reservations. In 1952 the only ways that Melangians had of becoming familiar with white behaviour was by working with or for whites and by seeing movies and watching TV.

To me, Lucy and Ricky Ricardo and Fred and Ethel Mertz on the *I Love Lucy* show, Ralph, Alice, Trixie and Ed on *The*

Honeymooners or George Burns and Gracie Allen were like neighbours I visited once a week. I saw what they did at breakfast or sat in their living room and overheard their conversations. Where else and how else could this have happened? While Max Bender and other white shopkeepers might have been genuinely cordial and exchanged a few niceties with a regular customer, I knew nothing about how people like Max lived or what he'd say to his wife. Radio and motion pictures didn't give us a regular enough dose of exposure to create the familiarity, the insider's view, that television gave us.

As liberal as Harry Truman was with his bills for public housing, socialized medicine, education as a federal, not a state, issue and his civil rights policy, there was never any suggestion that the races should mix socially. The GI Bill restored the interrupted education of men like my father and gave equal pensions to all Americans who had fought the war together, but nobody assumed that total integration would follow. Racial separation is part of American culture.

At six I wasn't aware of this, but I was soon aware that many children in my class had never talked to a Melangian before and some of them definitely didn't want to. Although John Wister school was close to our house, it was just beyond our local school-district boundary. Ikey got me enrolled there anyway. For the majority of my classmates and teachers, I might have been a visiting diplomat representing my whole race, because I soon learned that what I said and did was a reflection on other Melangians and if my classmates were going to overcome their assumption that they weren't as clean, as good or as clever, the onus was on me. For a six-year-old this is a heavy burden, but on instructions from home I did what I could to be my best self and come first in all things.

In spite of this and of being called nigger and other such names when it suited somebody, I did love my school and most of what went with it, whether it was history or social studies, spinster teachers or spelling bees. There was always some national hero's birthday or some impending holiday that gave us another excuse to hang up our pictures and create a display. Washington, Lincoln, Easter bunnies, Hallowe'en witches, Thanksgiving pilgrims, Christmas angels, fire-prevention week, keep-your-city-clean week, brotherly-love week. There was always something to celebrate and I wanted to be there.

I never felt as wonderful by the time I got to the school gate as I'd thought I was when I left home, and I was always uncertain if anybody would be brave enough to play with me in the school yard before the morning bell. I may have been the teacher's pet, but my classmates were still wary of me before they'd have a few hours to get used to me in class. By recess, it was usually OK, and if it wasn't, I'd stroll around with the teacher. Mainly, it taught me how to stand alone.

In 1952 when General Eisenhower and Adlai Stevenson were running for president, I overheard talk in the house that the Republicans were terrible and would bring a lot of hardship, but almost all the children in my class wore I LIKE IKE buttons to show that their parents were voting for him and his running mate, Richard Nixon. Being for Stevenson set me apart.

I didn't know much about the Republicans except that I'd heard they'd have us selling apples on the street corner. My mother bought me a grey jacket after the election which she said was an Eisenhower jacket. It nipped in at the waist and was of corduroy. It was a catastrophe and nearly made my life miserable, because it didn't look a bit like anybody else's jacket at school. I had enough trouble without it. Eisenhower had been a general, so I guess it was based on some army jacket of his.

Life seemed unaffected after Ike had won. I didn't have to sell apples, and he didn't make us go to school on Saturday, which was the other rumour I'd heard. Things at school were different but it had nothing to do with politics. I was often singled out to do special things like deliver a folded message to the principal, pass out the milk or read out loud when visitors came into our classroom. This made my classmates like me better. So, when Miss Courtney asked us to take a partner to file out in pairs holding hands, which we did going to assembly, recess or in fire drill, I no longer needed to pretend that it didn't matter that nobody wanted to hold my hand. I had a couple of friends. Even walking into the school yard in the morning ceased to be a crisis in my school life.

Playing with these friends was easier when I spoke with the

tone and rhythm of their speech, which was slightly different from mine and much higher pitched. I imitated their manners, too, their giggles and walk and the way they cocked their heads. I don't think I did it consciously, it just happened. At close range, I could hear their drummer and marched to their beat. As soon as I got home, I'd automatically revert to the old me. I spoke the way I was spoken to, and my thinking and body language accommodated my speech.

It was the beginning of a pattern, because at six, I led two lives which required two separate personalities. It wasn't a game or an act, though, it was more like a function. I lived between two nations – one Melangian and one American – and I adjusted to each.

During my first Christmas season at John Wister school I participated in the annual carol-singing at Grumblethorpe. Grumblethorpe was a house four blocks from school at 5267 Germantown Avenue, built by John Wister in 1744. (The year Johann Würster emigrated from a town near Heidelberg, Germany, he was nineteen and broke. Johann became a successful wine importer, anglicized his name and built a large summer house in Germantown. The three-storey house was originally known as Wister's Big House but John's grandson named the house Grumblethorpe after an English manor he'd read about in a novel. It has been refurbished to look as it did when John Wister and his family lived there.)

We sang our carols in the big front room. The blinds were drawn, so that the flickering light from the candles and the smell of Christmas pine and evergreens had a strange awesome effect, especially on a kid who'd not long been free of 23rd Street. I'd never seen anything like it and was dumbstruck.

Even though it was grand, Grumblethorpe was marked by Quaker simplicity. After carolling, we were shown around it in our usual file, holding hands in two lines. Our freshly shined shoes pattering across the floorboards made the only sound. We dared not whisper or touch the four-poster bed or the grandfather clocks. The drop-leaf tables and wooden chairs were less of a temptation. It looked as if nobody had sat in the winged armchair by the fireplace or eaten at the refectory table. The pastel-coloured walls were so quiet we were scared to cough.

Before we left, a white-haired lady chatted to us and gave us each a mug of hot chocolate with a marshmallow floating on the top. Another, similar lady passed out home-made Christmas cookies. I had never had chocolate to drink before. I stood as still as I could and was very glad my mother had put my hair in two ponytails even though I still had that silly braid on top. Edna had starched my grey and white dress which had a separate pinafore. The stillness there had a profound effect on me.

We had to walk past Grumblethorpe to get to the Band Box Theater, which wasn't a theatre, it was a cinema. Dennis and Pam and I were allowed to go most Saturday afternoons. A few times I went with Dennis by myself and we'd sit in the back row and stuff ourselves with buttered popcorn, Jujy fruits and Neco wafers, which seemed more the purpose of going than the movie. I always felt safe when Dennis was with me, because apart from the fact that the bad boys liked him, he was bigger than most kids his age and looked like the sort of boy you shouldn't mess with. I don't recall that anyone ever did.

Dennis loved the movies and comic books, and after we got a record player, he used most of his allowance to buy records. One of his favourite TV shows was *Amos 'n Andy*, which my mother thought should have been taken off the air for depicting 'Negroes' as ignorant. My brother used to provoke her by imitating the actors as soon as the programme ended. Dennis would pull faces, roll his eyes and speak an exaggerated Melangian dialect. Finally we were all banned from watching the show, but we loved *Amos 'n Andy* so we would sneak and watch it anyway. He'd turn the volume down and I'd guard the door for him. The telly was in the back room on the second floor so it was easy to get away with this.

There were hardly any Melangians on TV other than the cast of *Amos 'n Andy* and boxers like Sugar Ray Robinson. Once Richard Boone, who played the main doctor in a weekly hospital series called *The Medic*, had to treat a little Melangian girl. We all screamed with shock when she came on the screen. We'd never seen one of us in a television drama. Even the most regular police series, *Dragnet*, didn't have one Melangian criminal. There was a character called Rochester on the Jack Benny show, but it was very rare to see us on TV unless singing and dancing.

Our first major media star came through on the news in 1953. Her name was Autherine Lucy. She was a young woman who wanted so much to be free to study at the college of her choice that she took on the whole city of Tuscaloosa, Alabama, and finally the whole goddamn United States government so that President Eisenhower had no choice but to send her an army. I don't know why there aren't statues of her. She was our very own Joan of Arc and to see her on the television screen facing an avalanche of rednecks was unforgettable. For weeks after her appearance, our radio and television seemed to be tuned to nothing but newscasts from the moment Edna, Thelma or Ikey came home from work. Melangian neighbours who normally only exchanged hellos had a lot to talk to each other about.

I was stunned to see the hundreds of agitators jeering and spitting and name-calling while Autherine faced them. She never looked as if she was in a hurry; when the camera panned across her face she seemed neither angry nor anxious. She had that look of patience someone has when waiting for a bus they know is coming.

A couple of times since, when I've been up against bewildering odds and felt fear creeping up on me or dared feel sorry for myself, I've only had to think of Autherine facing the mob to put things in proper perspective.

As far as I could see, there was nothing uncommon about Autherine except her courage. The fact that she looked like most other girls of her age that ambled around the reservation on a Saturday afternoon made her confrontation all the more shocking. It could have been any one of us standing in her shoes when what looked like the whole city of Tuscaloosa was determined to keep her from entering the doors of a school which our taxes helped to keep open.

While this compelling national school drama played out, I'd start each school day like millions of American children by standing at attention after the bell rang to salute the flag. Led by the teachers, I'd recite the pledge with the whole class just as I'd been doing since my first day at school. I could say it in my sleep:

I pledge allegiance to the flag
of the United States of America
and to the republic for which it stands,
one nation*, invisible,
with liberty and justice for all.

*The words 'under God' were added by act of Congress in 1954.

Then we'd sit down and a passage was read from the Bible. I don't know how old I was before I realized 'invisible' was supposed to be 'indivisible'.

To salute you placed your right hand on your heart, although I was never sure I'd found my heart. The pledge said things that I knew weren't true once I'd seen Autherine Lucy and heard all the talk at home about what rights we didn't have.

I hoped nobody at school would ask what I thought about the Autherine thing because I wasn't allowed to lie. The teacher usually asked our opinions about current events, but I could tell from the way nobody mentioned Autherine in class that it was something we could not talk about. Patriotism was running too high to challenge it. America was like God. People believed in it.

When I discovered there was no Santa Claus, I think I cried. Part of my hurt was being robbed of my favourite myth and the rest was realizing that I had believed with all my might in something that older people knew all along was fake. I remember being told that since younger kids still needed to believe in Santa, I wasn't to tell them he didn't exist. I became an accessory to promoting a continuing myth and assumed I was doing the littler kids a favour by letting them believe a bit longer.

The same applies after I realized we'd been pledging ourselves to a myth about America. Obviously nobody wanted to deal with the truth, so as a child of eight I became an accessory, never exposing the deception, which everybody needed to go on believing in.

5
MOUNT AIRY AND CHESTNUT HILL

John Wister school mysteriously caught fire one Sunday night when I was in the second half of second grade, and I never went back there. I was bused to another school for quite some time.

Gradually the rougher elements became the majority in Germantown. Crap-shooters monopolized a corner of the street where we had to walk past them to the neighbourhood store. Some of them used to make passes at Ikey and Thelma. My mother was unnerved and called them gangsters. Edna called them riffraff and dared them to lay their hands on her. I suppose they were jobless as they were always there, throwing dice, calling bets and making idle threats to each other. 'Gimme a double, sir.' 'Come on baby, come on.' 'A five and a four.' 'Double or nothin'.' 'Take yo' hands off the dice. I'll shoot yo' ass.' 'You jive-ass mothafucka.' We could hear them halfway up the block.

Late one afternoon when Ikey and I were coming home from Charlie Chernoff's grocery store, all of a sudden a couple of police cars swerved up to the corner. As the police spilled out on the sidewalk, there was a melee and a shot was fired. It was like something straight out of the movies and I was scared nearly to death by the guns going off. But no one was hurt and I never found out who fired.

After my father's medical tenure at Boston State Hospital, he came to visit with his youngest brother, Ernest, and I was more worried about the two of them walking around the neighbourhood than I was about Edna, Thelma and Ikey. My father was so gentle. His soft voice always made me feel he needed protecting, whereas I imagined only a fool would dare lay hands on one of my mothers, who each had a wild temper.

The summer Blair and Ernest came to visit us in Germantown is the summer I remember there best. To sit next to him or pass him on the stairs was nearly too exciting. This was less because I had missed my father than because men rarely crossed our doorstep. Aside from the insurance broker who made a regular Friday collection of my grandmother's insurance premium, a couple of doctors making house calls when we were too sick to go to their surgeries, and a friend of Thelma's who took us on a family outing once to Bear Mountain, I can't remember men coming to our house. In those days respectable women didn't receive callers as they would today. In the 1940s and 1950s when I was growing up, the social and sexual role of women was entirely different. There was no parade of 'uncles' trooping through. The only uncles I had were blood relations like Henry, and he only made one whirlwind visit to see us after the Korean War ended before he moved to California.

Both Blair and Ernest had marked Bostonian accents. A Bostonian accent in the fifties was equivalent in American to speaking the Queen's English in England. It held a class distinction as much as anything else. For some reason a Bostonian accent implied that you were educated, cultured and well bred.

Blair didn't act as if he was at all impressed with himself, though. He made jokes which I didn't understand but I laughed all the same, following him about like our puppy followed me. When he arrived he'd brought us each a Timex watch and a pair of turquoise slippers with bronco riders printed on them. He might just as well have given me diamonds.

He had a big grey Studebaker parked in front of the house behind our grey 1950 Chevrolet. I hated to see him go outside the front gate, because I thought it was dangerous and couldn't conceive that somebody who never raised his voice could deal with danger. He'd been in the war, but fighting with guns I didn't imagine had anything to do with ferocious street combat.

I adored my uncle Ernest and thought he looked like Louis Jourdan, whom I'd seen in a movie at the Band Box. My father had never brought him before. Ernest was young and would scramble about on the floor, demonstrating some of his war skirmishes, showing how he pulled out his trusty sword when the Japanese attacked. I never believed that they used swords in the Second World War but I didn't tell him. To look out from the kitchen window and see him lazing in the blue hammock near the fat heads of Edna's orange and yellow marigolds made me wish he would marry Thelma.

Blair and Ernest took us to Valley Forge so that we could see where George Washington engineered America's victory against King George's army. Then they rushed back to their studies. Blair was already specializing in psychiatry. Ernest still had to pass his Massachusetts bar exam to qualify as a lawyer. I couldn't imagine what it would have been like to have a father living in the house all the time.

By Blair's next visit, we had moved to Mount Airy, which is the district beyond Germantown Avenue. In the late eighteenth century it originally attracted wealthy families who built country seats there, like Upsala, owned by the Johnson family descended from a German, Dirk Jensen, one of the original Krefelders who settled in the district. Like Cliveden House opposite Upsala, these local landmarks were always there to recall the past, those early European settlers and their struggle for freedom. The old buildings looked odd in a neighbourhood of 1930s terraced houses.

Cliveden House at 6401 Germantown Avenue was built between 1763 and 1767 and was turned into a fortress in 1777 during the Battle of Germantown when British soldiers used it to stave off George Washington's advancing troops.

I walked around the Cliveden House gardens when I went back in the summer of 1985. This English-looking estate occupies an entire city block of a Melangian urban community. The design of the façade of this mid-Georgian house was based on an engraving entitled 'A View of the Palace at Kew from the Lawn', published in London in the *Gentleman's Magazine and Historical Chronicle* in 1763.

Edna, Thelma and Ikey continued to work as they did throughout my childhood and Blair sent regular contributions. As much as anything, I think that they willed our progressive moves which always bettered our circumstances and improved the environments that we were growing up in. Like the move from 23rd Street to Germantown, the move to Mount Airy when I was nine made a great improvement in our lives. There were trees and tended hedges everywhere and the nearly new apartment complex across the road had the lawn mown regularly. My mother liked the neighbours and the neighbourhood. It was peaceful and the Melangian families thereabouts were as concerned about their children and their children's education as my mother was.

I was given more freedom when I started at John Story Jenks school in Chestnut Hill, and even though the Melangian children there could be counted on two hands, my classmates weren't reluctant to be friendly. There were many Quaker children in the school. That breath of freedom came in the nick of time, because the discipline imposed by my family in addition to the fear invoked on the streets had been inhibiting. Street life was pretty convincing proof that my mother was right – a dignified academic career was the safest future. At nine, I clung like my sister and brother to the notion that I would go into medicine like my father and therefore tried to maintain a high standard in my school work, whatever temptations I came across.

I remember the first time I was asked to write my father's occupation on a form at Jenks. I was confident that I could spell psychiatrist correctly. The teacher was more impressed with his occupation than my spelling and, like others then and since, she probably assumed that my home life reflected his professional rank. (In America, doctors make money. I was surprised when I came to London to discover that National Health doctors have the medical title but not the bank balance of their American counterpart.) I was a psychiatrist's daughter and this gave people the wrong idea about my family's income.

Times were visibly changing for Melangians in spite of the fact that Eisenhower made political apathy seem somehow respectable. The civil rights issue was like an eggshell that cracked after the Autherine Lucy case and segregation gradually continued to be challenged legally in the South and socially in the North, where habits rather than laws kept us isolated. Professional Melangian families moved to better neighbourhoods, although their white neighbours would make conspicuous attempts to keep them out and often moved out themselves if they failed.

As residential white areas got a few black families, the public school serving the vicinity reflected the neighbourhood's mix, and a school like Jenks would end up with ten or twenty Melangian children from upper-middle-class Melangian households. Even though Jenks was still a predominantly white school, I think it was relieved to have a token number of Melangian kids because this showed it to be participating in a developing mood among liberal Americans that it was time to be nice to 'Negroes'. People were getting more prosperous and more generous.

When I started at Jenks in the third grade, I made friends instantly with two little open-air girls who were top of the class and didn't mind my competition. They befriended me in the classroom and never pretended not to see me in the school yard. They dragged me along to their Brownie meetings and had me join their ballet class, though I didn't feel welcome there. They asked me to be part of their secret club, which was actually only the three of us. They were no less than best friends who invited me to their houses after school for tea, although they never came to mine. We did everything together except that I couldn't join them in their violin recitals. I never understood why they called their mothers 'Mummy' instead of 'Mommy'. I thought it was because they were Quakers. I tried to understand and imitate every nuance of their behaviour when I was with them. They spoke more precisely than my friends at Wister school. Soon I could talk exactly like them and I learned to find the humour in what they thought was funny, although it usually was corny.

Behind the surface of my polished manners of 'excuse me, please', 'I beg your pardon' and 'no, thank you' to virtually everything that was offered, there was a fanciful little girl who still knew the difference between a knife scar and a razor scar and was proud of knowing how to watch out for more than just the cars. But there was no need for my acquired street instinct at Jenks and no threats or fears lined the path to my house. The 23 trolley car picked me up from the corner of Southampton Avenue to cart me home in time for *The Mickey Mouse Club* and *Rin Tin Tin* on television.

Chestnut Hill was a solid white Anglo-Saxon Protestant community. The trees grew tall. The parks were beautiful. And the sun always seemed brighter there when I got off the trolley car. It was my neighbourhood during the school day.

Mount Airy didn't feel graced like Chestnut Hill and didn't have the village character of Germantown. The section we lived in near Mount Pleasant Avenue was very orderly with two-storey brick houses and canopied porches that displayed small flowerbeds and trimmed dark-green hedges. The big street-cleaning truck came once a week to spray the streets down. The neighbourhood looked well-tended but nondescript with block after block of these terraced houses, rather like certain areas of north London or north Manchester.

Occasionally, a kid pedalled down the sidewalk on a glossy two-wheeler bicycle or some toothless, brown-skinned, seven-year-old cowboys would bang-bang their way around a parked car. But there was never a baseball game played in the middle of the street and no one thought that opening a fire hydrant to let the water flood the street until the fire department came was a prodigious way to while away an evening. Dogs didn't dawdle unleased on the streets, and no fathead alley cats whined away the nights.

The number 23 trolley-car depot was a block beyond our house on the other side of the road, and when we first moved to Musgrave Street, you couldn't help noticing the rattle of the trolley cars on the track as they passed with their pole crackling against the overhead line. But this sound merely broke the silence. It didn't disturb the peace.

Our family nearly belonged. Pam was openly admired for her studious appearance when she rushed off early to school first thing, looking as if her mind was on algebra instead of boys. She'd be wearing her new glasses and clutching her briefcase, which was always stuffed and overflowing with books and homework. She'd started at the Philadelphia High School for Girls at 17th Street and Spring Garden, which admitted girls from throughout the city on the basis of outstanding academic achievement. Pam studied the bass violin, and on Saturday morning she and Dennis went to special art classes that were given to children selected from all over Philadelphia who had exceptional artistic talent. I was just as proud of them as Edna, Ikey and Thelma were.

Once Edna had started her new job, at a factory that made children's dresses, I was transformed from being starched and presentable to being 'turned out'. I'd like to claim that I wasn't made vain, merely extra confident in a wardrobe finer than anybody else's at school. Edna bought me each new model that came off the factory floor.

Ikey was in her element working at the local library as a librarian. She walked home through rain and snow and once through a hurricane with her arms full of books for us, which gave her a reason to write her own poems and read other people's, and I could get a reading of 'Invictus', 'Crossing the Bar' or 'The Ballad of Reading Gaol' any time I wanted. They were my favourites, though neither my mother nor I knew that 'gaol' was pronounced 'jail'.

Thelma remained our sweet unselfish aunt who cared about Ikey's children as though they were her own. She enhanced her good looks to the fullest each morning with a little help from Maybelline cake mascara, a trace of eyebrow pencil and rouge with a hint of dark-red lipstick to finish it all off. She and Ikey wore straight skirts with cinched belts and stilettos that you could hear click-click-clicking on the cobblestone street in front of our house as Thelma returned from work around 5.30 pm. It was no wonder that she and Ikey got an intolerable dose of whistles, especially during the summer months.

I was free to bang the screen door going and coming with a shout to name which neighbour I was rushing off to visit. My personality still changed between home and school. The two environments were separate but equal in my head and heart.

We were a strange family in some ways, compared to the people on television. Love was not a thing we discussed. Though we liked each other, we didn't call each other 'darling' and no one asked if you'd slept well when you stumbled down to the kitchen for a bowl of hominy grits or a fried egg. Sometimes we'd have a family pow-wow and decide that new resolutions were called for to make us practise at home on each other some of the good manners we exhibited outside. We could manage to adhere to the new rules for about a week, not raising our voices to each other, or speaking an unkind word, or leaping like Tarzan from the fourth stair into the living room.

There was a collection box to hold the penalty of a penny to be paid any time you used bad language or incorrect English or spoke dialect. It was always chock-full at the end of the week and went to the person who'd made the fewest faux-pas. My grandmother never played . . .

There was a certain amount of democracy in our house,

although hard and fast rules for the children like no cursing were never allowed to be broken. There was an assumption that we had as much right to an opinion and a vote in matters as the women. The word fair was used a lot, perhaps too much. It only confused me into thinking that life was going to be fair.

Television continued to be my teacher. Family sitcoms like *Ozzie and Harriet* and *Father Knows Best* not only kept me amused, they made me informed and aware of things that I was not exposed to through my own experience. For instance, women on the television were always crying, but I don't remember seeing my mother or grandmother cry through my childhood. For any upsets other than physical injuries, we were invariably told to 'save the tears'. It was almost a relief to fall down and skin a knee, because I could wail the house down without the least reproach.

One of the things that set us apart from other kids in the neighbourhood is that we weren't beaten. Even though people didn't yell out of the windows in Mount Airy or curse each other so that it could be heard by passers-by, we often overheard the parental threat of the strap or the belt and the screams and cries that resulted from such punishment, which my mother considered uncivilized and inhumane. We were never punished in this way and were thought lucky by kids who were. Edna would threaten us with the strap if we incensed her while my mother was out, but it fell on deaf ears, even if she stomped off as far as the back yard to pull a switch from the stinkwood tree.

We couldn't afford holidays, but I didn't feel that we were missing much, and at that time, family holidays weren't considered a necessity and planned with the feverish intensity that they are today. We had the odd day trip to Atlantic City or the Catskill Mountains, which broke the monotony. That we'd been somewhere and seen something was enough when school started and we had to write about our vacation. At Christmas we got enough presents to entertain us until a birthday brought some more. Most of the family's birthdays fell within a week of each other in the spring.

Apart from these minor deviations, we carried on like a lot of other families. We were just noisier. Mornings were absolute chaos. Any kitchen would be busy in the morning with a family of six, but when three of them are women, there's never enough space and our kitchen wasn't particularly large. The radio didn't blare as loudly as my grandmother claimed it did, but Dennis refused to switch it off so that Edna could think, and she refused to stop shouting about it so Ikey could think. There was always that beat in the background, for instance Bo Diddley singing 'Down Yonder, Down On The Farm' on the local Melangian station until it got switched to a station with Eddie Fisher or Tony Bennet crooning something above the din of the family rushing up and down the stairs trying to make their way to their separate lives. My mother developed the irritating habit of calling several wrong names before she hit upon the name of the person she really wanted to address. 'Pamala, I mean Dennis, I mean Marsha.' She did this so often that my aunt and grandmother caught the habit of it, too.

Fits and fights over whose turn it was in the only bathroom filtered downstairs into the kitchen through a crack in the floorboards to mix with the snitch of swearing that came with a last-minute touch-up with the straightening comb as one of the women singed her scalp in the rush of confusion.

'Was the cat fed?' 'Have you got your milk money?' 'Who took my last piece of chewing gum?' 'Put your front-door key in your pocket . . .' I can't think how anybody arrived in one piece ready to start the day. Luckily the long journey to school on the trolley had a calming effect.

There was nothing that I thought I needed that I didn't have except an atomic-bomb shelter stocked with neat little shelves of canned goods and folded army blankets and candles and a flashlight. Lots of people had converted their basements like this in case the Russians bombed us, a threat often implied in the *Junior Scholastic* and the *Weekly Reader* which we got at school. Instead, our basement was like an overstuffed attic with that oval portrait of my grandmother always in the way. Things were put down there when they had no other home and part of it was used as a laundry room. It was doubtful that it would ever become a bomb shelter, or even get a facelift of knotty pine walls and be called a den.

This is where my mother was one day, sorting out the coloureds from the whites to do a wash load, when I was called down to speak with her.

Ikey was standing on the platform near the washing machine when I bounded down the staircase. It was one of those old-fashioned washing machines that look a bit like a white pot-bellied stove with a separate wringer attached on top. No one ever went down to the basement unless they were doing the wash, and this made it the only place in the house you could be guaranteed a bit of privacy. It was lit by a bare bulb which hung down from the ceiling and cast spooky shadows.

When Ikey told me that Blair had been killed early that morning in a car accident, she wasn't crying. She was just piling the clothes into the washing machine. (I've detested doing laundry ever since.) Because she didn't really look up at me, I could tell that it was one of those times when I wasn't allowed to ask questions. If I blinked fast I could always keep back the tears so I tried that while I stood by the bottom stair waiting to be told what to do.

My father had never written to me. I couldn't rush upstairs to look at his handwriting.

There was no school that day because of a teachers' meeting, so Dennis and I went to the little green next to the library. It wasn't raining. The leaves had fallen.

Later that afternoon I was allowed to go to a friend's house. She had a Persian cat that had its own birth certificate, which I thought was the most wonderfully chic thing I'd ever heard of. My friend's mother must have found it very disarming when I looked up at her and said that my father had died that day. I didn't make a big deal of it, because I didn't want any sympathy. I just wanted to tell somebody.

No flowers arrived. And Blair wasn't mentioned again until my mother had to go to Boston for the funeral.

The mornings came and went with nothing to mark the change. This was something else that I was to learn not to talk about. I got so good at keeping secrets that I eventually learned to keep them from myself.

Music rescued me from secrets and silences just around that period. My mother had taken me to see Johnnie Ray once when I was about five. He was performing in a cinema with the curtains drawn across the silver screen so that it could double as a live theatre. He was supported by the Four Aces or the Diamonds – one of those groups with a name like a suit of cards. They came on before the main attraction wearing blue iridescent suits and sang. Three of them gathered around one microphone singing harmonies to the melody and managed at the same time to snap their fingers, smile and do little dance steps in unison. The lead singer had his own microphone and spoke to us between the songs while one of the three in back clowned around a bit as part of the act. The other two just sang and I suppose they did that well enough or the audience wouldn't have clapped so much.

Ikey had told me before Johnnie Ray appeared that he was deaf, so I felt very sorry for him when he came out with his hearing aid in his ear and sat down at the black baby grand piano. Our seats were in the balcony. It was dark everywhere except on the stage and we could see him perfectly, singing and swaying back and forth on his stool as he played the piano.

His blond hair was swept back and parted. Only one lock in the front moved, however much he threw himself around as he sang 'The Little White Cloud That Cried'. A few women sitting near us were crying and so was Johnnie. I imagined he was crying because he was deaf, which did seem very sad to me, but I didn't know what on earth those women were crying about.

The Uptown theatre in Philadelphia was rather famous for showcasing better-known Melangian performers. My mother said it was too dangerous to go there. Fights sometimes broke out in the audience, and on a few occasions gangs had scuffles outside after a show. So I didn't go to any more concerts, but when people like Eddie Fisher, Dean Martin or Sammy Davis Jr sang on the radio, I imagined them appearing on a darkened stage just like Johnnie Ray.

I had to rely on radio, television and my brother's collection of records for my music. When we moved to Mount Airy, it was not yet the kind of neighbourhood where people sang on the street corners, although we could often get within listening distance of the landlady's Holy Roller meeting, as a few spirituals filtered out to the street.

Music seeped in and around me at home for as long as I can remember and this may have been the initial reason for my passion for it, but I can say without doubt that it was 'seeing' music that eventually made it stick to me like cement glue.

A stocky, rather ordinary man with slick dark hair named Bob Horn hosted the 3 pm music show from our local TV station – *Bandstand*. He played the latest single record releases and talked to an invited group of guests after they had mimed to their record. He also introduced the teenage studio audience.

If I rushed home from school I could catch all but the first half-hour of *Bandstand*. Tearing out of my fourth-grade class as soon as the final bell rang, I'd nearly get myself run over by the cars on Germantown Avenue because I'd spotted my trolley coming and couldn't wait for the traffic lights to change.

Unfortunately, the programme time interfered with my friendship with the open-air girls and their after-school teas as well as my ballet practice at home to my scratchy 78 record of Chopin's Polonaise. Watching *Bandstand* made me want to practise the mambo and the bunny hop instead, because that was what the fourteen- to eighteen-year-old audience was doing. That, and the bop. I'd been dancing since the hucklebuck, but never with the frenzied fever to get it right. I suppose that having a teenage brother and sister introduced me to teenage tastes early, but it was music that whipped me into my premature adolescence.

I was still wearing braids when I started bopping about the dining room in front of the television imitating teen attitudes with my head filling with notions about 'earth angels', 'thrills on Blueberry Hill' and other fairy-tale romances nailed to a four-four beat. I felt I was missing a ponytail, bobby socks, a cardigan sweater worn backwards and a felt skirt with a curly-haired poodle on it wearing a diamond-studded collar. I also had to find a partner to dance with as Dennis refused and Pam would arrive home loaded with homework and disappear straight upstairs to study.

Five afternoons a week for at least an hour each day I was mesmerized by *Bandstand*. I gave my undivided attention to the vision and sound of what they were calling rock and roll, which sounded like a pokier version of the rhythm and blues I'd heard on jukeboxes on the reservation and on the Melangian radio station. I don't want to give the impression that I was getting lost in it, though. If anything, I found myself in the music, because somehow it satisfied all my secret needs.

Rock and roll's simple childlike passion poetry had various smudges of joy, pathos and sentimentality which I felt or was starting to feel but couldn't express. The lyrics were repetitive like the commercial jingles that regularly interrupted my favourite TV and radio shows. There was a throbbing rhythm which was sometimes almost menacing and had an element of the reservation about it. Melangian dialect was often used for the lyrics and Melangian groups like the Platters were as important to the music as white stars like Bill Haley and the Comets.

In the early days of *Bandstand*, Melangian teenagers used to participate. When the camera scanned the audience, which was invited to dance to each record that was played, the Melangian couples were by far the best dancers, doing the most intricate variations of spins, twirls and fancy footwork and never looking as if they'd just graduated from an Arthur Murray dance course.

As *Bandstand* was broadcast live from South Philadelphia, which was a rough part of the city that had more than its share of gangs, slums and delinquents, it attracted teenagers from that area, so the dancing audience didn't look like a contrived showcase for middle-class kids. They had something of 'the street' about them.

The show was off the air before Ikey, Thelma and Edna got in from work, and they didn't disapprove of my watching. My mother was only in her midthirties at the time, neither old enough nor old-fashioned enough to denounce rock and roll as a sinful or negative influence, which was a growing complaint about it among very conservative adults. She and Thelma liked the music in the house.

They were as enthralled as we kids were when Elvis Presley first appeared on *The Ed Sullivan Show* one Sunday night, gyrating like a rhythm-and-blues singer. When his bumping and grinding below the waist was banned from the screen on a subsequent show, it made a tremendous stink, turning his censored performance into real box-office and TV-rating appeal. It made people talk about him. I can't remember how many appearances he made on the show, but there were several at a time when Ed Sullivan had the most popular variety programme on nationwide television. The censorship made Elvis's appearances newsworthy. The papers were full of reports and I guess it was the first time that television and journalism married their interests to make a rock idol.

Edna was a bit distressed by the newspapers' claim that Elvis's style was original, because she said rightly that it was really the Melangian rhythm-and-blues singers' performing style. But she could have screamed about that until the cows came home and nobody would have taken a blind bit of notice. It was his white version of the form that made it provocative and caused white teenage girls to scream and want to pull out his hair and their own. Others imitated him and his style and helped his brand of rock and roll surpass teen-cult status to become a national phenomenon.

Bandstand was so influential to the promotion of this teen music phase that it was picked up by a big network and became a nationally broadcast television show. It was renamed *American Bandstand* and a young MC named Dick Clark replaced Bob Horn as the star presenter.

When the phase became a craze, Philadelphia was on the map again. *Bandstand* spotlighted a growing trend in America to recognize teenagers as a breed with their own style and culture, and the weekly allowance to be consumers. To say you were from Philadelphia in the mid-1950s was probably like saying that you were from Liverpool after the mid-1960s. The place name projected a certain teen-cult music status, not only because of *Bandstand*, but also because many of the popular teen idols like Frankie Avalon, Dion, Bobby Rydell, themselves teenagers, stepped out of Philadelphia city-centre high schools into the media frenzy building up in America about its teenagers.

Ten years after the Second World War, parents may have been relieved that they could afford and tolerate rock and roll, and regarded it as a minor cultural nuisance that was temporarily captivating their war babies. Even though I was a postwar baby, I was ready to be captured, too.

My passion for music and the culture that grew out of it was not my only interest. There were other elements of my life, like getting good grades at Jenks school, which held me back from becoming a wholehearted bobbysoxer. But I had no reluctance about putting my dolls and my roller skates in the basement to show that I wouldn't be playing with them any more. And I found new friends in the neigbourhood who wanted to master the latest dance steps as I did.

I was nearly delirious when I spotted my first adolescent pimple and had to buy my first tube of Clearasil, which was new on the market and being advertised on television and in teen magazines.

Wasn't there a whole generation going through it? I was just taking an early grab at the tail of pubescence. It pulled me into the pandemonium of teenage culture so fast that there wasn't a chance for me to wave goodbye to childhood before it disappeared over the horizon with some of my more agreeable traits in tow, such as wanting to please adults. As can be expected, my mother wasn't thrilled about my quick personality change. It made her nervous and angry to see me running up and down breathlessly while I chased the spirit of something that was invisible to her but galvanizing and hypnotic to me.

The teen cult was like the call of the wild. It beckoned me first through music. Rhythm and blues and rock and roll had an insidious penetration. Sometimes I'd hear a song that I couldn't get enough of from hearing it a few times on the radio, so I'd buy the record and listen to the same song over and over and over again. It manipulated me like a mantra with the lyrics about puppy love and such, accompanying a beat that excited me to the point that I was either transfixed or transported to another zone.

I had become so good and convincing at marching to other people's drummers that it was a shock to me and my family when music let me hear my own. I was a handful and couldn't be constrained any more by a harsh word or criticism of how I looked or behaved. I didn't want to look like a nice little girl and refused to wear clothes that didn't have a look of flair and independence. I would have teetered around in stilettos if only I could have got away with it.

First it was music, then it was clothes, then it was boys. Or first it was music, then it was love, then it was boys. I'm not sure. All I know is that while I was jumping up and down dancing in the mirror to the beat, not being in love just didn't seem good enough. I pulled my cinched belt tighter and waited. Falling in love with love came before falling in love with somebody.

It's a wonder that I kept my studies up, but I did. One day the school principal called my mother to find out why I was wearing lipstick to my seventh-grade class. This came as a bit of a shock to poor Ikey, who sent me to school looking as refined and dignified as possible. She never realized that on my way to catch the trolley car in the morning I slipped into a telephone booth en route and made a few subtle alterations. Like Superman, my persona was transformed by my get-up. I'd come out of the telephone booth with my skirt hitched up by a belt to a much shorter length, my hair swept to the side in a winsome braid, and at least two thick layers of Westmore's Oooh-La-La Orange on my lips. The iridescent lipstick cost 49 cents at Woolworth's. I kept it in my briefcase.

My whole demeanour changed under the 'Oooh-La-La' spell. I wanted to be noisy and boisterous and saw nothing appealing in being dignified. I didn't want to imitate open-air girls except in their occasional company. Instead I wanted to mimic the DJ on WDAS (the Melangian radio station), whose fast, hip monologues derived from the reservation dialect. The friends I made in the neighbourhood were happy to do the same thing and were impressed that I was good at it.

My musical preference reflected my love for music from the reservation and its dialect. I didn't want to sing along with Bing Crosby and Grace Kelly or 'The Yellow Rose of Texas'. I wanted to moon about to Frankie Lymon and the Teenagers, Little Anthony and the Imperials, and the Flamingoes. Anybody with that sound of a cappella singing that I used to love to hear on 23rd Street was for me.

Dennis thought that I looked and acted a bit ridiculous but he did enjoy my departure from childhood. We didn't have the same taste in music, unfortunately. Our allowances would have gone further if we'd wanted the same singles, but he was more into Little Richard, Chuck Berry and Fats Domino. They were all right but hardly made the kind of music that you could stand in a dark corner and do a slow stroll to, which was what I wanted to do.

I was a nightmare for my mother, and it was probably a shock as much as a relief that I qualified for entry into the Philadelphia High School for Girls when I was thirteen.

Pam was going to the University of California in Berkeley, where Uncle Henry lived, after her graduation from the Girls' High. Ikey took the day off to go to Pam's graduation, and took me. I hoped the fact that she graduated summa cum laude from the best school in the city made her trials in Germantown pale.

My sister and brother hadn't been infected by the music craze the way I was. With Pam in the all-city orchestra and Dennis going out for football and track, I guess they didn't have time. Dennis was going to Central, which was as scholastically competitive as Girls' High. There was hardly time to think about much other than studying, although I kept boys and music high on the list of priorities after I started there.

The Bivins family lived across the street. Mr Bivins was a detective in the downtown police force and his daughter Lynn was my best friend, along with Jean and Gloria Scott who lived a few blocks away. Lynn was a beanpole and although being tall and thin was not considered a plus on the reservation, where having big legs was the great physical attribute, Lynn was very popular with the boys. She had a younger sister, Patsy, who was born with Down's syndrome. When Lynn's mother went out, we were often expected to baby-sit for Patsy, who at eight couldn't converse or follow instructions. But she had the sweetest nature and was easier to mind than a baby as long as you didn't leave her on her own for a minute.

As soon as Mrs Bivins went out, boys were invited in and invariably there would be some necking in the kitchen beside the refrigerator, shielded from view in case someone walked in unexpectedly. Patsy would sit patiently waiting and watching. We were sure that she couldn't tell and she seemed a harmless enough voyeur. What we didn't bargain on was that the sight of two adolescents kissing and groping next to the refrigerator would make such a lasting impression that she tried to imitate us in the presence of Lynn's mother intermittently for months after. Mrs Bivins never quite figured out what Patsy was doing rubbing up next to the refrigerator.

Lynn, the two eldest Scott sisters and I never considered more than necking. We didn't even deign to talk about anything else.

There were four children in the Scott family and Mr and Mrs Scott both worked to keep them all fed. It was the girls' responsibility to take care of the house and even the youngest, Helen (who has since become one of the singers in the Three Degrees), was well trained to do the cleaning and cooking. The three girls and their younger brother Robert were all pretty, especially by Melangian standards, with their green-grey eyes, fair skin and tawny hair. Mrs Scott, whom they got their good looks from, suspected that boys would be endlessly banging on their door. What she didn't imagine was that we would go out looking for them while all our parents were out at work.

Ikey probably hoped that if she was lenient and patient, my new personality would disappear as mysteriously as it had appeared. She tolerated new habits like smoking cigarettes as long as I restricted them to the house. I'd enjoyed sneaking a smoke with friends but didn't find the experience half as gratifying when it came around to doing it at home.

I don't know if the girlfriends I entertained found as much resistance from their parents to our fast noisy talk as I did, but it was certainly easier for me to get on with the life I was making for myself before Ikey, Edna and Thelma got home from work.

When Edna lambasted me for thinking that I was a woman, she wasn't far off the mark. I'd put a wiggle in my walk and my head was full of love lust. My 'fast' ways were encouraged by my older friends but beneath the new, worldly exterior, my intentions were harmless. I didn't really want to do any more than a bit of necking under a red light bulb in a darkened room with some new heart-throb of mine from the local playground who, I'd decided, was the beginning and the end of my life . . . for a week or two. We girls loved sauntering by the nearby playground where the teenage boys were always sweating in the heat of a basketball game or lolling about at the edge of the court waiting for a chance to play. We pretended not to notice them as we drifted past slowly enough to be seen in a pair of short shorts or a tight skirt, hoping to attract the attention of our latest forecourt fantasy. (That priest who accused me of switching down the aisle at St Elizabeth's must have had a premonition.)

Suffice it to say that by the time I sat in front of the

television watching John F. Kennedy win the nomination to run as the Democratic candidate in the 1960 presidential election against Richard M. Nixon, I was a fully fledged teenager. I felt terribly sophisticated while I chomped chewing gum and smoked an Alpine mentholated cigarette and waited for the party returns.

Dennis was ready for college that summer and had been accepted at the University of California at Berkeley like Pam the year before. My mother decided that with both of them at college on the other coast, we needed to leave Philadelphia and move west. I was horrified by the thought of being wrenched from my beloved city. I didn't think I could cope without my favourite TV show and my favourite radio station.

Television, radio and the industry that manufactured teen culture had fashioned me far more than anything that was fed to me at school except the talk about freedom and equality, the principles of which I used as an argument against my mother's protests that I didn't have a right to do with my life as I wanted. After all, she said, wasn't my life her life too? I didn't think so.

She proved me wrong when she packed me onto a propeller plane and dragged me to the other side of America.

6
THE DREAM MACHINE

Although I didn't want to go to California, my imagination painted a vivid image for me of Oakland, the city we were moving to. I expected it to look like the unidentified towns which were the backcloth of the family situation comedies I regularly watched while I grew up 3000 miles away. They usually depicted a pretty suburb: a mini Beverly Hills, divided by neat front lawns on quiet tree-lined streets with the splash of a freshly painted ranch-style house with a garage that had a basketball net conveniently attached to an overhead wall so that the kids could play.

I wasn't an avid moviegoer, but I had enough beforehand knowledge of California to be wrong about it. In my head was the clichéd vision – blazing yellow sun, picturesque orange groves, palm trees against a blue sky. I could see a swimming pool and the languid masses of draped bodies slung across deck chairs as they browned like toast under the sun. An unspoken wealth supported the whole canvas.

California might just as well have been in another country. Our only connection to it was that each Christmas, Uncle Henry used to send Edna a voluptuous basket of fruit from California where he'd been living since he'd retired from the navy. The fruit was always a glamorous array of wrapped citrus with something exotic like a pineapple on top in coloured cellophane with a big bow around it. (Once a basket arrived with a dark green thing in it which I had never seen before. Edna claimed that she had in Florida, but I didn't believe her. I was sure she was just saying this to impress us and that the avocado pear wasn't a pear at all and was poison.)

The journey to San Francisco airport took about sixteen hours and we had to stop off once to refuel. At one point during the flight, the pilot told us to look at the Grand Canyon. I did so reluctantly. I'd never been on an airplane before, but I can't say that I appreciated my first experience, because I was too caught up in sombre remorse: I was sick from the ache of leaving friends behind and believed that the only reason destiny was pulling me westwards was to help Ikey interfere with a budding romance between me and an eighteen-year-old boy. It was July 1960 and I was not a bit happy about the prospect of a future in California.

That first afternoon we drove through Oakland was sunny – too sunny for my liking. A heat of light burned the sidewalk. There was no imposing residential monument of history to interest me and no orderly strips of red brick houses with dark-green hedges to match. In fact, brick must have been at a premium, because every house and building seemed to be made of stucco.

I'd only been out of the North once, when the Bivins family took me on a weekend jaunt to visit some of their relatives in North Carolina. The flat dullness of the small nameless Southern towns we drove through left me with the same depressed feeling that I had when I looked at Oakland for the first time.

There wasn't one lawn or ranch-style house to be seen as we drove down Grove Street. It looked like an architectural free-for-all. No building seemed planted in the sidewalk with solid old East Coast permanence. Instead the ticky-tacky greyish boxes with storm windows looked as if they'd been thrown on the pavement and designed with less imagination than my first Lego attempts.

More sky than I'd ever noticed before hung down. It was barely the palest blue and was dipped in dry heat. The air seemed no cleaner than the sidewalk.

I wanted to cry and probably would have if I'd thought that it would do any good. But the truth was that I was there to stay. I knew my grandmother had had the right idea when she ground her heels in and refused to join us for the move west. I longed to be back there with her, lounging around in big-city civilization.

I also felt Ikey's disappointment and could see it registering in the dull glaze of her eyes as she stared from the car window listening to her brother explain how she, Thelma, Pam and I could temporarily cope with a one-bedroom apartment above some shops at the corner of 55th and Grove. He wasn't quite right. It wasn't so temporary.

I was still living there when I started Oakland High School in September. My mother had used someone else's address to enrol me in a school located in a classier district than ours. Although the two buses I had to catch to get me there were tedious, I much preferred the early-morning punishment of the long bus journey to the alternative of going to the local high school, which was not only rough but had a lousy academic standard. I still had my sights on university. The neighbourhood surrounding Oakland High was straight out of television, and the trees and flowers around the campus made a pleasant view from the school window. The student body came from the local district.

I still didn't want to know about any of it. My heart was bound to Philadelphia and I lived from day to day throughout that first Californian summer just waiting for the postman to bring the letters that rarely came.

I used all my effort to remain uncommunicative when I enrolled at Oakland High. I assumed a foreign accent when I spoke and most of the time I refused to speak (keeping up the accent was quite difficult). I decided I was surrounded by hicksters and avoided any exchange with them. The accent was a mixture of French, Spanish and German, depending on my mood and inclination.

Of the 3000 pupils in the student body of my first year, only about twenty-five of us were Melangians. So however invisible I pretended to be, my colour as well as my being from the East Coast gave me a distinctly different look. (An Easterner was noticeable in those days before travel and the media started homogenizing the whole country.)

Ruth Pchelkin was about forty-five. She taught English and liked her job. I don't know whether she found me pathetic or ridiculous with my foreign accent but she never questioned me about it. She just assigned me to the remedial speech class at 8 am, which soon cured my impediment. Because I had to leave home before dawn to get there in time, after a few sessions I was eager to prove that I could speak English as well as anybody else.

Mrs Pchelkin was easy to look at while she waited for answers. She had bright blue speckly eyes that always seemed to pick up the light even when there was none to pick up. She was a handsome woman, too substantial in build and robust in her attitude to be called pretty. She wore suits with a whiff of feminine scarf around her neck and had a collection of practical walking shoes. Her dark greying hair was knotted in a heavy bun at the nape of her neck. At the front it fell into a soft wave at her temple, so it didn't look severe. If she bent down near you, you could smell the pat of powder on her face which took the ruddiness from her cheeks and which never caked in the smile creases at the sides of her eyes. She looked dry no matter how hot it was in the portable hut which was our excuse for a classroom. Mrs Pchelkin smiled a lot but I don't think I ever heard her laugh – not that she gave you the feeling she was holding it back. Perhaps it wasn't in her to go that far.

Most teachers forget that you're forced to look at them as well as listen to them, but Mrs Pchelkin didn't give the impression she ever did. Somehow she seemed ready for us when we came into her class and wasn't intimidated or irritated by our sophomorish wit or contrary opinion.

I wanted to read the books she asked us to read, not only because she proved that it was impractical to criticize a book unless you had read it, but simply because she asked. She encouraged us to write essays that didn't necessarily put our grammar in check but rather put our thoughts in order, and we dared tell her what we really thought without her acting as though she was paid to change our minds.

Mrs Pchelkin might have been the one who put it in my head to run for class president.

My foreign accent had taken a bunk by the time I stood up in front of the class of 900 to deliver a speech that Dennis had helped me write. He had helped a couple of his friends with speech awards by adding a bit of his humour. No doubt I won the election because I made everybody laugh, brazenly standing up there at the speech-giving assembly acting as if I wasn't nervous.

Being president that first half year made quite a difference to me. I didn't quite put away my dancing shoes, but had to be responsible and set an example in a school that took student politics to heart . . . freshmen cake sales, brunches, dances and sports. Some American high schools make a serious affair of that kind of student council activities. Oakland certainly did.

The civil rights issue had been building throughout the fifties. In the South Melangian protesters marched, had sit-ins, and demonstrated in the face of violence. Apart from the major confrontations, there were my own minor encounters. Once I was invited to a girlfriend's for dinner. Her elderly grandmother held the purse strings and was head of the household. She was from Texas. A big family argument ensued when I arrived and the grandmother stormed upstairs saying that she wouldn't have a nigger eating off her good china.

Nobody could pretend that America was not still divided by the same old rift. The issue that the Germantown Krefelders first protested over in 1688 was not yet resolved.

On 19 October 1960, a Southern Melangian leader, Martin Luther King, was arrested in Atlanta, Georgia, with fifty-two others for insisting on his rights to sit and eat at a lunch counter. He was sentenced to four months' hard labour. The senator from Massachusetts, John F. Kennedy, who was also the Democratic nominee for president, negotiated through his brother Robert for King's release with the understanding that such a move would ensure him of the Melangian vote in the South, particularly where Melangian voting rights were still not taken for granted. It seemed reasonable to assume when Kennedy won the election a few weeks later by 120,000 votes, a margin of only 0.2 per cent of the population, that Dr King's endorsement had been instrumental in putting him in the White House.

America didn't regret it. Kennedy introduced a style that was more important than his politics. Art and intellect had a place in his White House. He assigned government posts to Melangians when he spoke of equality. His wife was seen as his equal and they both made humanitarianism seem as essential as cornflakes.

I adjusted quickly to California. It wasn't difficult to be a human being there during Kennedy's reign because, as Americans started to imitate him and his wife Jackie, being 'Negro' didn't cause regular racist confrontations. Racism became less acceptable and was opened to political discussion. I began to realize how politics affected daily life.

My diddybopper days were over. While I had a seething passion for music and dancing, Californian teenagers were more into beach parties and surfing. I still managed to divide my life between WASPish alliances and Melangian ones, and was greatly assisted by the telephone in developing a few clandestine affairs. Whites and Negroes didn't date then. Boys at school weren't brave enough to ask me out, but they called me every night on the telephone, and discussing homework was their acceptable excuse. I didn't appear to have a boyfriend all through high school, but at night my phone would always ring and it would be some blue-eyed boy wanting to discuss physics.

I was caught up in the business of high-school life and hardly ever watched television any more. I loved 'A Letter from Tina', which was Ike and Tina Turner's first hit, and doing the Slauson shuffle, a dance worth sweating over. I enjoyed bouncing around at an all-girl slumber party and screeching in the car on Saturday night at the drive-in movie. I went to varsity games or the lunchtime dances organized by Ben Fong Torres, our social secretary (who went on to become associate editor of *Rolling Stone*). I no longer carried that burden of deception about justice and equality that I'd felt since the days of Autherine Lucy, to make my white friends and classmates feel comfortable.

There was a sweet girl at school named Susie. She was immediately friendly during my first semester at Oakland and it was impossible not to like her a lot. We stayed good friends throughout my high-school years. Susie was a chirpy, all-American girl from one of those soundly middle-class families who are so ideal they cease to be ordinary. Her father was a doctor and her mother most likely made attending civic groups an occupation. Susie and her older sister were effervescent but hard-working cheerleader types and deserved to be liked and admired in spite of their sugary niceness. They were devoted to each other and looked alike. I never got invited to their house, but I guessed there was home-made jam in the refrigerator and a cocker spaniel that was trained not to beg at the dinner table. The family seemed straight out of *Life* magazine.

Susie had to stay at school late sometimes for cheerleader rehearsals. It must have been one of these nights in the middle of a school week that she was dropped off and walked into the house alone to find her mother and sister who'd both been bloodily murdered by some madman that tied them up first. I'll spare you the details.

I can't remember if a school friend phoned to tell me about it that same night or if I read about the tragedy the next morning in the newspaper, but like most of the student body, I was in a state of shock.

Susie had to spend the next few nights at the home of a girl in our class but she only missed a few days from school. Her eyes were red-rimmed sometimes, but she tried to smile at people whose curiosity made them stare. Susie looked a lot like Jackie Kennedy, and she carried off her mourning with similar dignity.

I was sitting in my French class on 22 November 1963 when the news came over the Tannoy above it that our president had been shot. There was a momentary freeze before the room buzzed with whispers and some girls started crying. Boys didn't cry then, it wasn't masculine.

The news came over the tannoy at the end of our school day and I took the long bus ride home alone. I turned on the TV to get the up-to-the-minute report.

Our president was murdered. Ikey hadn't come in from work, and I didn't know what to do with myself. All that had happened during his thousand days in office raced around in my head as TV newsreels took us back through his short career. His incumbency and the term of his presidency not only marked my high-school years but my transition from East Coast adolescent to West Coast teenager.

Kennedy had introduced the 24th Amendment which wiped out the poll tax that kept Melangians from voting in the South. And he had pushed the power button that sent 200 US marshals to Oxford, Mississippi, to help a Melangian boy named James Meredith register at the all-white state university. It seemed incredible at the time that two people were killed and 200 injured so that one human being could assume his rights to sit in the same classroom with others. The momentum had been building up for three years to the summer of 1963 when 200,000 protesters marched on Washington for equal rights. We felt the wind of change.

I hadn't been able to mourn my father's death or my distress when shortly before Kennedy was murdered I'd overheard a conversation about Blair's suicide. Suicide. The why and how weren't to be discussed. I shouldn't have been listening was all I was told. My mother and I weren't getting along well enough to talk about my father and what made him end his own life. So I buried the fact and never expected answers or got any. Seven years later, tears couldn't change any of it. But I still shed some, and those I hadn't shed for Blair were there for Kennedy.

7
EVERYTHING'S NOT EVERYTHING

I found out before I graduated from Oakland that I'd got into the University of California. My grade point average had remained high and I did well on my college boards, so it was no surprise that I was accepted. Although it was supposed to be a good school and had an excellent teaching staff, it was too close to home for me, so I wasn't thrilled.

Our family remained divided after the move west. The six of us never lived under the same roof again. Dennis and Thelma stayed in Oakland after Ikey and I took a flat in Berkeley. Pam had her private rebellion and quit Berkeley to make a life for herself in San Francisco. Because of an illness and no doubt a touch of loneliness, Edna had given in and moved to California in 1961. She was living with my Uncle Henry and his wife Margaret.

I'd taken a little job towards the end of my senior year at high school as a waitress in a late-night coffee bar in Oakland, called the Egg Shop and Apple Press, which presented poetry readings and unknown local folk singers. I found out about it through two sisters, friends from my school, who occasionally did a little folk turn there. I didn't make a lot on tips because it didn't seat very many people. There were just a cluster of small round tables in a darkened basement with candles lighting each. It was never packed but never embarrassingly empty.

I can't think what possessed me to ask if I could read poetry there, but I had the audacity and it was agreed.

In those days North Beach in San Francisco had a high tourist profile. Carole Doda was dancing topless with her newfangled silicone breasts, Laurence Ferlinghetti's bookshop was a well-known hang-out for 'beat' poets and beatniks, and there were clubs where live jazz was played. It was generally considered a hub of alternative culture. While I was still at high school I went there a few times, but I hadn't read *On the Road*, didn't know who Jack Kerouac and Dean Moriarty were and didn't much care.

A beatnik could not have thrived in our rah-rah high-school atmosphere with kids rushing enthusiastically to varsity football games. You didn't see anybody at Oakland High walking around in handmade leather sandals, sloppy over-sized sweaters, and long lank hair which formed the beats' unisex uniform. (The maijuana that was found growing under a pine tree on our school's front lawn had nothing to do with the beats' social rebellion as far as I knew, and I wasn't much interested. I guess it was dug up and disposed of. But nobody was arrested.) Oakland was not the town for beatniks at all. You had to drive to Berkeley or San Francisco to see them.

Dennis introduced me to some of his friends at Berkeley who were three or four years older than I was, with their own apartment near campus. I wanted the same freedom. While my high-school friends worried about what they would wear to the senior prom, I was secretly looking for an apartment to share and summer work to pay for it.

Before graduation, I paid my first month's rent to share a spacious apartment on the north side of the Berkeley campus with two college girls. I'd hardly got my cap and gown off before I said goodbye to Ikey. Independence was mine.

No sooner had I moved into the apartment than one of those friends of Dennis's loaned me a Vespa motor scooter for the summer to help me get back and forth to the Bell Telephone Company where I had landed a job operating the IBM billing machine on a night shift.

I started doing the odd poetry reading at the Egg Shop and Apple Press. I wanted to look the part of somebody who reads poetry to a bongo beat, so I only wore black and got Edna to make a poncho from a big square of Mexcan fabric, and ordered a pair of handmade sandals. I bought dangly hand-made earrings and wore my hair hanging as straight as I could get it with the help of some chemical hair-straightener. None of my friends at Oakland High would have recognized me.

I was preparing for something, but exactly what wasn't clear, until one balmy night I was speeding home on my motor scooter. While I waited for a set of traffic lights to change, two big motorcycles pulled up beside me. Since they weren't

Harley Davidsons and the two guys and their girl passengers didn't look like Hell's Angels (who already had a bad reputation in northern California), I returned their greetings. But it wasn't really like me to accept their invitation to follow them to a party. I managed to trail behind them for a couple of miles to a coffee shop called the Cabale Creamery on San Pablo Avenue in Berkeley, which made the Egg Shop seem like a synthetic suburban version of the real beats' hang-out in San Francisco. When I got there I feigned nonchalance but stayed close to the door.

There was hardly any light and it took some time for my eyes to adjust, so I could see that the dark corners of the hot dingy room were empty. The leftover cigarette smoke suggested it had been full. Somebody played a kazoo on a stage next to the bar. The place was anything but salubrious. I didn't want to stay and was figuring out an excuse to leave when I was introduced to the two owners, a small Melangian man named Carrol Perry and his tall blond partner, Howard Ziehm. The lights came on and Carrol said that after he had counted what was in the till, we should all go to a party.

Though I played the part, I knew I was out of my depth as soon as we arrived. I saw a cigarette being passed round which I was sure was a reefer. I'd seen one in a documentary about heroin and marijuana they'd shown us at school. I knew that a thin hand-rolled cigarette that left a sweet smell of incense was probably marijuana. I imagined I'd pass out if I had a puff as I'd seen in the documentary, so I managed to move on before it was my turn for a smoke and drifted around the small apartment where the party was held, nursing one after another of my Kent cigarettes. It was immediately apparent that the less said was best. My imitation of their 'cool', 'way out', 'too much' and 'like' easily rolled off my tongue by six in the morning when the party ended. This beat crowd that adopted me that night were mostly sophomores and juniors at Berkeley who lived off their well-to-do families but endlessly complained about them. Three or four were fully fledged junkies whom I tried to avoid, because they were drowsy types always looking for a loan. I needed my money for rent and was saving as much as possible so that I could move to the other side of the Berkeley campus where my new-found friends lived. The south side of campus was near

Telegraph Avenue, which was the heart of Berkeley street life.

The wild thing in me was emerging once again, and this time it wasn't courting the beat of rock and roll and rhythm and blues. I was excited by the left-wing ideas about society and politics that my new companions 'hipped' me to. As far as music was concerned, their musical tastes and mine remained completely separate, so mine got starved. I didn't have a taste for folk music at all and couldn't fake one. Sometimes a few old blues singers performed at the Cabale Creamery, as well as a Melangian group called the Chambers Brothers, real brothers who sang and accompanied themselves. Their blues was always a divine relief to my ears after an overdose of Bob Dylan, Phil Ochs and Joan Baez.

I knew that when the fall semester started at Berkeley I would have to trade these social companions in because they had the makings of students who were not likely to take studying seriously. All the while I ran around with them that summer I tried to remember that I was Melangian and they weren't, which made our future prospects very different. I liked the masquerade, but I protected myself from illusions. Civil-rights skirmishes regularly took place in the South, reminding me that all Americans were still not treated equally. And it wasn't paranoia but reality that indicated to me that our job opportunities were going to be unequal, too.

I'd started on the pill at the beginning of that summer of 1964. I dressed myself up, called myself Mrs and strolled into a makeshift family-planning test centre in Oakland. The pill was quite a new thing, and although I had no immediate intention to give up my virginity, having protection was practical in case the spirit hit me to do more than I was doing, which was nothing. Yet. The guys at the Cabale Creamery were always trying to goad me out of my sexual inactivity as it was not modern.

When the fall semester started I had moved into an apartment on Dwight Way with another student, Ellen Calvin. Her father, Melvin Calvin, was a Nobel Prize winner in physics and a professer at the university, so I imagined she'd be serious, which would help me to be. To pay my rent, a friend of Dennis's gave me a job at the school library, and it seemed that I had organized my life well enough to deal with the undergraduate year ahead.

I was saving drugs for Saturday nights and my only daily vice was lunching too long on the Terrace, which was the campus cafeteria, or dining too late at the Forum, a new coffee shop on Telegraph Avenue.

Once again I was stuck with a high profile on campus as there were about 120 Melangians in the Berkeley student body of 32,000. (I'm not including the African students because they were totally a world apart.) My race was an important factor at the time, because the Berkeley campus was politically alert and the student and faculty community was particularly intelligent and earnest about social conditions in America. The civil rights movement caused some people to make a special effort to be friendly to Melangians to compensate us for some of the injustices. White Americans like Andrew Goodman and Michael Schweener joined the Student Nonviolent Coordinating Committee (SNCC) or the Congress of Racial Equality (CORE), and picketed and protested in the North and South against racism. That summer Goodman and Schweener were brutally murdered together with James Chaney, a Melangian. They had all been working on registering Melangian voters in Mississippi.

It was a rare period in America. Political apathy was considered mindless and repugnant. There was an enthusiasm about committing yourself to what you believed should be the order of things. Maybe this seed was planted after the Second World War and grew as people gradually admitted that political apathy helped exterminate 6 million Jews. Certainly a lot of my activist friends on campus were Jewish. Or maybe the shocking atrocities connected with the civil rights movement made apathy unacceptable.

It was in this politically committed atmosphere that our campus got caught up in a conflict that became a major crisis and set a precedent for a spate of student protests around the country.

During the 1964 fall semester at Berkeley a ban was put on the student privilege for campus political groups to offer up their pamphlets and dialogue from tables lined up by Sather Gate, one of the main thoroughfares on campus. The ban was challenged and a police car drove on campus to arrest one student. Police were not popular and the idea that a student was being arrested for ignoring a ruling that some claimed encroached on their freedom of speech incensed students who probably didn't care one way or another about the ban.

They sat down in front of the police car to prevent it taking the arrested student off the campus. In a show of student solidarity, others joined, until about 3000 students were sitting in front of and around the car over a 72-hour period. The newspapers called it a sit-in, which associated it to other respected nonviolent protests taking place in the country and in the South particularly. The Free Speech Movement grew out of this.

I was on my way to my work shift at the library and like others was angry that a student was being arrested for opposing a regulation that justified no more than an administrative reprimand. We 'arrested' the police car with a student and two policemen inside. It couldn't move for three days as we sat there, slept there, sang and chanted, and listened to speeches delivered by politicos who addressed us over a loud speaker as they stood on top of the police car.

One student speaker stood out from the rest. His name was Mario Savio, a maths student. He was articulate and had the capacity to keep us rallied and yet keep us calm, which was no mean feat considering the pool of energy that we embodied. In association with other student leaders, he negotiated on the arrested student's behalf between the school administrators and the police, and was tireless in resolving what threatened to become an ugly confrontation between police and students. Fire hoses were poised and ready to be turned on us when a temporary truce was finally called that meant we could all go home.

We sat there for three days listening to speaker after speaker with our eyes cast up like hungry children. There were few dark-skinned faces in the crowd. Certainly mine must have stood out from the canvas of all those white ones. I wasn't more than a few deep from the front of the car and when it was suddenly over, Mario gestured to me to wait. He walked straight towards me while the throng of students from the sit-in dispersed. People were stretching and bending and dusting off the stiffness from positions they'd been in for so long.

Mario's voice was very soft when it wasn't commanding and his shyness triggered a slight stutter. Our eyes made a timid embrace. There was nothing bold in his manner and whatever commitment and aplomb that gave him the right to captain the Free Speech Movement had disappeared.

I liked his wanting me, although I wasn't sure why he did. He approached me almost apologetically with his head bowed and shoulders hunched under a tweed jacket. I made every gesture slowly so I wouldn't frighten him. There's an ache and a tension that ooze from the fear of a rebuff. I touched the cuff of his jacket and brushed his hand – not by accident.

It was hard to believe that he was Italian. His skin was pallid and his frizzy hair the palest tan. He stood more than a head taller than I and was boldly built but none of it was muscular. His strength was in the bank of ideas stashed in his head. I knew that he wouldn't lose the piece of paper with my address that he shoved in his pocket. But I didn't know when to expect him.

He was Catholic and I felt his guilt torturing him when he turned up at my apartment. It added a shrill note to each glance and embrace.

There was something unspoken between us that was understood from the first. We both knew his private passion shouldn't interfere with what he had to do. He had a serious media profile that had to stay unblemished for the sake of FSM. The slightest departure from a straight, narrow path could be misused to damage him and the work he had to do for the movement. He was older than me. I was a freshman, a spade chick.

I was good at keeping secrets. So was my flatmate, Ellen Calvin. She was a conscientious sophomore who carried herself like a ballerina and swept her long wavy hair into a tight bun at the back. Our ground-floor apartment on Dwight Way was a couple of blocks from Telegraph Avenue, the main street that led to the busy Sather Gate entrance to the campus.

We divided the flat so that Ellen had a large bedroom and a small kitchen. I had a living room, and a small separate bedroom. My bedroom was once a sun porch. We lived privately in our separate quarters, and shared a bath. By student standards, it was a luxurious space. Ellen didn't know about Mario's first visit. I longed to tell her that in the middle of our fumbling embrace I heard someone playing a harmonica. At first it was faint. As it got louder, I realized that a thin, curly-haired English major named David who was a folk-music fanatic was serenading me from outside the sun porch. Telling him to go away wasn't effective, and he'd brought a friend. Mario was too well mannered to ask what the hell was going on. I tried to ignore David's harmonica playing. When he climbed the tree next to the sun porch, I had to beg him to leave.

Very early one morning during the following week, Ellen found Mario asleep in the front doorway of our apartment. She was too discreet to ask why. I didn't know myself. He had turned up in the middle of the night, afraid to ring the bell. He was painfully shy when he wasn't talking to a group or a crowd.

Mario started my addiction to men who have the capacity to stand alone and roar and claw like tigers but who are also brave enough to expose themselves privately as doves. He also introduced me to the delicate extra buzz that a secret affair gives me.

I was infatuated with him. At the time, I thought I was in love. It never crossed my mind that I may have been one of many girls. When he stopped coming around, I stopped thinking straight and didn't want to be in Berkeley or within a whisper of the Free Speech Movement, which galloped along apace. I took a plane to New York, attempting to leave behind whatever destructive mental paralysis I was in the grip of, and I was on the East Coast when the movement's second confrontation with the administration ended in massive student arrests.

Running away to New York seemed romantic but it turned out to be scary. I had very little money, knew no one, and arrived in the dead of winter when people were generally in a bad mood because of the snow. Carrying my heavy army duffel bag and with a paperback called *The Journals of Albion Moonlight* peeking out of my coat pocket, I traipsed the streets of the East and West Village looking for a job that I never found and going through money like water. The shabbiest hotel was expensive and every Tom, Dick and Harry that offered a crummy blanket and a space on their floor wanted more favours than I believed they had a right to – pill or no pill.

New York was not Berkeley, and student travellers weren't greeted with a spliff and a smile. I was out of my depth strolling around the Bowery gaping like a tourist. The only way that I could figure out how to avoid the frost and the string of pushy advances I seemed to invite from some of the vacuous boys who hung around Greenwich Village was to move in with a Californian girl I happened to meet near Washington Square.

She turned out to be a friend of a Berkeley friend. I figured she was 'cool', but she had an unsavoury habit of enticing men into the flat and checking through their pockets and valuables. I was sure one of these guys was bound to come back to the apartment and mistake me for her or imagine that I had something to do with it, so I moved out and decided to try Boston, which was less seedy. I thought I'd find a waitressing job in one of the cafés along Charles Street.

There was a student connection in those days between Berkeley and Cambridge, Massachusetts, and I hoped to stumble on someone I knew from Berkeley. Some of the people I used to hang out with at the Cabale Creamery came from Cambridge. And I hoped I could find my father's brother, whom I hadn't seen since that summer on Ashmead Street in Germantown.

I felt lost but wouldn't damn myself by owning up to it. My heart was still in Berkeley and I knew I would have to go back. I was only away for six weeks when my money started to run out and my family was hedging me back to school. No one had a great deal of influence though, because I had been living away from home and earning my own rent and spending money since I left Oakland High.

I came very close to having a couple of major scrapes with men in Boston. I wasn't a mild, malleable girl who could be persuaded into one-night flings, but I must have looked that way sitting bored and alone in coffee bars listening to folk singers banging away on an acoustic guitar and singing their protest songs. My experiences with Berkeley activists had led me to believe that boys took you back to their apartment to sit up all night smoking joints and arguing about politics. But the guys I met in New York and Boston figured a girl bumming about on her own was to be had. Enlightened girls went on the pill, and it was assumed they'd make use of its protection.

The change slipped up on us in the mid-1960s. The availability of the pill didn't just cut down on unwanted pregnancy, it made sex before marriage acceptable until it got to a point where casual sex was an evening's entertainment. There was a dicey period when it was hard to decide what to do. It seemed that the whole moral code of sexual abstinence before marriage was just a form of birth control.

I was relieved to get back to Berkeley where sex wasn't an issue, it was a fact of campus life.

I took an English course taught by the English poet Thom Gunn. He came to class on a motorcycle, wearing a black leather jacket and looking like a graduate student. He made you want never to miss an English class, but he also made full concentration difficult.

I was determined not to let any distractions get in the way of my studies. Many of my friends who had been arrested during the second Free Speech Movement uprising were also making every effort to keep their heads down.

My only thrills were music and drugs. Amphetamines were illegal but available and students relied on them around exam time to cram. We were so close to Mexico that pot was neither difficult to find nor expensive to buy. It was sold in little matchboxes and was so cleaned of seeds that it looked like catnip. Peyote was about, too, but acid was the supreme hallucinogen, reserved for special occasions. People were serious about taking acid – the circumstances and purpose of the trip were important. Scholars like Richard Alpert and Timothy Leary gave it their blessings.

Psychedelia was born out of artists' impressions of hallucinogenic images. To be weird was to be wonderful. Mysterious and quixotic behaviour was not only acceptable, I knew people who worked hard at it. The label 'hippie' hadn't been coined yet, but 'beatnik' was wearing thin.

Middle America resisted Berkeley's alternative culture and social rebellions and laws still resisted civil rights for everybody. Peace protesters of the fifties and early sixties, like Martin Luther King, were accused of compromise by a growing number of angry young Melangian voices that had probably been soft-spoken until they realized they would never be heard. I had first met Huey Newton at the flat at 55th and Grove. He came visiting with a friend of Dennis's. Huey Newton showed no sign of anger or militancy in 1963. I remember him as being stolid and quiet and rather beautiful. I could hardly believe it when his face started appearing around London on Black Panther posters. I suppose the Oakland Panthers were made up of other boys like him who got fed up waiting.

Stokely Carmichael eventually became another militant voice. He came to Berkeley once, when he was still in favour of passive resistance, to speak at a rally. He was a leader at the time of the Student Nonviolent Coordinating Committee and was highly respected for his work in the South. Passive resistance down there was dangerous, because racists often attacked, maimed or even murdered the young protesters who tried to effect a change. I guess Stokeley must have seen so much racist brutality that it forced him to reassess his tactics. (As recently as 1985, he was refused entry into England because of his politics, with an implication that he was likely to stir racial unrest.)

Banner-waving wasn't just a way to spend an afternoon. We believed it would change things, although sometimes I'd come away from a political demonstration or rally and wonder. Jerry Rubin was an activist on campus and was one of the organizers of the last protest march I went on, in 1965. We marched through Berkeley to show our solidarity against intervention in Vietnam. Three years later he was tried as one of the Chicago Seven after a demonstration at the Democratic convention.

During the summer of 1965, Ikey married Allison Hennix, a gentle giant from Shreveport, Louisiana, who smilingly tolerated Ikey's preoccupation with her family. I adored Allison. They bought a house in Kensington on the Berkeley border. I decided to start a play group. I'd always loved babies and kids and it seemed like a sensible way to make the money I needed to pay my rent the coming semester. Ikey and Allison let me turn the spare room off the garage into a playroom and I set about building the tables and buying the rest of the things that the children would need.

I got friendly with the young mother of one of my little terrors and we decided to share a place together after the summer. She wasn't a student, she lived off her alimony, which was extravagant by student standards.

Towards the end of the summer, we'd regularly hop into her big convertible and go to San Francisco, which was only a twenty-minute drive away. We must have gone to see a LeRoi

Jones play called *The Toilet* five times. It was through a friend of hers that I saw Lenny Bruce and met his wife Honey and fell into the occasional company of Allen Ginsberg and Peter Orlovsky, who took me to my first sitar concert. One of the good things about Berkeley was that the campus attracted a lot of people, known and otherwise, and it was acceptable to take them at face value.

There were endless alternative 'brotherhoods' stationed in Berkeley. They were more than cliques. I wanted a peek at them all, and being a 'spade chick' probably helped to make me welcomed everywhere. I knew how to make myself belong, but at a certain point, I'd stand back and examine and end up being an observer.

However adaptable I was, the reservation was like the 'old country' to me. My root was there and this governed my sensibility and kept me separate. It didn't affect my friendships but it did make me experience life from a different vantage point. Maybe I didn't belong in the academic community at all. Something gnawed at me, but I kept trying to shrug it off.

I wanted to specialize in psychological anthropology, and assumed that when I finished at Berkeley I would go to the University of Michigan at Ann Arbor, which had one of the few departments in the field. In the meantime I was determined to blot out the feeling that something was missing.

I tried living with a boy one semester. Cohabitation was all the rage, although few of us let our parents know that we'd shacked up. Joe was gentle and very kind to me. I'd originally met him during the Free Speech Movement. He was an English teaching assistant working on his master's degree in English. He had a good friend named Jonathan Cott who was also in the English department and came to see us a lot. (Jonathan was one of the people I kept in touch with after Berkeley. He interviewed me for *Oz* magazine in the sixties and went on to become a major contributor to *Rolling Stone*, the magazine started by Jann Wenner, who was also at Berkeley while I was there.) Jon and Joe were stabilizing factors, temperate good students with whom I could talk about T. S. Eliot and get wrecked on a jug of mulled wine on a Saturday night.

* * *

My restless energy found an outlet when I went to a screening of a Kenneth Anger movie called *Scorpio Rising*. It was the first film I'd seen that used a background of contemporary rock-and-roll and rhythm-and-blues hits as a sort of lyrical commentary. I wanted to get up and dance, but everyone sat motionless in the darkened university hall that was being used as a screening room.

I bounced as little as possible in my seat, but it wasn't easy. I hadn't been so excited since I don't know when, and it felt as if I'd woken up from a long, long sleep. I needed to bop but refused to admit it. I was hellbent on proving that I was a serious student. (It wasn't that I didn't want to read Jean Genet and Ken Kesey or sneak into Michael McClure's lectures at the California College of Arts and Crafts. It wasn't that I didn't think it was worthwhile to demonstrate and wave protest placards or sit on the Terrace at lunchtime and listen to arguments about Kierkegaard and Kant. I didn't hate struggling through my statistics class and nearly enjoyed my psych lecture when I got there in time to get a seat. It just wasn't completely satisfying. Caviar won't do when you want fried fish.)

I was surrounded by people who had passions which were either academic or political or both, and I'd convinced myself that because these things were important to society they automatically should have been important to me. I tried and tried to take on the tones around me, and sometimes it seemed to work. I'd slipped back into my old syndrome of holding my ear so close to somebody else's drummer that I couldn't hear my own.

At this stage I'd gone beyond adopting my friends' language and manners. I'd done this so much since early childhood that it came naturally. I could think and speak white American and affect all the mannerisms that went with it, as naturally as the words. Though there were only rare occasions to use reservation dialect, when I was back East it got an airing, and it flowed through my brain from time to time. It wasn't that which I felt I was missing.

What I didn't know was that my passion for music was valid, and that I didn't have to apologize for it.

I didn't think about any of this while I was watching *Scorpio Rising*, because the feelings always come long before I can begin to verbalize them. I just felt a surge to jump and shout and whoop it up.

I hadn't met any rock-and-roll or rhythm-and-blues fanatics at Berkeley. Dennis remained one, but the campus was enormous and our paths rarely crossed even though he was there while I was. We also hung out with very different types of students, and no doubt he didn't approve of my friends.

I spent most of my spare time with activists whose passion was politics, and the music that played an important role in the political movement at Berkeley was folk music. Protest singers strapped to an acoustic guitar or harmonica making some socially relevant statements had an enormous following, whereas Bobby Blue Bland, James Brown and Bo Diddley weren't the stuff of budding intellectuals.

A change in musical taste was becoming apparent, and drugs probably had a lot to do with it. People got high and wanted to sit around listening to music. Motown hits gave rhythm and blues a blue-eyed, lighter feel, and the student interest in English rock bands made their rock acceptable. Groups like the Beatles, the Rolling Stones and the Kinks not only had a sound that differed from American rock and roll (even though that's what they were imitating) but also had a look that was different. They weren't beatniks or radicals but they didn't look or dress like the 'straight' man on the street. Their hair wasn't simply long, it was styled and fashioned. Their clothes mattered.

By 1965, not only had the Beatles' popularity penetrated America, but psychedelic experiences manifested a music of their own. To cater for this growing interest, gathering holes opened in San Francisco, like the dances at the Fillmore Auditorium presented by Bill Graham. He organized the first on 10 December 1965 as a benefit for the San Francisco Mime Troupe. At the Fillmore I saw the Jefferson Airplane with lead singer Signe Anderson, who was replaced by Grace Slick after the band's first album. A collective of people known as the Family Dog ran a dance at the Longshoremen's Hall. The dim, smoky dance halls were glorified on a Saturday night by moving coloured lights, strobes and a DJ who played songs by British as well as American groups.

What seemed to happen in Berkeley in 1965 was that a few

cultural elements associated with the music fed off each other and the artists who made it, the fans who bought it and the venues that served them. The combination had an impact which spread fast, and the same thing was happening in other places at the same time. It affected clothes, thinking, art and fashion and was youth-orientated.

Going to Fillmore on a Saturday night was not merely going to a dance. There was an element of masquerade about it too, because what we wore there suggested our drug consciousness as well as imitating the fashions of popular singers and bands. People danced to show that they were out of their heads, as they often were, not to show they were good dancers. 'Finding the meaning' and 'getting the message' from a song was important, although the habit of listening for meaningful messages in the lyrics more than likely evolved from the interest people had in the lyrics of protest songs. It all went together spinning round and round, gathering up people and pieces until we were on the edge of a cultural revolution.

Radio pumped it out. Television let you see the music you were buying and the fashion worn by the hit makers. Kids had the money to buy the records, fashions and drugs and pay the door fee at the right venues. It wasn't just another brotherhood, because the media backed it and the consumer element in it made this growing cult highly profitable. I was soon tempted away from the political activist crowd at Berkeley and I spent more time alone or with friends who were tuned into pop music as music and art. I didn't do it consciously because I didn't know what I wanted. But I knew what I didn't want, and I didn't want to have to listen to folk music.

Around that time, another popular indulgence which may have developed out of drugs and a fat safe economy was the fact that people examined themselves and their environment. A lot of asking who am I, why am I here and what am I doing went on. Psychology and psychiatry were popular, and it was fashionable for students to trot off to see their shrink as well as expanding their consciousness with drugs to get a more introspective view of themselves and life.

Trust me not to be different. I took an acid trip and while I was looking at the multicoloured snowflake patterns moving on the wall and listening to my Bessie Smith collection, I thought it must be wonderful to sing. The thought drifted and was replaced by others.

A friend of mine who lived in the flat upstairs was there at the time. I called him Baby John because he had a pretty baby face. We'd shared a flat on the north side of campus during the previous semester and I'd harboured various degrees of lust for him but fortunately nothing had stuck. He was the kind of calm spirit it was good to have on hand for an acid trip.

I had a few revelations about myself, and after the drug wore off, I decided it was time to come to terms with the fact that I wasn't committed enough to what I was doing, and I wanted to go away and think.

Baby John was the first person I told that I was taking off and going to Europe. It was just going to be a term's break. But I needed to think. I'd be lying if I said I knew what I was doing at that point or that I really had a plan. I only knew I had to sell my car and books and get hold of some money. I had a little Simca – nothing special, but I could raise enough cash on it to buy myself a plane ticket.

I felt that I had to go. I don't know why. Something seemed to be pulling me, nudging me all the time.

I liked Berkeley and I had many friends. But I knew I had to find something in me and I couldn't do it so close to home.

8
FREE AT LAST

'What the hell do you think you're doing?' was all Ikey wanted to know when she heard I was leaving. It was a question she invariably asked when she could find me, which wasn't often. Living in my own apartment and leading a life entirely separate from hers gave me a fiercely independent attitude.

I didn't know *what* I was doing as clearly as I knew what I wasn't doing. I realized that the less I said the better, because people asked questions about my intentions and I had no pat answers. A few people thought I'd flipped out. There were certainly enough acid casualties floating about – people whose psychedelic trips kept them trapped in their hallucinations long after the drug wore off. I wasn't one of them.

By the end of February 1966 I had got rid of my apartment and books and had a cheap ticket on Icelandic Airways from New York to London. I'd decided by then that Paris was where I was headed and that from London I could easily hitch across to Europe.

It was going to be cold on the Continent and I needed some warm clothes. I'd made two good friends in Berkeley who were both from Beverly Hills. Patti Herzfeld and Andi Luria were extremely chic by student standards. They subscribed to *Women's Wear Daily* and introduced me to Rudi Gernreich clothes and shoe fetishes. You could have opened a shop with the shoes they had between them. I occasionally borrowed a pair when we went dancing at the Fillmore. I stayed with them before I left Berkeley and upon my departure they'd loaded me down with some of their castaway clothes which I gratefully added to the stack I'd been collecting.

A lot of my companions that last semester were from LA and when I'd been down to visit a couple of times on one of those $11.99 air fares, I'd met some people I wanted to see before I left the States.

I waved goodbye to Berkeley and headed for LA with two suitcases stuffed with donations of winter clothes and a 1940s box-shouldered silver fox fur jacket that a fellow student named Larry bought for me. It made my bags very heavy to have all those extra pairs of shoes Andi and Patti had chucked in, but they were worth their weight in gold, as it turned out.

I had traded in my torn jeans and long hair that past summer. I didn't want to look like a radical any more and got my hair sheared short at the barber's. When I started wearing eyeliner and lipstick again, it was a clear sign of a new phase.

I didn't look out of place on Sunset Strip. There was a fundamental difference between LA and Berkeley. People expected to impress you with what they had, not with what they knew. The cloistered cosiness of academia was unimaginable in the dazzle of neon lights and go-go dancers on the Strip after dark. Brassy cars cruised the broad streets. But there was not a sign in Hollywood that Watts had had riots the summer before. I stayed just long enough to spend more money than I should have on a few more trendy items of clothing.

By the time I got to New York, I could hardly carry my suitcases, which had to be supplemented with two paper carrier bags. I was wearing an innocuous camelhair coat and dark brown lace-up shoes and hoped to God I looked straight and sedate, because I'd been warned you got searched at customs if you didn't.

I nearly didn't want to catch the plane out of LA. It hit me there that I was taking a big chance hoping I'd find a job in Paris. I didn't speak much French. And I didn't have my return fare. I had to charm my way round paying overweight baggage charges. I couldn't afford them. I had a five-dollar bill left when I boarded the Icelandic DC–8 going to London with stopovers in Reykjavik, Iceland and Prestwich, Scotland.

On board it took a good deal of earnest deliberation to decide whether to buy a carton of Kent duty-free cigarettes or give up smoking. The man next to me was gabbing on about how I wouldn't see a 25-cent pack of cigarettes until I got back home and, while I didn't want to waste a dime, I was already too nervous about not having money to give up smoking. So I broke down and bought a carton as they wouldn't sell me a single pack.

The airport at Reykjavik looked like a deserted air base. There was one big solitary hangar standing alone in the snow. It was too cold to feel the wind blow as we disembarked. We were stuck in the terminal so long that the airline had to serve us a complimentary breakfast. Passengers were getting antsy with the waiting. I'd only ever been inside big airport terminals and Reykjavik's was not only small, it looked like a dismal bus terminal. I refused to be dismayed and sat by myself, as I didn't spot any other student types on the plane.

I slept like somebody in a coma between Iceland and Scotland. There was nothing to see in the air or at Prestwick airport.

Coming in over London I expected to see one of those aerial views of Marble Arch that you get on a tourist postcard. Instead I saw the symmetry and order of slanted rooftops and brick houses against grey, grey cloudless sky, or maybe it was all one big cloud. It looked like nothing I'd seen but I couldn't pretend it looked exciting.

When our DC–8 taxied in at Heathrow airport twenty-three hours after we took off from New York, the passengers had lost that neatly pressed image. It was too early in the morning for anybody to look and act their best.

I worked out what to say if the elderly man at the narrow immigration desk asked me why I only had $1.83, and my thoughts were tripping over each other and my heart was pounding so fast it made me forget to paste a smile across my face, which I had thought would help. Not only didn't I have enough to take a taxi into the city, I didn't quite have enough for the bus. I could always walk or hitch. I suspected none of it would be a problem if I followed my nose.

When you know absolutely nothing about where you are or who you've got to deal with, only the most obvious things worry you. I had no idea about English rules and regulations or the joy that a 'job's worth' might get from upholding them.

I'd tried to dress myself like a very straight middle-class American college student who travels abroad with a walloping big allowance, but the immigration officer still asked how much money I had. I smiled and tried to look perky when I said $1.83 and used the same ploy when he asked if I had a return ticket. (I knew it wasn't good to lie about things like that in case I was asked to produced the goods.) He listened to my rubbishy story about my parents having my money sent through American Express and looked at me over the top of his glasses when he asked me to step to the side.

Shit.

Every soul on the plane had gone through while I sat trying to look casual in an area sectioned off by a glass partition. When another official joined my immigration officer, I smelled heap big aggravation.

It didn't take them long to break from their pow-wow to explain that not only was I being refused entry but I was being shipped straight back to New York on the next American carrier and would be charged for the full fare by the American embassy, who would temporarily foot the bill. Well, this wasn't the time to smile and act cute. I took on a very serious air when I told them that my grandfather was an important man and I suspected racial discrimination and this would not be tolerated by my family . . .

The detention centre in the lower depths of Heathrow had two matronly women sitting at a desk. They looked like prison wardens, and when they locked me in a room with a door that had chicken wire over its small window, I felt as if I was in the clink. I knew a lot of kids who'd been arrested for demonstrating, so being jailed didn't disturb me. The thought of winding up in New York with $1.83 did.

Another 'detainee' was shown into the room; she was Finnish and had come in from Paris. She was crying, which seemed like a big waste of energy. After one of the wardens brought in a Fortes menu, I suggested to the girl that we go on a hunger strike. She said she was too upset to eat anyway.

When I told the warden I was on a hunger strike, she said food would do us good and asked if she could telephone somebody for us. I didn't know a soul in London and wasn't planning to stay there for longer than was necessary but I'd taken a couple of names and addresses given to me by Berkeley friends, including that of the brother of an English girl in my anthropology class.

We had tried Martin Hill's number for the umpteenth time when he answered, explaining that he'd just stepped in from his job in the City. He told me he'd got a long letter just the day before from his sister Caroline saying that he should expect to hear from me. Otherwise, I was a total stranger to him and I certainly had no right to ask if he could help get me out of the detention centre. To this day I don't know why or how he managed it.

He'd rushed straight out to the airport, still in his pinstripe City suit and brown suede shoes. He was so terribly English that when he said 'terribly', which he said often, it sounded like 'tedibly'. I had to listen very closely to him as he drove me into London in his Mini, or I couldn't comprehend enough of what he said to respond. Of course, I gratefully understood when he offered to let me sleep off my fatigue at his place.

Martin's flat in Norland Square could have been in paradise but was in Holland Park, London, England, which was even better.

I found it hard to believe when I woke the next morning that there was no heating apart from a little gas fire and that the scalding hot water came out of a separate faucet attached to a small gas geyser on the wall that sounded as if it was about to blow up every time you turned the hot water on.

Even the most incidental object was worth looking at from the moment I lifted myself out of that first deep night's sleep, and I didn't force myself to try to take it all in.

Outside I wasn't looking for anything, I just wanted to feel my way around. Street names and districts brought nothing to mind. Marble Arch, Piccadilly, Hyde Park, Shepherd's Bush. Nothing was familiar. Everything was so entirely foreign to me that there was no sense of being lost. It was like being in an enormous museum without a guide book.

I walked because I didn't have the money to ride and my feet burned with the wet penetrating cold, but that couldn't keep me from tracking miles across central London wearing out the soles of Andi's and Patti's shoes, which seemed to guide me as Dorothy's red shoes guided her to Oz.

I was mesmerized by the blanket of calm everywhere, even in the busy atmosphere of Carnaby Street and the King's Road. London seemed to dwell in a permanent state of very late autumn, although weatherwise there was no mistaking that it was the dead of winter. For sky, there was a film of smoke, grey without the slightest hint of blue in it. Some days the sky seemed to have exceeded its overhead limit and drifted down to ground level. It hung like a big curtain veiling the landscape and tricked your eye into seeing everything in the distance in black and white. There was no sun and no one expected one.

The people looked whitewashed. So many men in bowler hats, so many women in the parks pushing enormous high-sprung perambulators. So many belted raincoats. Rolls-Royces and Minis and compact cars and black taxis and red buses tearing around the roundabouts. Much of London looked like Beacon Hill in Boston to me, but I sensed nothing of New York. On the streets nobody made passes or was rude or looked as if they could be bothered to do anything but mind their own business, which was all right by me. (I wish I could say the same thing about Martin's room mate. As the flat was his, too, I left to avoid hitting him over the head with a milk bottle or something when he made one more drunken late-night pass.)

When I drifted one night into a Hampstead pub, I was surprised to see a familiar Berkeley face among all the foreign ones. He offered me a place on his floor, the first of several that helped me survive those first couple of weeks as I made new contacts.

Being from Berkeley in 1966 was like having a master key to the student underground. The university had a good reputation and the notoriety of the Free Speech Movement had added a radical activist image that cast a beneficial light on me. Other students were impressed to find out I intended to bum around Europe penniless. It had a note of wild adventure about it. The rejection of material wealth had grown in importance among my friends who equated money-mindedness with a low consciousness. It had been awfully timely and convenient in Berkeley that everybody I knew wanted to look poor while I had no alternative, but when I arrived in London, fashion dictated mini-skirts, bell-bottom trousers and geometric haircuts.

I don't know what I would have done without the fox-fur jacket Larry Mellman gave me or the shoe donations from Luria and Herzfeld. Around Chelsea you really felt that what you wore was important. Not that I wanted to hang around Chelsea that much. I was more into Notting Hill Gate and Hampstead, where there was a strong allegiance between American students who were either studying here or taking time off, as I was, or had dropped out. It was a protective community. Their generosity was immediate. Nobody waited for you to look hungry – food was shared with open-house hospitality from one bedsit to the next. We converged like orphans from the English storm, fluttering and chirping and nesting together to create our own extended family. I made some friends during this period, like Steve Lovi, a well-travelled film student, and Kaffe Fassett, a painter from Big Sur, California, both of whom I still see.

Sometimes I seemed too lucky to be merely lucky, the way people offered me a place to sleep and kept me from starving. Sharing went along with rejecting material wealth, and the students who got dollars from home were the quickest to be generous.

Before the six weeks' leave of entry stamped in my passport at Heathrow had run out, I had made a coterie of American and English friends, and realized there was too much to see and do to leave. Not having money was neither an embarrassment nor an inconvenience. I knew I wouldn't starve in London and applied for an extension. Paris had to wait.

There were other factors that made things easy for me. I was after all a girl, and in London there was not just the appeal of being a Berkeley student, but also that of being a 'spade chick'. What suddenly made this an asset? Was it the civil rights movement, Donyale Luna captivating the fashion world, Sidney Poitier, Aretha Franklin being heralded as queen of the vocal chords, James Baldwin, or girl groups like the Ronettes and the Supremes looking cutesy and accessible? 'Spades' were 'in' like a fashion, although it was impossible to assess it in this way at the time. We thought that things had changed and that society generally would eventually imitate the alternative culture and make racism passé. 'Spades' weren't seen that much on the London scene but we were a welcome lot, and this made a difference to how I survived. I lived from one crash pad to the next, sometimes landing in a lap of luxury, like the time I spent with Tim Street Porter's parents in Blackheath.

Tim was a student at the Architectural Association who had travelled to Berkeley and made friends there. His telephone number was one of the few that I'd been given. I was glad to have it and his parents welcomed me. They were ideally

English, proud of their garden, and were the first people that I heard talk about the Second World War as though it was a real part of their lives.

Marjorie and Cecil Street Porter lived in a big three-storey house with a crescent drive. Cecil was an underwriter at Lloyds and marched off in a bowler hat in the morning. Marjorie waved him off and minded the fort. It never crossed my mind until recently, but their house on Pond Road was like Grumblethorpe inside except you were allowed to touch things. The grandfather clock and handmade quilts, the antique chairs and polished tables had their own history. It was an unconsciously handsome house, and wonderful to be in, especially when Marjorie stuck a hot-water bottle in my bed.

As the weeks became months, I can't remember how many different places I stayed in, but each one was a new buzz and an education. At only one crash point were sexual favours expected in return for lodgings. While I wasn't totally put out by this, I wasn't thrilled to bits, especially as the man was impotent and refused to believe it. He didn't come home often, as his work took him away, so at least his futile attempts weren't an exhausting daily exercise. I have genuine compassion for impotence as long as men don't abuse my tolerance. He wasn't holding a gun at my head, so I moved out.

I was never enthusiastic about casual sex. Invitations to share somebody's bed were frequently offered, but I maintained my fast-footed independence by sleeping alone on hard cold floors.

That's just how I was sleeping, at Kaffe Fasset's, when I was helping Steve Lovi and some of his fellow American students from the London School of Film Techique shoot an experimental movie. It was one of those 16-mm black-and-white affairs with obscure but meaningful references and it was being shot at David Hockney's flat in Powis Terrace. There was a young English art student appearing in the film named Caroline Thompson Coon, who offered me a room complete with my own drawer space in her basement flat.

Months before I moved into her Shepherd's Bush flat, Caroline had recorded a demo. She had a shrill, feminine voice that would have been perfect for singing Gilbert and Sullivan. If the right record producer had got hold of her, she might have become a singer instead of a painter and eventually an activist. She had a passionate nature, and once she committed herself to something, she would throw herself into it wholeheartedly. She did this with Release, the organization she helped to start in 1967 to assist people when they got busted for drugs. Trying to help a West Indian boyfriend of hers deal with a minor possession charge, she became aware that people were ignorant of their rights and what to do when they were arrested. I was at her flat one afternoon when she arrived home to say that the telephone number was going to be used as a help line. People could phone when they were busted to get information about how to get a lawyer and deal with the police.

Caroline came from a wealthy farming family in Northamptonshire and was educated at the Royal Ballet School, which concentrated her education on dance. This left her sensitive about her literacy. She was conscious of her limitations and when student friends of mine came to visit me at her flat during the summer of 1966, I noticed that she was insecure. As Release mushroomed, with Caroline as its spokeswoman, she educated herself. Within a few years, she was not only well read, she had turned her hand to writing.

She was my first English friend. Sharing the flat with her introduced me to English frugality. Switching off the lights every time she left a room, turning the gas heater on in a room only when we were in it seemed most peculiar to me. Coming from California, I took basic amenities for granted, and it took years before I was able to imitate the habits of people who'd experienced rationing during the war and after it.

Caroline had an interesting assortment of admirers: the art critic Edward Lucie-Smith, the poet Christopher Logue, the painter Derek Boshier. She liked being at the heart of what was going on in London. I always felt that she would have been taken more seriously as a writer and activist if she hadn't been pretty. She was a coquettish, voluptuous brunette in the sixties and became a sleek fastidious blonde in the seventies and eighties. The impact of her personal flair seemed to undermine her credibility.

She is one of the people I met during my first few months in London that are still my friends.

Caroline's was the first place I parked with intentions to stay a while, and although I hadn't yet tired of floor hopping, it was a relief to have all my clothes in one place and be able to put a return address on the back of my air letters.

With summer approaching, London decked herself out in a floral dress. I'd never seen anything like the cherry blossoms and rose gardens. It made everybody giddy. The English become a different race when the sun shines. They get frisky in their shirtsleeves and speak without being spoken to.

When we all were nearly thawed out from the bitter winter, I realized that something strange was happening. I was being considered and treated as an American and a foreigner. My accent was unquestionably American and people often made fun of the way I said things like 'bath' and 'aluminum'. Complete strangers would hear me say something and ask where I came from with enthusiastic anticipation that I'd answer with a fantasy word like Hollywood or New York or Detroit. (Detroit was on the map after the success of Motown.) People called me American because among other things I talked like one, dressed like one (though I tried not to), grew up celebrating Thanksgiving and Hallowe'en and thought cricket was a form of baseball. They were curious about America and wanted to talk about it.

I didn't have to be on a 24-hour guard to defend my race and its rights. In America, dealing with all the subtle variations of racism could be a full-time job. While the English have their own form of racism, my nationality superseded the colour of my skin.

I was staying at Caroline's and trying to figure out how to get a job other than baby-sitting for the clothes designer Alice Pollock, which is what I did to feed myself. Tim Street Porter had introduced me to Alice, who had the Quorum boutique with Ossie Clark on Radnor Walk off the King's Road. With their help I was able to keep getting Home Office extensions on my passport. I'd also worked out that it took the Home Office so long to refuse an extension that waiting for their ruling could be a three-month extension in itself. Eventually I had to go to Paris and return, getting a stamp at Dover.

When I got back I bumped into an English friend, David Dugdale, who had studied at Berkeley and returned to England to collect an inheritance after his father died. David and his American wife, Linda, were my age and childless but Linda was new to London, wanted companionship and someone to do light chores. They asked me to be their au pair girl in exchange for my own room in their luxurious modern flat in Kensington. I had a weekly wage of £2.50 and thinking time. I shared my friends with them.

I still didn't have a plan and didn't have the gall to admit to myself that I wanted to sing, although I ruminated the notion in the back of my mind. It seemed far-fetched and impractical, but in 1966 a brave brash stab in the dark, grasping for the unknown and the unfamiliar, wasn't uncommon. Music was a strong political force and to sing seemed as romantic and as brazen a departure as my spirit needed.

I guessed it was best to explain nothing and just do it. I decided to put an image together and asked Alice and Ossie to lend me an outfit from the Quorum boutique to go with my Vidal Sassoon haircut, false eyelashes, big red plastic hoop earrings, red pumps of Caroline's, and I was away. Again.

Steve Lovi took some pictures of me on the train tracks at the end of Caroline's garden. I didn't know one musician and no one I knew did, not even somebody who played guitar as a hobby, so I had to practise singing by myself. There was a full-length mirror on my cupboard door at David and Linda's. I used to stand in front of it singing whatever came to mind. I suspected I wasn't an Ella Fitzgerald, but that technical style wasn't popular anyway. I didn't have any preconceived idea about how or what I'd sing, I just wanted a recording contract. I needed the effrontery to tell people that that was what I wanted to do, and, figuring out how I could start from nowhere, I didn't question whether I could sing or not.

Although London was brimming over with music, I wasn't too taken with the music that English groups like the Beatles, the Animals and the Rolling Stones made. I didn't rush to see them on *Ready Steady Go!* (although I did make the effort to see Otis Redding). Once I went to a Rolling Stones concert at the Royal Albert Hall, because Ike and Tina Turner were supporting them on the bill. The audience liked Tina but went totally berserk when the Stones came on. This seemed ridiculous to me, because Tina's performance was so much stronger, with her cluster of Ikettes diddybopping behind her. They did everything but somersault and show their behinds. I'd been to see James Brown perform in a smallish theatre in Walthamstow and people clapped with the reserve and respect you'd expect at a piano recital while James screamed and sweated and threw himself about the stage doing the very same act that would have had them standing on their seats at the Uptown, the main Melangian venue in Philadelphia.

I always maintained my link with other American students in and around Notting Hill Gate, which is how I happened to stay at David Hockney's flat in Powis Terrace. He had left an art student friend of his, Dale from Denver, to take care of it while David was teaching for a term at Berkeley. His drawings weren't regarded by us with any reverence and it was not odd to open a drawer looking for a pen and have to range through some forgotten Hockney sketches. One day an American friend of Dale's dropped by for a visit. Her name was Susie and I don't recall how our conversation turned to her wanting to sing and that she was going to audition for a blues band fronted by Alexis Korner. I'd never heard of him but she said that he was looking for backup singers, and suggested we audition together.

We rehearsed a Cream song called 'Sleepy Time Time', a twelve-bar blues with hardly any melody or lyrics. Unaccompanied, we practised this one song endlessly and when we could get anybody to listen, we'd try it out on them. I hate to think what it sounded like, because neither of us could work out a decent harmony.

Once we arranged to sing it for Joe Boyd, another American in London at the time. He was an impresario of sorts but hadn't begun managing or producing bands yet. I asked him to meet us for a listen at a friend's house on Oakley Street in Chelsea, where the kitchen echoed. Susie and I were so loud that we had Joe Boyd stand in the street outside the open window.

Alexis Korner's audition was held in a basement club. He was a small man. His size made him ageless, although I realized that he was a good deal older than I was at twenty. He had a dark gypsy look about him and you might have mistaken him for Greek or Italian. His dark hair was partly concealed under a cap and his face was framed by heavy sideboards. He was friendly enough and didn't look at all horrified while we were singing. He announced our pay in the same breath that he announced that we had the job.

Five pounds a week was twice as much as I was getting as

an au pair. I was ecstatic. I was in an English blues band. Alexis called it Free At Last.

Alexis had built up a solid blues reputation while he and Cyril Davies fronted a band called Blues Incorporated. A lot of established players had performed with them at one time or another, and it was quite a coup that I landed a job with him. What counted in my favour was the assumption that all 'spades' came out of a gospel heritage and had developed a good set of lungs. Musicians took it for granted that I had spent my childhood Sundays in a reservation church. As it turned out, I could sing but couldn't pitch. Nobody complained, because they always had their guitar amplifiers turned up too loud to notice that I needed a couple of bars of music to settle into the right key.

Susie couldn't get to rehearsals on time and it was plain that her lax time-keeping wasn't well received by Alexis or his drummer, Gerry Conway, or the bass player, Binky McKenzie. So, when Susie told us that she'd decided to nip off to an Israeli kibbutz a week after rehearsals began, I think Alexis was relieved. The fact that he decided not to replace Susie spared me the anxiety of having to blend my voice with someone else's.

For a lot of bands on the English music scene in 1967, Chicago blues was more influential than American rock and roll. I started meeting musicians through Alexis, who eulogized blues artists I'd never heard of before. There wasn't anything patronizing in their overt passion for 'spade' blues heroes like Robert Johnson or B. B. King, and some of the artists they raved about they couldn't believe I'd seen live at the Cabale Creamery. High on the list of English blues fanatics was a musician named John Mayall, who trailed me home one night after he'd come down to check out one of Alexis's rehearsals. He had a Chicago blues singer named Eddie Boyd with him, who was doing some recording with John's band, the Bluesbreakers. I'd never heard of either of them, but John seemed pleasant enough and I was relieved he'd come to my door, because I needed to replace a light bulb and wasn't quite tall enough. John Mayall was a bear of an Englishman, a modern, eccentric Thoreau. He wore buckskin clothes that he designed and stiched up on his sewing machine. They made him look like Davy Crockett without the coonskin cap. His shoulder-length hair and beard were the same colour as his buckskin and his moccasins, which he'd also made by hand. The tan tone of it all gave you the impression he was tan, too, although he had that English whiteness, which continued to look strange to me even after a year away from California.

John did everything, made everything, and was everybody to himself. He required far more space than he had after he'd convinced me to move in with him. The fourth-floor walk-up that I shared with him, not far from Alexis's flat on Queensway, was small but the built-in furniture he made gave the impression that it was larger than it was. He not only made the benches and cushions that fitted them, but also everything else in the three rooms. The bathroom converted to a fully equipped darkroom and he took all his own publicity pictures, including ones of himself.

I don't know how we managed to stay together for the few months we did. He was stubborn and I was wilful and I don't expect either of us was in love or had delusions about our affair lasting. He was an extraordinary collector of things and thought I was right for his collection. I was caught up in my blues-singer guise when he first met me and no doubt he was taken off guard when I showed myself in different lights.

Both of us were on the road doing our separate gigs while I was living with John. His band was popular at colleges and clubs and got booked for one-nighters throughout the week. At the time Aynsley Dunbar was the drummer with the Bluesbreakers, with John McVie on bass and Peter Green on guitar. John handled all the vocals but coaxed Pete into singing a slow number by himself. This was no mean feat, because Peter, a brilliant sensitive guitarist, was shy about singing solo though he had a sweet voice.

Seeing Pete virtually shrink at the microphone was good therapy for me because it showed me that a song sung however sweetly didn't sound as convincing when performed without confidence. Peter's voice was more melodic than John's, but he was timid when he sang. He didn't push. Eventually this became the essence of Peter Green's vocal style and made it special.

I knew how hard it was to take the microphone and face the audience. I cringe when I recall how shy I was on stage at first.

Admittedly, it didn't last very long, maybe the first two months of gigs, but I must have been a ridiculous sight. I used to walk on with cigarette, not just because other musicians did, but because it was something to hide behind. I was so at a loss for what to do with my hands that I insisted on playing a tambourine. Somehow Gerry Conway coped with my banging away all over his beat. I kept good time at the start of a song, but by the end, my arm would tire and I'd slow down a bit. I'd get so carried away banging that tambourine I'd be miles away from the microphone singing my little backing bits to myself. Alexis was patient.

I learned more about performing at John's gigs than I did going to my own. I tried to see as many of his as I could when we didn't work on the same night.

John had a big Wurlitzer organ which weighed a ton and had to be lugged in and out of gigs, but unlike Alexis's band, the Bluesbreakers had two roadies. Alexis only ever had one, and we had to help him carry the gear in and out. The others didn't like me to be seen hauling the speakers and amps, but I was as fit as anybody in the band and didn't want to be treated like a wilting lily.

John had trouble with his band during the period I was with him, in 1967. First, Aynsley Dunbar had to be replaced. I can't remember whether he quit or was fired. His successor was an extremely tall thin drummer named Mick Fleetwood. Mick and I struck up a hearty friendship right away. He had a schoolboyish sense of humour and was a prankster. John didn't take to his drumming and thought that Mick's drum feel was too pop-oriented to suit a blues band. It all got very hairy.

The Bluesbreakers possibly felt they had to live up to certain expectations after Peter Green replaced Eric Clapton who broke away and formed Cream. It was important to them to maintain the reputation and following they had before Eric's departure. I was really too new to the business to understand what pressure John was under, but I tried to be supportive without getting involved. It was a very intense period for the entire band and with Pete living in the flat downstairs from us with his girlfriend Sara, I avoided conversations about the boss and the band.

Once I visited Pete and he told me he was considering a

move to Chicago so that he could work with some genuine blues players and hang out with them. I could only imagine this small temperate London boy getting his ass kicked in Chicago, and I tried to put him off in no uncertain terms. He was full of romantic notions.

Soon after Mick Fleetwood got fired, Pete and McVie left. They'd decided to form their own band, which they called Fleetwood Mac.

John dealt with their departure very well. He wasn't a man for remorse. Had I known anything then about northern Englishmen, I might have put his stolidness down to that. He came to bed every night with a pencil and pad and would take a phrase, turn it into a song title and add it to the list he was compiling for a new album he was planning, *The Blues Alone*. He was extremely economical and didn't waste pen, paper or ideas. I know he wrote a few of the songs for me or about me, 'Brown Sugar' ('I got a taste of brown sugar, gonna leave white sugar alone'), 'Brand New Start' and 'Marsha's Mood'.

John played all the instruments on that album, wrote all the songs, designed the album sleeve and took the photograph of himself for the cover. It was impossible not to respect him for his single-mindedness even though it was hard to live with. To have the opportunity of seeing how he wrote songs, managed his band and kept his eye on every aspect of the business was like taking a course, and I only ever met one better teacher.

He had a few quirks. Sometimes he would come back from a week on the road with a hunger to see movies. He'd get out the newspaper and plot a movie marathon that would mean we'd see three movies in one day, four if I was unlucky. I'd be bonkers by the time I came out of the last cinema. Movie marathons were one of his favourite entertainments, and if I was working and couldn't go with him, he'd go alone, heading off on his bicycle with his long hair pulled back in a low ponytail. The bicycle was odd-looking with extra small wheels, and to see him pedal off with his buckskin flying in the wind . . . well, what can I tell you?

He had the most redeeming laugh. It burst right from deep in his stomach and showed his teeth, which were like I imagine a real cowboy's, long and a bit crooked with a few missing along the side. He was a very rough-cut diamond but a diamond all the same. And I was hardly a pearl.

While I was still trying to keep my geometric haircut

chemically straightened, it started to fall out. This happened before I met Alexis, when I was living between Caroline Coon's and my au pair residence. Caroline complained that I should stop combing my hair in the kitchen, because it was always all over the floor. I swore blind I wasn't guilty, but the next time she swept the red and white linoleum tiles she thought that I'd been at it again. Finally I realized that my hair was falling out – in every room. It took a long time for bald patches to appear because even cropped as short as it was, it was thick – thick.

When it was impossible to cover the baldness with the hair that was left, I had Linda, whom I au paired for, cut it off. We only had cuticle scissors in the flat that night so we cut off what was left with them. My only consolation was that the wig I soon bought to camouflage my bald head was much easier to manage than my own hair.

By the time I moved in with John, I was wearing the wig, which I kept on even in bed. I don't remember his asking me to take it off. Not that I would have. Living with John didn't alter my sense of independence, which was strengthened by the five pounds a week I made from singing.

Through being in the group and sharing John's life, I was engulfed in music and surrounded by people who lived by it and for it and never questioned the validity of it. I was able to convert what had been my teenage passion into an occupation and this gave me an obsessive determination to work at it. I was consumed: listening to songs, imitating sounds, postures and gestures of performing. I wanted to understand the art and business of making music, in every sense.

I was among Englishmen who acknowledged my race's contribution to music and understood its roots. My colour represented a cultural fact instead of a political issue. I was indeed free at last.

Free At Last was booked on a short blues tour with Champion Jack Dupree, Long John Baldry and Jesse Fuller, who must have been the oldest blues muscian on the road. He claimed he was only seventy-two, but I didn't believe a word of it. He was always making passes at me, tottering about backstage and winking at me. At the end of the tour, Long John Baldry asked me to audition for his band. I couldn't quite believe it, because he'd certainly had enough opportunity to hear me sing, but I didn't quibble over his offer, and my audition was arranged.

Free At Last had never stopped struggling, and Alexis relied on his income from doing commercial voice-overs to keep the band going and feed his wife and three kids. There was always the suspicion that bookings weren't healthy enough to keep us on the road. I was too indebted to Alexis to sneak off, though, and when I confronted him about the possibility of my leaving, we both used Baldry's increased wage offer, £35 per week, as my valid excuse.

Baldry's band was more on a par with John Mayall. They were both booked by the Gunnell Agency, which also owned the Flamingo Club in Wardour Street. Like most of Gunnell's London-based acts, Georgie Fame and Geno Washington biggest among them, Baldry had a healthy gig schedule and a substantial following, left over from his previous band, the Steampacket, which had featured Rod Stewart and Julie Driscoll in the line-up. Baldry's backing band, Bluesology, was a five-piece band that included a singer. Baldry wanted to augment the group with a girl singer and a brass section.

When I went to his audition at the 51 Club, Great Newport Street, the band was rehearsing. The place was so small that the Farfisa electric organ wouldn't fit onto the stage. Nor did John, whose head was practically touching the ceiling of the basement club even though he was standing on the floor. All over the walls were pictures of bands and old blues musicians whose faces I didn't recognize. I was introduced to the band, but only the keyboard player, Reg Dwight, and the guitarist, Neil Hubbard, stayed to play for my audition.

I leaped onto the stage in my fox-fur jacket and my wig. This was not actually a committed blues band like Alexis's or John Mayall's and I was looking a lot more flash than would have been appropriate for Free At Last. When we toured together, I had noted that Baldry always wore a suit and tie and the band wore satin shirts, bell-bottoms, and anything else that was sold on the King's Road for followers of fashion.

London was still gripped by pop music, fashion and obvious changes in the balance of social power. The media brandished the term 'Swinging London'. I gathered that for a barrow boy to think that he too could drive a Rolls-Royce and buy a town house in Knightsbridge next to Lord So-and-So was a new assumption. It was endorsed by glittering examples of working-class success stories like those of the Beatles, Twiggy, Mary Quant, Michael Caine, Vidal Sassoon and a very long list of others, whose world status blared as a constant reminder that anything was possible. People felt it more strongly in the music business than anywhere else and it made them surer of their chances. Anything could happen.

I acted very nonchalant standing on that itty-bitty stage in the 51 Club as Neil and Reg went through a list of Stax and Motown songs they could play. I didn't know any of them, thank goodness. Neil went for a drink but Reg persevered. Then I offered to sing unaccompanied. (The divine thing about a capella singing is that you don't have to pitch, which was one of the things I couldn't do.) Before anybody had a chance to make another suggestion, I just started in singing.

I stood there bold as day and sang Little Anthony and the Imperials' version of 'Love Is A Many-Splendoured Thing'. The one rare thing about my voice was how loud it was. I threw in all the vocal turns that Little Anthony did himself back in 1958, and if you'd never heard him do it you might have been fooled into thinking that I knew how to bend a note. Why on earth nobody stopped me is a mystery. If I'd been watching, as Baldry and Reg were, I wouldn't have been able to stop myself from laughing. But Englishmen are so polite, aren't they?

Baldry gave me the job.

Soon it wasn't enough that I had a job, I was impatient to be good at it. Even after months on the road with Baldry, I was frustrated by the limitations of my voice, although it had improved a hundredfold since that audition for Alexis. With the music charts full of Melangians, particularly Motown and Stax artists, I was expected to be able to hit and hold those high notes. People mistook it for a racial aptitude. The fact that Bluesology had once backed Patti LaBelle and the Bluebells on an English tour didn't help my confidence.

I had a time finding songs that suited my range, and we preferred doing obscure songs to covering top-ten hits. Reg Dwight wrote a couple of soul imitations for me, and I went to his home in Pinner to learn them.

Reggie still lived with his mother and stepfather in the

suburbs and wasn't wily like the other musicians in the band, who always wanted to go out drinking, 'pull chicks' or be 'with the lads'. He looked the image of the boy who played Piggy in the film *Lord of the Flies* because he was stocky (verging on plump) and wore gold-rimmed glasses. Reg was always dissatisfied with the waves in his reddish-brown hair, which was cut in a fringe at the front and curled at the nape of his neck.

Usually when the guys in the band ragged him, he took it well, but sometimes he'd lose his temper in an ineffectual tantrum. The fact that his mother and aunt came to our local gigs at clubs like the Marquee excluded him further from being one of the lads. And while merely cohabiting was accepted as standard, Reggie got engaged. He had an unusual sense of humour and used to make noises like the Three Stooges and coin phrases like 'peedy grig' for 'greedy pig'. It didn't leave him friendless, though, and he palled around with a young half-West Indian, half-English guitarist named Caleb Quaye.

Towards the end of my six-month stint with the band, after we'd all decided to split up, Reg introduced us to someone he'd started co-writing with called Bernie Taupin. They were taking their songs to Dick James Music, and Reg hoped to become a singer-songwriter although some of the band members disliked his vibrato and discouraged him from singing harmonies while we were on the road together. I had no idea what band he could join after Bluesology, and it seemed bizarre that he decided to use our sax player Elton Dean's first name and call himself Elton John.

John Mayall and I broke up before he finished recording *The Blues Alone*. Once I'd started working with Baldry, I was on the road as much as John was. It was obvious that our days as a couple were numbered. He was cutting an album literally by himself, and I charged about forcing myself into a shinier mould to suit my new gig. There wasn't enough space in John's flatlet for his ambition and mine. He hadn't designed it for that.

John also had the task of putting a new band together. His final addition was a pretty blond baby-faced guitar player who turned up at the flat to audition without a guitar, and landed the job using one of John's. His name was Mick Taylor. He was a quiet gentle young guitarist whose personality didn't clash with John's and his playing was a real asset to the new line-up.

There was never a raised voice or a harsh word between John and me (although certain silences are noisier than all the screaming and shouting in the world). We took a perverse pride in the fact that our separation was ideally organized and friendly.

After living with John and spending over a year in London, I was starting to realize that the difference between English and American wasn't merely in the accent. The subtle nuances make them different languages and there was a danger that something I'd say in American meant something else in English. On the road with Baldry, I'd listen to musicians talking to each other and I'd imitate their sounds and expressions in my head. The English I was learning was the near-cockney which had gained credibility with the shift in working-class status. To add effect, a smattering of swearing was thrown in here and there. For instance, 'Hey, man, how the fuck are you?' was a pleasantry.

I liked being on the road with the band. It was an education in everything. I was not only in another country, among a different race, and immersed in a life style peculiar to the music business, I was also a girl playing in a boys' game, and an ex-student who had to suppress the habit I'd picked up at Berkeley of wanting to discuss everything in depth. 'Shut up' was a necessary directive to myself, if I was to fit in. The music business was another brotherhood, a society removed from anything I'd known, which I was committed to by virtue of work.

Through gigging I saw most of England as I rode with Bluesology up and down the motorway in a red Commer van, stopping only to eat beans on toast and greasy egg and chips in the 'trannies' – the nickname for transport cafés.

In 1967, there were a large number of club venues all over England as well as town hall, college and university dates that employed bands, and there were as many bands on the road scrambling for the gigs. The motorway, the A roads and B roads were buzzing with vanloads of young eager musicians who weren't just creating music for the sake of making a living, they made music for the sake of music, and with the latter intention, the quality and standard of musicianship flourished. You'd play on a bill with an unknown band one month and the next time you played with them, their playing standard might have improved unrecognizably. This may have been down to better equipment, a change in the line-up or the direction of their music, a change in their management, or sudden support from a record company.

We were booked to do a gig at Nottingham, third on the bill with Jimi Hendrix topping and the Kinks as second support. By today's standards this was a small venue, the hall probably held 600 people, and it was pretty packed. There weren't enough dressing rooms and the ones they had were holes – so we sat around with the Kinks and waited to go on. I'd only ever done gigs with John where we topped the bill. Hendrix slipped into his dressing room and didn't come out until it was his turn to play, which was not how I'd seen bands behave backstage.

He walked out on the stage to no screams but some soccer calls, plugged in and was off. The audience pushed to the front. I was standing by the side of the stage waiting for the moment when he pulled the guitar up to his mouth and played with his teeth, as I'd seen him do at a newly opened London nightclub called the Revolution. This was not a handsome boy, not by my standards, but his performance was incredible. He turned the guitar into a phallic extension of himself and played with such a sense of deliverance that it wasn't just the music that was art, his delivery was a dance, a style that was sexual art itself.

I bumped into him a couple of times after that at the Speakeasy in London. He said 'Heah, girl' in perfect Melangian. That dialect sounds divine, especially when I hear it outside America.

Hendrix had only begun.

Bands needed money to present their music and their image. But aspirations to be rich and famous were not the main motivation. The world economy caused no one to worry about tomorrow. Young people didn't save money and the booming English industries, related to fashion, film, music and drugs, relied on our spending. (People probably spent more on drugs than they spent on the rest combined, although there are no statistics to prove it.)

I stopped doing drugs as soon as I left Berkeley. I had enough trouble with the Home Office without worrying about getting busted, which would have resulted in my immediate deportation. It often made people uncomfortable that I didn't do drugs with them but it was one discipline I imposed on myself that I refused to adapt for somebody else's benefit.

When the pressure of the Home Office left no alternative, I got married. My husband-to-be, Michael Ratledge, was also my best friend, really. When I met him for the first time he was practising in a club in Soho called the Zebra Club where he was playing keyboards for his band, the Soft Machine. We immediately sensed that we had a lot in common. The music business had a rough edge and there weren't many people in it that I came across who were from universities. Mike had a degree from Oxford and though he was very English, in many ways I felt more comfortable talking with him than with the other musicians I knew. He even had me rehearsing with the Soft Machine for a week after I left Baldry, because Robert Wyatt, who was drumming, was also the lead singer with the band and wanted someone to relieve him. My singing with the Soft Machine didn't come to fruition, but marrying Michael did.

Our wedding, on my twenty-first birthday, was unusual. We overslept and nearly missed the appointed ceremony at 9 am. I didn't have time to do more than throw on a yellow cotton dress and black patent shoes; there wasn't time to fool with stockings or my wig.

John Mayall was our only witness. When we discovered we needed another, John ran and got a little old bespectacled lady who was selling flowers at a corner barrow to be our second. She looked as pleased as punch as she came walking into the registry office, wearing one crumpled black glove with the tips of the fingers cut off so that she could handle money more easily at her stall.

I think she was a little shocked to be participating in a mixed marriage with the bride and groom not looking their best. I got the giggles as soon as she replaced the shocked look with a timid smile that made her the only one of us smiling. She stood posed in her coat with her hands clasped, next to John in his buckskins, who loomed two heads above her. I sat next to my husband, who was wearing dark sunglasses even though there wasn't any sunlight to speak of inside or out.

I should have known when Michael left for St Tropez to work with the Soft Machine that I wouldn't see him for nearly eight months. He fell in love with a model from Texas and they returned to England together. I liked her and was glad that Michael was happy. We didn't bother to get a divorce, and remained good friends. He was a perfect husband by being my husband in name only.

After my week of rehearsing with the Soft Machine, the Gunnell agency asked me to join a band called the Ferris Wheel. Three of the musicians were West Indian and two were English. With the prospect of getting more of an opportunity to sing than the Soft Machine offered, I took the Ferris Wheel job.

When I realized that I was trapped again by that same old assumption that I was a budding Aretha Franklin, I didn't waste any time before asserting that I wasn't gospel trained and wasn't likely to sing like it. They took this in their stride, but it was quickly apparent that I wasn't progressing, singing with this group. I was ready to do original material and the band was committed to covering hits. Not wishing to leave them in the lurch, I found a singer called Linda Lewis to replace me.

I retreated alone to my £5-a-week Holland Park bedsit and tried to determine my next sensible move. I came down with glandular fever which forced me to do nothing but stay in bed, where I had more than enough time to think. Kaffe Fassett was living two floors below but I am extremely antisocial when I'm ill and didn't want to see him or any of my other American friends, like Steve Lovi, who lived in the neighbourhood. It was during this hibernation that Kaffe, who was a painter from the West Coast, popped up to say that he had started knitting that week and wanted to know how to cast off. I wasn't the girl to ask, but what started as Kaffe's hobby became a profession that he's now renowned for around the world.

My illness gave me time to think, and I concluded that to use my opportunity in music to its fullest, I should be writing material as well as singing it. I also considered that I should learn an instrument and borrowed an old bass from John

McVie through Mick Fleetwood, with whom I had remained friends. McVie was supposed to teach me a few bass riffs. I intended to buy an amp as soon as I raised some money. The bass sat in the corner of my room collecting dust while I tried to find work.

I decided to get an au pair job so that I wouldn't have to worry about food and rent and could use my spare time to write songs and learn the bass. Without some sort of visible progress, I couldn't excuse not returning to my studies at Berkeley. My notion about bass playing was interrupted by eventual employment.

When I was finally well enough one Saturday, I went to the Portobello Road anticipating to bump into familiar faces and ask them if they knew of any au pair jobs. Nobody did, to my dismay, but Roger Croutcher – who was an aspiring director in the theatre and lived across the road from me with a writer named Nicholas Wright – told me that there was a show called *Hair* being brought in from New York. They were holding auditions in the West End and I should try for it.

When I called the Shaftesbury Theatre the following Monday, I was told that the auditions were virtually closed and that they only needed to case a 'Black' girl. I explained that I was just that.

I was asked to sing two songs for the audition and to bring the appropriate sheet music for the piano accompanist. I took the keyboard player from the Ferris Wheel instead, after considering that an accompanist might not show me in the best light. It probably seemed rather flash that I'd brought my own piano player, but my intention was merely to be safe.

I'd never been on a proper theatre stage before but I had performed on so many different types of stage up and down the road that I wasn't daunted by the expanse of the Shaftesbury or the darkness of the stalls, where a few people sat hardly visible but totally audible.

Mike Snow, who'd come along with me, was in one of his superior moods. It was all right for him to be extremely confident – he wasn't auditioning. But having him there was a bonus, because he was flash and had a great sense of attack even when there was nothing to attack with.

I can't remember what I sang or if I thought I sang it well. We were told to come back after lunch, which was a pain, because we hardly had enough money for a coffee and sandwich on Denmark Street, a couple of blocks away from the theatre. And it meant that we'd have to walk there in the drizzle of rain. This may not sound particularly difficult, but I was worried about my hair, which I'd gone to great lengths to style in big soft curls which were fashionable.

I had vowed I would never straighten my hair again after it fell out. While I was on the road with the Ferris Wheel it had grown back entirely, and I buried my faithful wig at the bottom of a drawer believing that it was very passé to wear one. I resented the time and effort that I had to spend styling my own hair, but as it was important to my overall image, which was part of my gig, I tolerated the inconvenience. Barely.

My hair had a mind of its own in the rain, though, and the finer the rain, the more catastrophic its effect. My big soft curls could balloon to triple their size with a fine drizzle, and there wasn't a hope in hell of stopping this process once it had begun. Living in a rainy climate was the bane of my life. Why had nature bestowed on me more hair than the law should allow?

The few blocks' walk to Denmark Street and back had just the Jekyll and Hyde effect I feared it would have. I walked out of the Shaftesbury Theatre looking curly-headed and schlepped back with my hair like a busby. I rushed to a theatre toilet in a panic to see what damage had been done. Hardly a curl was left, and the more I brushed, the bigger and bushier the whole mass got. I'd just have to audition looking like a Queen's Guard.

It takes balls to sing when you feel ugly.

Not only was I recalled, but the stage manager asked if I could please wear my hair like that again at my next audition.

Mike Snow couldn't make my final audition so I took an acoustic guitar player, a Canadian named Steve Hammond. Dressed like a secretary, I sang 'The Shadow Of Your Smile'.

Had the world gone mad?

I was given a small part in the show after four auditions with my busby, and in the meantime I got fond of the effortlessness of my new hairstyle. I could go to bed with it 'buzzed', and it hardly changed by morning.

9
PURI NATURABILIS

When I joined the rehearsals for *Hair* at the beginning of August 1968, a lot of the cast had been rehearsing for the show in the spring of that year and had been given a break. When the rehearsals resumed with a few new people in the cast, like myself, the management was assured that the opening date would be fixed as soon as the Lord Chamberlain's post as theatre censor had been abolished.

There must have been about twenty-three or twenty-four kids in the cast. Most of us had never performed in the theatre before but nearly everybody except me had agents and managers or knew something about theatre, Equity and contracts. I just knew what the weekly salary was and that one of the producers, James Verner, was responsible for arranging my Equity card. Supposedly, my contract was being drawn up. I asked no other questions and considered myself lucky to be employed.

The new job brought a change in my life overnight. I was suddenly in the theatre and not on the periphery but at the centre of it, rehearsing a show that was already a hit on Broadway and which I quickly came to realize London was anxiously waiting for. I was less impressed by all of this than I was relieved to know I had a salary coming in to pay my five pounds a week rent. The benevolence of the mid-sixties had already started to thin by 1968.

I met two extraordinary men during the *Hair* rehearsals, Galt McDermot and David Toguri. Galt wrote the music for the show and had come to London from New York to whip the cast into shape vocally. Galt was between thirty and forty. He had a sincere paternal manner and could not have been mistaken for a hippie like Jim Rado and Jerry Ragne, who together wrote the book and lyrics.

Galt had a short-back-and-sides haircut and wore

unimaginative suits and ties like a bank clerk. He'd sit down at the piano with a careful pensive air as if about to play at a church organ recital and, without changing his demeanour, he would rock out a rhythm on the upright piano that moved me to sing better than I believed I could. Galt was a keyboard wizard, and his daily exercises with us helped me find my voice.

David Toguri, a Japanese Canadian, originally came to London as a dancer in *West Side Story*. He took us through our rigorous daily exercises to prepare us for rehearsals with American director Tom O'Horgan who had also directed the Broadway production. Toguri's hawk eye immediately spotted a poor movement. His ability to explain how to correct it made his criticism invaluable. He taught me about stage presence, body dynamics, and reacting on stage with control: things that I'd never thought about. To work with him and the company of players was some days like being in a large encounter group. It was intense physical and mental therapy. David helped us to function as a unit and gave us the sense of how important it was to remain individual at the same time.

Through David and Galt I discovered how to perform without fear. I still had reservations about my singing but once I could accept that individuality was as important to a performance as energy and that the combination was valuable, I stopped worrying about my voice. To sing and dance was a joy instead of being just a challenge. I had a new confidence.

Close to our opening, when I heard from a couple of sources that I might be replaced because the producers were not sure that they could get an Equity card for me, I realized that working with David and Galt had already altered my sense of myself as a performer. The rehearsals had been worthwhile in themselves even if I didn't find I was on the stage on first night. Everyone had a contract before I did. At the time, it didn't give me any comfort to know that the job wasn't secure, but after I was photographed as a member of the cast, my contract was quickly issued with a smile.

Hair was an ensemble production and the entire cast was on stage throughout most of the show. For the audience I was identified as a character called Dionne, but I was only required to be myself. I was featured in a song called 'White Boys' which was a spoof on the Supremes, performed by me with two West Indian girls doing backup. We were dressed in one enormous blue sequined gown and wore blonde wigs. Melba Moore sang the song in New York, and if they were looking for someone with a two-and-a-half octave range, I was not the girl.

I had no delusions about the production. Whatever it may have represented off Broadway, by the time it opened at the Shaftesbury Theatre, it was a commercial venture. It was the issue of nudity that made *Hair* seem more of a social landmark than a theatrical success.

On the preview night, Eamonn Andrews broadcast a show from the Shaftesbury stage. Zsa Zsa Gabor was one of his guests, as were the entire *Hair* company. I grew up with the Gabor sisters as the forerunners in the fifties of glitz, glamour and the risqué. I was surprised when Zsa Zsa Gabor claimed that the show offended her. We took it in good humour and tried to get her to join in a song with us, whereupon she stormed off the stage. She must have tripped on something, though, and spoiled her dramatic exit by tumbling down a few stairs with her dress flying over her head when she landed at the bottom. The boys in the cast rushed to pick her up. The television cameras missed it, of course.

While experimental theatre had used nudity in stage productions, the commercial theatre didn't attempt it until *Hair*. When the London production opened, one night after the Lord Chamberlain's control of theatrical censorship ended, the English media headlined the advent of nudity on the West End stage because the entire company of *Hair* appeared starkers in a dim light for all of ten seconds at the end of the first act.

Hair was a musical about young American idealists who rejected the conservative materialistic society which fostered war, racism and an imprisoned libido. These kids were committed in spirit and life style to peace, love, freedom and a drug-expanded consciousness, and like the American Indian they revered the natural order of the cosmos and man's place in it. No doubt this brotherhood evolved out of the serious striving for a liberal alternative society which marked communities like Berkeley, but these passive idealists were labelled hippies, which had an aimless connotation.

Through *Hair*, conservative middle-class theatre-goers

were exposed to the innocence of the hippie subculture. The musical made issues like drug-taking, casual sex and draft-dodging seem less ominous and made the long-haired appear less of a threat to society. Be-ins, free love and banner-waving were part of the hippie way of life. For them, taking their clothes off was an act of liberation as well as an assertion that the human body was not in itself pornographic.

The actual moment when the entire cast rose naked before the first night audience isn't memorable to me, but I did feel when I talked to people and read the next day's press that it was hypocritically exploited. While I accepted that nudity was a valid and crucial element of *Hair* as originally conceived, the media attention to our naked exposure was sensationalist.

Nudity was the star of *Hair* even before opening night. I was quite prepared to use my naked body to help challenge theatre censorship and exhibit the liberation of mind through body, but if the media and public reaction were anything to go by, there was too much of an atmosphere of titillation and voyeurism attached to that naked moment. They seemed to be missing the intention so I didn't take my clothes off after that.

While we rehearsed the show, the large cast became very close and there was something genuinely tribal about our relationship to each other. The company, which included Paul Nicholas, Michael Feast, Sonja Kristina, Sheila Scott Wilkinson, Diane Langton, Elaine Page, Peter Straker, Oliver Tobias and eventually Tim Curry, shared a stage without any of the jealousy and competitiveness that I have since come to accept are natural to actors and theatre companies.

It was not unusual for the entire cast of the show to be invited somewhere after the performance and on a few occasions we obliged, having been asked by the management to go as a company. Paul Nicholas and I were very good friends, as we've remained over the years. We trundled along with the rest of the cast to a late night premiere of *Duffy* starring James Fox, James Coburn and Susannah York. We discovered that the reception was a costume affair, with a prize of £250 for the most bizarre outfit. A lot of the guests turned up completely rigged out. One person was painted silver and looked like a tin man. I allowed myself to be goaded into the judging arena as it seemed that the *Hair* company was seen to be antisocial by not participating. I felt as if I was in

Crufts dog show walking around in a roped-off ring observed by the judges, who included James Fox. It was as close as I'll ever get to knowing what a beauty contestant must feel like. I felt like a complete fool. As I was wearing my normal day clothes it seemed all the more ridiculous that I should be marching around in the circle with people in strange costumes. I was stunned when the judges announced that I was the winner. It was shocking. They awarded me seven weeks' wages merely for making a spectacle of myself for ten minutes.

I was always uncomfortable about getting more attention than others in the cast. Since I didn't play one of the six featured characters, it seemed peculiar that the *Hair* publicity was so often linked to me. 'Hi. This is Chrissie,' which was my line early in the first half, was hardly a show-stopper. It may have had something to do with my willingness to deal with the press, which meant extra work and no extra pay. Suddenly to work with the best photographers and fashion editors was an education. It never dawned on me to refuse a photo session because it was too early in the morning. I was on time and amenable and considered this part of my job. Others made more of my having my picture in the papers than I did.

I appreciated my press but was wary of the celebrity offered to me. During rehearsal, when people speculated on which one of our talented company would emerge from the show, I hadn't been considered. Without a contract, I wasn't sure that I would be performing on the first night. I guess if I'd had secret aspirations about wanting to be a star, the fast build-up of publicity linking me to the hottest show in town would have registered differently. I merely felt guilty and embarrassed that I had hogged so much attention, especially as a couple of members of the cast seemed to feel that they had more right to it.

After our opening night, Wendy Hanson, the *Hair* publicist, told me that Pamela Colin of American *Vogue* wanted me to do a photo session with Patrick Lichfield. I was flabbergasted, and doubly so when I later got flowers and a note from its editor, Diana Vreeland. What I presumed would be an anonymous head shot in American *Vogue* turned out to be a four-page spread with a written profile.

I was considered Black and Beautiful suddenly and my busby and I established a new London fashion. Admittedly, I had changed my hairstyle, which made a statement in that it was exceedingly larger than the style they called the natural. But otherwise, I was the same old girl with the gap between her teeth who never could get thin enough.

Black had become beautiful as race riots burned their way across urban America. After the Watts riot of 1965, militancy gained momentum. The raised black fist symbolized a threatening demand. 'First Watts, when Beverly Hills?' was not an unrealistic concern, and when H. Rap Brown, of the militant Black Panther Party, said that violence was as American as apple pie, how could anybody challenge his statement? Dr Martin Luther King was assassinated on 4 April 1968. While Americans were still reeling from that horror, Bobby Kennedy was senselessly murdered sixty-two days later, which gave the conservatives another excuse to blame liberalism for the nation's madness. By the end of the year those conservatives put the Republicans back in the White House with Nixon holding the whip. We gallivanted on the London stage singing about peace and acting out the burning of draft cards when 540,000 troops were committed to Vietnam.

What happened in my country deeply affected me. It disturbed me that in America, sixties humanitarianism was dying while I sang about it so far from home. I wanted to believe that some of the thousands who saw the show took home its message as well as its melodies.

Full-page newspaper interviews and fashion covers took my life by surprise. Unemployment and stardom exchanged places so fast that I hadn't had time to move out of my bedsit. People who would otherwise have considered me invisible made efforts to include me in their gatherings. I was socially naive. (The first time I met Princess Margaret at a party, I commented at length on the smallness of her feet. As far as I was concerned, I was making conversation.) I enjoyed how much my scope expanded with the addition of celebrity, but I still knew the difference between a knife scar and a razor scar. *Hair* may have been an event on opening night, but it was £35-per-week employment, and that made it a steadying factor.

We performed six nights a week with Friday and Saturday matinées scheduled so close to the evening show that the management had to send out for sandwiches because we didn't have enough time to get our own. Somehow the energetic pace had a tranquillizing effect, and if our energy lagged, the company doctor was on hand with a vitamin shot. Between the show, the social cesspool and the publicity roundabout, my essential self survived.

But it took concerted effort. With journalists, photographers, socializers, taxicab drivers, shopkeepers, *Hair* enthusiasts and strangers in the street suddenly telling me I was wonderful and giving me special treatment, it was necessary to keep a close check on conceit. I discounted my sudden celebrity in the same way that I had trained myself to disregard being debased because of my race: I considered that other people's opinions of me weren't always rational.

I didn't want to be called a star. It made me uncomfortable. I was prepared to acknowledge that I'd stopped being invisible, which is a quality most human beings retain throughout their lives in spite of the heroism it takes to endure their day-to-day existence. I'd become visible under the magnifying lens of the media which can distort the image for better or worse, and I was lucky that it was for better.

However I dealt with my celebrity, it was still the stuff of fairy tales. Cinderella's story had nothing on mine. Designers gave me clothes, film producers gave me offers, newspapers wanted my opinions, and men of every description wanted my telephone number. Anonymity was a thing of the past. My busby, called a natural or an Afro, made me instantly recognizable.

By the time the 'Black is Beautiful' slogan leaped across the Atlantic, racial integration was fashionable in London. Without explanation or apology, Black-and-white couples were acceptable, and it was the norm to have a few Blacks dotted around a party. At the time, it seemed to be part of a progressive trend towards a more integrated society. There was no way of knowing that this trend was a fad that would fade like the slogan.

When my brown face was high-glossed on the 1968 Christmas cover of *Queen* magazine, there was the distinct feeling that 1969 was going to be a special year for me in London.

But I never expected that Paramount Pictures would be flying me to Hollywood.

Richard M. Roth, then a producer in Paramount's television division, had seen my American *Vogue* spread and wanted me to test for a TV series. The *Hair* producer said that in spite of my small part and low salary, they would not release me from my *Hair* contract to costar in an American TV series. To be on the safe side, when my round-trip ticket arrived, I didn't let anyone in the company know that I was flying to Hollywood.

Planes take you out of the world. I had a chance to think about what had happened to me in London and what could happen in LA. I sat on my own wearing the complimentary Pan Am flight bootees, drinking the complimentary champagne, in the nearly empty first-class compartment. Although I was enjoying the experience as an escapade, I remember thinking that I didn't ever want to believe in first class; I didn't want to become someone who believed in money.

A slinky black limousine was waiting for me at LA airport and shimmied me off to the Paramount office of young Mr Roth, who nearly dropped dead when I greeted him with a broad grin. As my mouth was closed in those *Vogue* photos, he had no way of knowing that I had the gap and he reacted as if I was missing a front tooth.

He carried his remake of me off with chivalry and personalized attention. In genuine filmland style, Richard whisked me straight to a cosmetic dentist who designed a plastic fitting to snap snuggly over my two front teeth, hiding my gap. We then zipped over to Hollywood and Vine to see if I could be fitted for a wig in Max Factor's. I was happy when they had nothing big enough.

I don't know whom I looked like during the screen test, but it wasn't anybody I recognized. A real stodge had done my make-up. Whereas my normal day make-up was as extreme as anybody's in London, with lower and upper false eyelashes and heavy dark-grey and white shading on the eyes, Hollywood TV wasn't into that yet. The make-up artist tinted my eyelids with matronly light-blue shadow and painted the thinnest possible trail of eyeliner. It might have been just the thing for Margaret Rutherford, but it didn't do a lot for me.

They really wanted the me from Oakland High, but I didn't like her anymore. I was able to act that role for the sake of a screen test, and I could tell that it would have had to become my full-time identity if I were to fit in.

In general, I wasn't comfortable. I hadn't sensed the relief of being home that you expect to feel when you've been away for two years, and I wasn't unhappy when the time came to check out of the Chateau Marmont and fly back to London. But first I made an afternoon detour to Ikey's. My mother was still happily married and living with Allison in their house near the Berkeley border of Kensington. My sister Pamala was studying and lived next door with her husband and little daughter, Stephanie.

The *Vogue* spread had quelled my family's rampaging fear that I was a hippie dropout headed for failure and destruction, but my mother still wanted to know when I planned to re-register at Berkeley so I could start working towards a career.

I had left London on a Friday morning and by the following Tuesday night I was back on stage with the rest of the company singing 'Aquarius'. I felt that I was home where I didn't have to conform, and where if anything was expected of me it was to be individual. I needed that. There was one luxury that London celebrity afforded me: the freedom to be myself without a single apology for my gap, my freaked-out hair, my brown skin, my slave-class ancestors or my radical views.

Soon after my American trip an offer came from a record plugger called Tony Hall. He wanted me to sign a production deal with him which he planned to link to a contract with Track Records. I signed on the dotted line after my introduction to Kit Lambert, who co-owned and ran Track.

At our first meeting, Kit was wearing a full-length raccoon coat. He moved down the aisle of the Shaftesbury Theatre with the sure-footedness of someone used to having things all his own way. Had he been an actor, he could have easily played Napoleon. He had the right stride and urgency to portray a little dictator. That should have put me off but it didn't.

When we went out to eat, I discovered that although he unquestionably believed in the privileges of stardom and the advantages of money, he was decidedly anti-showbiz in the established sense. The latter suited me fine. His prickly carelessness hovered near bad manners and made him seem devilish, which was entertaining. His upper-class English and clever banter left me certain that he was nobody's fool. He was entirely unsanctimonious about Robert Stigwood and this made me laugh a lot. Robert was the major producer of *Hair* and I was used to hearing his employees discuss him with cautious restraint.

Kit's dark curly hair was eye-catching but something about his expression kept him from having a kind face. He didn't have the vaguest air of physical vanity, though it was quite definite that he was vain about something.

I found our late supper nerve-racking, because Kit didn't actually converse; his thoughts were racing too fast for him to listen. It was useful that I'd learned to tolerate such habits at Berkeley and, forgetting how tedious this can get, I relished the company of someone who was mentally speedy. 'Speedy' turned out to be the operative word for him, and 'late' ran it a close second.

I was excited that Kit wanted to take me on. He wanted to sign me to his label with his other three bands, Jimi Hendrix, the Who and Arthur Brown, and he also wanted to manage me. He had no girl yet on his small label and no intention of signing any others. The fact that he was certainly not interested in women was refreshing. I didn't want to get involved with somebody who had designs on me. I was only worried about the ructions he would create around me at the theatre, because he insisted that I should leave the show, and my contract had another six months to run. He assured me it could be settled with a telephone call to Robert Stigwood. As it turned out, Kit left the dirty work of dealing with the *Hair* management largely up to me when he had me leave in April 1969. There had been other changes in the cast, so my departure wasn't tumultuous.

I guess I believed that Kit was totally compos mentis because I'd met enough students like him who played at being verbose. He was by no means a dullard, although I slowly found out that a lot of what he said was a repeat of some verbal performance he'd given before. In one ream of monologue, he'd pick his words to cajole, irritate, instigate and control. No doubt Kit was the closest thing the rock-and-roll business had to Oscar Wilde. One minute it was a conversation, next it was Kit's firm offer of a record deal with one of the strongest independent new labels in town. I was glad I hadn't landed that TV series.

A pageant of new faces came into my life as soon as I signed to Track in March 1969. I started looking for material to record with Tony Visconti, an American producer who agreed to do my first album. While I was still in *Hair*, Tony's patient nature made it very easy for me to slip back and forth between the two different mentalities that I needed to accommodate the music business and the theatre world. I'd walk out of the Shaftesbury and drop my tribal, effusive 'Hello darling' self and switch to my cooler 'Hey, what's happening?' manner.

My rock-and-roll image immediately required a definition. Tony had me listen to all kinds of music so we could find songs and establish a direction for my single. He was producing a band called Tyrannosaurus Rex, which was in fact only two boys, with one of them, Marc Bolan, doing the writing. Tony thought some of Marc's material might suit me.

I was sitting in the control room of Trident studios. It was dark apart from a dim stream of light that bounced back through the window overlooking the recording studio below. A small figure walked into the room. His cascade of dark curly hair locks commanded notice and he was wearing girl's shoes that looked like tap-dancing shoes, roundish-toed with a strap. His dark T-shirt with scooped neck and three quarter sleeves was also a girl's. He didn't look outrageous, just terribly pretty. I blushed and he smiled, but not at me, although I felt I had his undivided attention while he greeted everybody else.

Sometimes it's immediately obvious when two people are going to be together. It was that way with Marc and me before we spoke. We both had that feeling . . .

I personified things which Marc rejected. He was reclusive, macrobiotic, and professed aversion to success. He had no money and acted as though he was opposed to it on social grounds. Maybe his choosing to be with me was an indication that he was changing. Tony Visconti believed in Marc and continued to produce his records when Marc made his transition from an ethereal sound to mainstream rock.

Marc was a cautious boy creature whose whole philosophy was as soft as the palms of his hands and his lips which fluted the poetry that filled his head from his other world of unicorns and gypsy elves. Our relationship wasn't passionate, it was a delicate sigh, a whispering that belonged to a moment in time when love could be taking an acid trip together or extending a flower plucked from someone else's garden to a stranger passing in the street. Not that we did. Neither of us being into drugs was one of the things that made it easy to be together.

Marc looked like a flower child. Flower Power and flower children represented idealistic sentiments about peace and love associated with the hippie movement. For a short time Flower Power was brandished in the media and commercially exploited like a carbonated drink. Marc and I didn't consider ourselves hippies or flower children, but believed in man's capacity to govern himself peacefully.

We agreed about this, but we didn't see eye to eye on everything. He teased me about my success. I almost believed he spurned it, except he brought it up too much. Even without his prodding, I was unsure of my talent and uncomfortable with the privilege of my celebrity. To Marc, my visibility was commercial, and this wasn't appropriate for the serious art of music which he implied was validated by obscurity. His undercover enthusiasm for the Ronettes and Melangian girl-group vocals made his protestations about pop and rock success seem hypocritical.

I cut his songs 'Hot Rod Poppa' and 'Hippy Gumbo', and he sang on one of my sessions. Having the same producer made us feel we were in the same camp, and we were really very supportive of each other musically.

I remember hearing the changes in Marc's writing, particularly after he bought a kiddie's electric piano from Woolworth's. There was a repetitiveness in his lyrics and a bounce in his melodies which didn't have the ethereal quality of his acoustic songs. Around the same time, I hired a stereo for him, because he didn't have one when he moved from Blenheim Crescent into a flat above some shops in Little Venice. The sunlight broke through the front window there, and I would sit reading while he jangled on his new toy.

There were these and other moments of bliss, but our being together caused a schism in his life (or there was a schism in his life which was amplified by our being together). After a while, I didn't want to try to figure out which any more. I was looking for material and working in the studio and he was preparing to go back on the road. None of his friends were meant to have him for long, and it was my great fortune to have had him to myself for a time while he was such an outlandish thing of beauty, who satisfied my need for a stroke of innocence.

It was somebody in the publishing division at the Beatles' Apple office, newly opened on Savile Row, who suggested I consider doing a song from the first album by Dr John the Night Tripper. From it, Tony Visconti and I finally agreed to do a cover of a track called 'Walk on Gilded Splinters' as my debut single. This was in the days when an entire backing track could be put down in one session and sixteen-track recording seemed advanced. Rick Wakeman played piano, and Tony used a young Malaysian drummer named Ricky Fataar who had just arrived in England from South Africa.

The song had an eerie quality, because it was about gris-gris, better known as voodoo. Tony had a part written for a cor anglais which added an unearthly sound. I recorded the vocals on a separate night. It was extremely hot in the small vocal sound booth, so we taped newspaper to the window on the door of the cubicle and I sang in there nude from the waist up. There was nothing that I did that made Tony bat an eyelid.

The record went into the charts and I was asked to perform it on *Top of the Pops*. I nearly went into the annals of English television history when I appeared wearing a tight bolero top which, unbeknownst to me, allowed my breasts to poke out from the bottom every time I lifted my arms in a little voodoo conjuring motion.

While I was performing the song I could see Pete Rudge from Track madly flailing his arms at me from offside one of the cameras. I had no idea why he was doing this until I finished singing and he told me that I'd been exposing more than I'd planned to with every arm lift. I was hardly the one to be overly sensitive about such an innocuous exposure, not only because of my part in *Hair* and my nude spread in *Vogue*, but I had also done a nude session with David Bailey that we were using to promote the record.

I had met Bailey socially and by then done too much modelling to imagine that a session with him would have been different from the rest. I liked him and his girlfriend, Penelope Tree, a young New York model that he was living with when I went to his studio in Primrose Hill, which was also his home. I wasn't shy about taking my clothes off and asked for a heater to be put on. Nudity was as common as sliced bread in 1969 when David and I did that session. People took their clothes off all the time. The act had changed from being an expression of one's liberation to indicating a consciousness of man's natural state, to showing sexual freedom, to displaying abandonment, and had finally become just something to do. It makes me laugh now to think about it, but it was as fashionable as macrobiotic diets and burning incense. Body painting, too, was seen as an art form. When the *Daily Telegraph* commissioned Ralph Steadman to paint a royal crest on my breasts for the cover of the colour supplement, I realized that nudity was no longer the stuff of alternative culture. It had moved to the middle of the road.

The accidental appearance of my breasts on TV caused me to be seen as being provocatively wayward. The reports and complaints that were aired, with photographs of me in my errant bolero-length suede jacket, gave me more exposure, but this time with the slant that I was a bad girl. (My association with the wild boys signed to Track was further evidence.) Not that this adversely affected my single. We were ecstatic that it was a minor hit.

Soon after this I came into the Track office one Friday afternoon to be told by Peter Rudge that Jo Bergman, secretary for the Rolling Stones, had telephoned on behalf of Mick Jagger to ask me to be in the publicity photo to promote the band's next single, 'Honky Tonk Women'. The picture was going to be of a girl dressed like a sleaze bag standing in a bar with the Stones and they wanted me to be the girl.

I'd just had a record success, was putting my own band together to go out on the road, and had my image and reputation to think about. Representing my race, and more specifically Melangian women, always had to be considered

Marsha, Mick and Karis.

Emma Shouse Hunt, Marsha's great-grandmother.

1968.

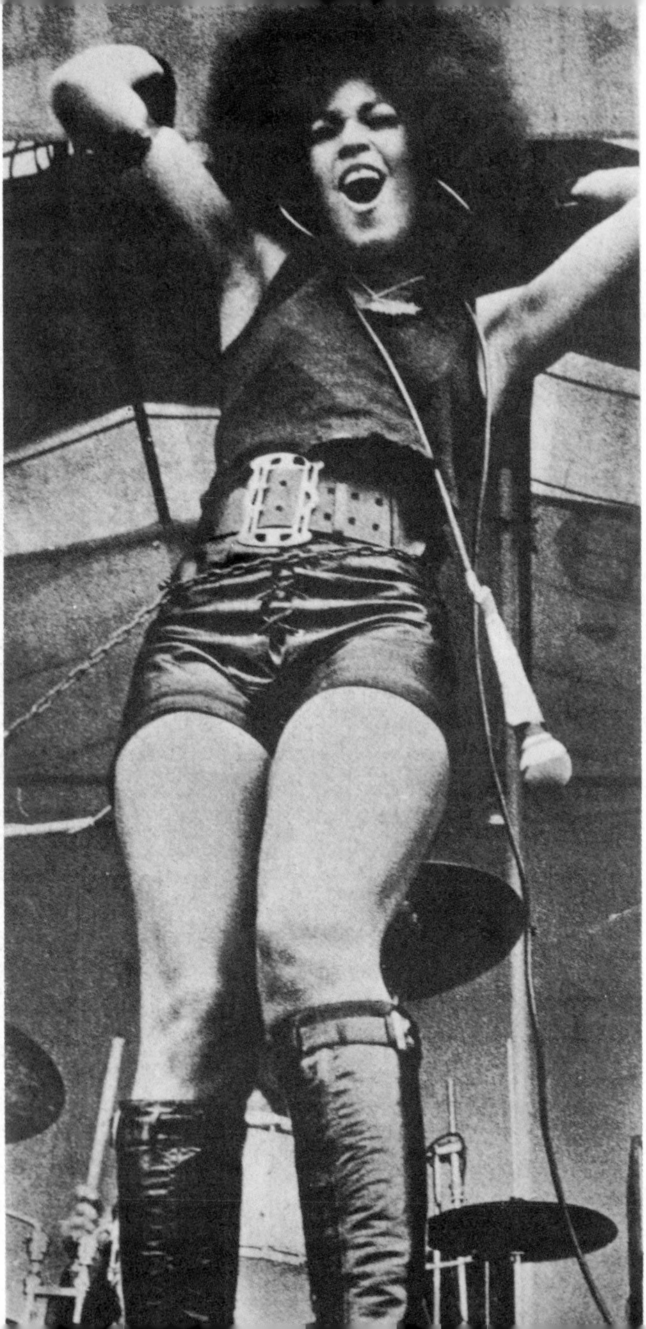

1969

November 1970.

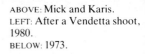

ABOVE: Mick and Karis.
LEFT: After a Vendetta shoot, 1980.
BELOW: 1973.

Hollywood, 1978.

PRINTED TIGERS
OF THE 1980 SEASON
TREES AND MEMORIES

APRIL 1983
ROOT
EARTHA KITT
profiled in ROOT with
DENIECE WILLIAMS
Dionne Warwick
and Frank Bruno
THE STATE OF
BLACK BRITAIN
FLAT RACING REVIEW

bazaar
BEAUTY ISSUE
THE
NEW MAKE-UP
AND
HOW TO PUT IT ON
DIRECTORY OF DECORATION
PART 1
EDNA O'BRIEN???
&
MARY McCARTHY!!!
SEX
IN
THE
STABLES

HUNT
39.030. DIE NEUE HIT-SINGLE
"THE OTHER SIDE OF MIDNIGHT"
PRODUZIERT VON PETE BELLOTTE
NEUE LP 69.052
NEUE MC 669.052
MARSHA

because of my visibility. The last thing we needed was for me to denigrate us by dressing up like a whore among a band of white renegades, which was an underlying element of the Stones' image. I tried to get in touch with Jagger to say 'thank you, but no thank you.' He returned my call very late and suggested he come round.

Mick arrived after midnight at the Bloomsbury flat in Endsleigh Court where I was temporarily staying with a designer friend named Brian Godbold whom I met through Sammy Lopez. Little Sammy, as he was known, was a Mexican American and one of that LA coterie that had waved me off to Paris back in 1966. He arrived in London the following year, became one of the Beautiful People who dallied about town in chic restaurants, and was tempted by the abundance of social excesses that were available. He moved out of Brian's one-bedroom flat as I moved in, taking over the living room and the leather Chesterfield sofa, while I searched for a permanent home of my own.

Endsleigh Court was the kind of block that might once have been a superior 1920s hotel, with its nearly impressive reception and its layers of long windowless corridors lit by overhead strips which were not quite bright enough and cast unfavourable shadows on the nondescript runner carpet and the nonspecific paint colour on the walls. The lighting did nothing for Mick's English complexion.

He was framed by the doorway as he stood grinning in a dark coat with his hands pushed down in the pockets. He looked so unlike any photograph I'd seen of him that had it not been for his phone call, I might not have been sure that this caller was Mick Jagger. He drew one hand out of his pocket and pointed it at me like a pistol. His silly 'Bang' was precisely the icebreaker we needed to get over my ungracious hesitation before I invited him in, not sure how to salute a notorious rogue who rings me just before midnight and suggests he pop round on a pretext of loneliness.

There's no doubt that this was an odd way for two people to meet. The unlikelihood of the circumstances gave us the opportunity for a long conversation. We had to talk – there was nothing else to do, sitting in the small living room, after Brian coyly introduced himself and tee-hee'd off to bed. Maybe I gave Mick wine, but more than likely he got endless cups of tea. I certainly didn't offer a joint, though it would have been the thing to do, and made it quite clear that I was not into drugs. I wouldn't be surprised if he now claims that he didn't even get the tea.

He wasn't beautiful or even striking, and after Marc's mythical good looks, there was no pretending that Mick was. He sat in the mirrored alcove giving me a back as well as front view of his lank shoulder-length hair, which was darker than I'd imagined it, making his skin look sallow. He apologized for the spots (but we all got them). His redeeming facial feature was his infectious grin, which was utterly boyish and openly direct and made me less wary.

It was a relief to find out that he wasn't at all like any musician I'd been up against, and to think that he was the same person who had such a wide-boy image intrigued me, because there was nothing of the wrangling poseur about him. He was direct and straightforward and his London accent got less harsh as the morning crept in while I listened to him talk about anything and everything. We rallied old stories to find common ground. He functioned in the fastest lane of rock-and-roll music but, having come to it through the blues, knew cronies like Alexis. Like the London blues crowd, he had a respectable knowledge of Melangian root music. He even understood Melangian dialect and spoke it as well as I could speak cockney – well enough for us to catch each other's humour. I could throw a Melangian phrase at him and he'd hurl it back, sometimes with an authentic twist, to make me squeal with laughter which I tried to check so that I didn't wake Brian. Mick loved my belly laughs and wickedly tried to evoke them when we should have been speaking barely above a whisper.

The fact that I was free to talk about something political or socially relevant without his expression clouding over and his thoughts drifting off to a pair of tits in a pub was encouraging. It made me take notice of this stranger, whose media visibility had given a false impression that had to be dismantled, and who had walked in from out of nowhere to mark his time with mine. I believe he was actually lonely and the fact that he was able to admit it made him more man than I. He was riveting.

I didn't know why he stayed so long and even though I realized that he had come to look me over, believing that he might take a bite, I had received him out of sidewalk curiosity expecting to find him predictable. Instead he was in all ways a surprise. He wasn't typically white, or English, or rock and roll, and made the effort to be straightforward and decisive about most of what he said. It made our conversation easy on even mundane matters like family. He had feelings and he exposed his emotions with such defencelessness that I wondered occasionally if he'd forgotten that he didn't know me. How could he know that I was the right person to tell and that even now I wouldn't betray my promise that what he told me that night was between us?

When he walked out of the door at six or seven in the morning, I didn't expect to see him again, although he said he would call. I figured that I was just another night on the town and the secrets that he shared with me were indiscretions spilled like white wine on the carpet, expected to dry after the party was over and to disappear without stain. He actually needed to talk to someone, and maybe he found my ability to listen as unexpected as I found his to speak openly about what was on his mind. He was in a bad situation at home and with his band that had no easy solution.

He didn't subject me to a babbling stream of drug consciousness, or a fitful confession to relieve guile and guilt. Mick didn't talk down to me in the way musicians often tried to, disguising chauvinism beneath a tone of ribaldry. He held no prejudices which he needed to cover up to talk about racial politics, and he was aware of the devices that kept the world in a mess. My ignorance about matters that he was versed in didn't put him of, and it was rather foolish of me to think that after we made love he wouldn't come back as soon as possible.

Since childhood, my straddling a black-and-white world had left me stateless and I didn't presume that I'd come across anybody who could empathize with my sense of belonging to both worlds. Perhaps my assumption that he understood me was wrong, but I don't think so. Not that night.

Whenever he called after that, I knew that he didn't just want to see me, he needed to talk, and I felt a responsibility towards him and his problems because we were not so much lovers as friends. There were no silly cat-and-mouse games. He knew that I adored him and that he could depend on me.

In spite of the fact that I couldn't hold his success or mine in high esteem because it seemed superficial, he realized I respected him as I respected myself. I was always straight. He could rely on that. One source of his worry was that his live-in girlfriend, Marianne Faithfull, was dependent on drugs. Perhaps the fact that I was cold sober was my attraction.

I've tried then and since to understand why he came to me. He must have had a selection to choose from. But he came like a golden eagle with a broken wing, and I suppose he believed that I had the willingness and capacity to bandage it up and help him to soar.

Our relationship was another stimulus that catapulted me into a new throng overnight. Around the time Mick snuck into my life I had decided to use White Trash, a Glaswegian band signed to the Apple label, as my backing band. We usually rehearsed in the Apple studio getting ready for my solo debut and a spring tour that had been booked after the success of 'Gilded Splinters'. I was fully my own person and music gradually gave me a sense that I could continue to grow in it and use it to express myself and channel my energy, which seemed to get more ferocious with the demands of work, play and my new secret life.

Once Mick popped into one of my rehearsals with White Trash, and I could see how awed the band was by his being there although they tried hard not to show it. It made me realize that whoever Mick was privately, his media visibility left him so magnetized and magnified that people weren't likely to relate to him beyond that. In private he was a person, but in public he was a music product, and he automatically adapted to serve his public image. It was a necessary reflex, but one that he never needed to exercise when he was alone with me. He was shrewdly manipulative as a commodity, and I was glad that there was no call for me to cope with that. Our complete privacy sheltered me from the product and only exposed the person. Being a product myself made me realize how important it was to strike a balance between being a commodity, a media abstraction, and a human being. It was hard work to be as visible as he was, and apart from making music and dealing with the creativity and business involved with that, he was virtually managing the Stones. It's no wonder that a lot of people in rock and roll who were under similar pressure opted for staying stoned, which was a good way of not dealing with any of it. He resorted to that too, but never with me. I may have been another kind of drug.

In our sequestered friendship, I was sturdy and steadfast: butch is what he called it. There was nothing namby-pamby about me, and I tried to be ready with some laughter, wit and common sense whenever I welcomed him back to our private world. Our relationship wasn't really about romance or even passion, which was everywhere for the taking. I felt that it could thrive by my being supportive. I loved to see him run free. It was all very sixties – very Kahlil Gibran. In the state Mick's life was in, it must have suited him. I needed my own independence and didn't expect him to relinquish his.

To live with someone that you care about can destroy a relationship. The sore state of marriage in our society is proof of it. Two people can have a totally satisfying relationship living apart and maintaining their independence. Cohabiting can mean that you live too close to be comforting.

Back in 1969, the sexual revolution was pumping out all kinds of hypothetical variations on the theme of male/female relationships. My ideas were moderate set against free love and communes and other alternative relationships which were up for experiment. For someone like me who had grown up in a matriarchy, the ideal of a man and woman living together seemed nice but unnecessary. I never envisioned myself as the sort of girl who would dangle from a man's coat sleeve or find any gratification in being Mr Somebody's wife, and by 1969 this wasn't considered unusual or impractical. I made no secret of it in my public and my private life.

While I rehearsed to go on the road backed by White Trash, the Stones were reassembling their ranks and Brian Jones (who was said to be putting a band together with Alexis) was to be replaced. I told Mick about Mick Taylor and sheepishly went to John Mayall's Fulham house to find out how to get hold of him.

At the Stones' concert in Hyde Park on 5 July 1969, I was rather proud that Mick Taylor proved himself to be a worthwhile addition to their line-up. But that Saturday concert, which was going to be a launch for the band without Brian, also served as Brian's memorial, because he was found dead in his swimming pool four days before it. What should have been an open-air showcase for the Stones with Taylor on guitar had emotional overtones with Mick first reading from Shelley and releasing 10,000 caged white butterflies from the stage to commemorate Brian. The atmosphere was tenser than the Granada television cameras showed, but Mick in his white dress had an air of flamboyance that overshadowed his strain and distress. Marianne Faithfull sat on stage with the other wives, girlfriends and Stones' entourage. Her long blonde hair had been hacked short, a self-mutilation which indicated to me that she wasn't in a good state. This was confirmed a few days later when she overdosed in Sydney. For Mick's sake, I had hoped that she would stay on top of things.

I was booked to do a gig at the University of Manchester that night and should have been motoring up the M1 by the time the band appeared on stage, later than expected. One of Mick's assistants who knew about us and wanted to be helpful had placed me in an obvious spot: perched 30 feet in the air on a scaffold attached to the left-hand side of the stage. I was worried that Mick wouldn't understand if I disappeared in the middle of his all-important gig so I stayed longer than I'd planned. From our aerial vantage point I was too nervous about being late for my own gig to appreciate the sight of all the people in Hyde Park, a gathering of rock fans including hippies, flower children, freaks, students, teenagers, straights, you name it. I had never been a Stones fan and in spite of my relationship with Mick, I always had a hard time at his concerts getting excited about the music, though I came to appreciate it eventually.

Later that night, when I got back from Manchester, Mick came to see me. I was glad that I'd been at Hyde Park to show that I was behind him. It had been a long taxing day for him. And me. It was a relief that it was over, that he'd triumphed and that the Stones were back in business doing live gigs.

The next hurdle was our parting in the morning in time for Mick to catch a plane to Sydney, Australia. He and Marianne were booked there to do a film, *Ned Kelly*, directed by Tony Richardson. I laughingly shrugged off Mick's last kiss. I hate goodbyes especially when the lump in my throat threatens to get the better of me. That day it rained harder than I'd known it to in England. It was as if the heavens sympathized with me.

After arriving in Sydney, Marianne took a near-fatal overdose of pills and went in a coma. I was frantic, because I didn't think that Mick had the stamina to deal with another crisis. I had seen him so dogged, but there is only so much a person can take.

On 9 July, David Ruffell from the Track office escorted me to Germany and on to Casablanca to do a television gig as part of the country's celebration of the king's birthday. I was reveived like a visiting dignitary, although the local children looked at me with my hair combed on its end and ran as if they'd seen a Martian.

I didn't really expect Mick to keep in touch with me while he endured the filming in an Australian winter with Marianne hospitalized. I doubted he was the type to write, but he still flummoxed me with surprises.

His letters and phone calls during his absence strengthened our friendship which was more sensitive and delicate than I had expected. He wrote laughing, sad, pensive, deep, observant, touching letters to me, the friend he called Miss Fuzzy, and the wonderful thing about them is that they captured the essence of him at that time when he was still unjaded. I have them all except one I've mislaid which he scribbled with his left hand, because he had injured his right during filming. A gentle letter came dated 'Sunday the moon', written on that 20 July when the world watched by televised satellite as America's three astronauts landed on the moon, 239,000 miles away. The two of us spent a fortune phoning each other. Once he called to say that he'd got an idea to write a song about me called 'Brown Sugar'.

I was gigging while Mick was away, and cutting some more material for my album. Kit took me into the IBC studio, where he recorded the Who, to do three tracks with Pete Townshend, Ron Wood and two other Small Faces, Kenny Jones and Ian McLagan. Ronnie and I did a vocal together on 'Wild Thing', but it never made the album because Kit lost the tape. With the success of 'Gilded Splinters', Kit had decided he should produce me himself. He dismissed Tony Visconti, claiming that the material he'd produced wasn't strong enough. Though Kit was a great producer for the Who, he and I were badly matched. Once he was nearly three hours late for a vocal session. The backing vocalists and I were fed up and worn out from waiting by the time he turned up with the audacity to be in a vivacious spirit. I had to talk myself into a state of calmness, because I was actually in a crazed fury.

The relationship between Kit and me had been badly affected from the moment his partner, Chris Stamp, returned from the States. Chris was angry that Kit had taken on an artist without consulting him. I was caught in the middle of the power politics, which they seemed to resolve by making me the fall guy. Chris was Terence Stamp's younger brother but exhibited none of Terry's guru calm or 'good vibes'. (Chris was always on about somebody's vibes.) One of Chris's redeeming factors was his loyalty to Mike Shaw, the Who's lighting man who was a boyhood friend of his. Mike had a motor accident delivering the Who's equipment in 1966 which had left him paralysed. Chris had kept him on the payroll, found a job for him at the office and made sure he had attendants.

As the pressure built at Track, I did think that Kit and Chris put up a good front, that they were collected and dealing with it all. They still had the Who, Jimi Hendrix and Arthur Brown, as well as myself and a one-hit band called Thunderclap Newman who were protégés of Townshend's. But the bravado covered up a lot of panic, par for the course in the hit-and-miss music business.

Kit and Chris used to expect me to eat the rubbish they wouldn't have dared serve up to their male bands. Their juggling my producers and not being consistent about what direction my album was taking was detrimental to my career. I'd been in the charts and should have pounced in again on the heels of that initial success and the publicity derived from it. My visibility from *Hair* was worth a lot in the record business, where bands used gimmicks and hype to be seen. When Chris came back from the States to find Kit had signed me, he offered my management to David Ruffell and Peter Rudge.

Peter Rudge was married to a school teacher named Frankie who kept him under control. Pete was a pudgy, sweet-natured boy. It was hard to believe that he was a Cambridge graduate although he was certainly bright. He was an innocent when I met him, but there was a glint of ambition in his eyes which sharpened when he talked deals. The majority of the Who's tour activity relied on Pete, and while Kit Lambert and Chris Stamp are always associated with the band's early progress, Pete was the person I heard hustling to get them into venues like the Metropolitan Opera. Pete was in the office by eleven executing the good ideas that Stamp and Lambert had. Together with David Ruffell, he formed Muipo management. (Muipo is opium backwards.) They would have been exceptionally effective managers, but while employed at Track they had neither the money nor the independence to be decisive. In 1969 when Mick was looking for a replacement for Jo Bergman, an American secretary who helped him handle the Stones' affairs, I suggested Pete for the job. A couple of years later he was working for Mick, booking all their big international tours.

David Ruffell, kind and efficient, was the receptionist when I started at Track. Sitting at the front desk, he was a welcome sight. I was confident that David and Pete were genuinely concerned about my musical direction and might do a more competent job than Chris anyway, but what he really hoped to do was humiliate me by giving my career over to his office staff. Chris was constantly goading me and trying to provoke me and I don't think he ever imagined that I was holding back the vitriol that I one day showered on him. Even I was shocked when I finished, but it didn't resolve anything. Shouting rarely does. Subsequent to that shouting match I adopted a take-no-shit attitude in the office that I'd believed I could suppress in England, which was still registering in my head as a sprawling Grumblethorpe.

I finally had to accept that I needed a temper in the record business, because for all the camaraderie on the surface, the business had a ferocious dog-eat-dog element. On the road I didn't feel it so strongly, except in band politics. A band can turn on one of its own like a pack of wolves.

In 1969, the brotherhood of English rock bands was like a drugged soccer league. I was one of the few girls who had joined it by fronting a hard rock sound and getting out on the road with an aggressive band. This got me into the league in spite of my being a girl, but Chris acted as if my entree via fashion and theatre was a crime that eliminated my right to play. I wasn't fazed. My passing up the joint and the snort of coke also made him want to leave me sitting out the play on the bench. He was also one of those chic street people, both Black and white, who thought they had a right to determine who qualified as 'Black' when Black militancy was in vogue.

These things are sent to try us.

My sharpened edge transferred from my office persona to my stage identity, which became hard-hitting, boot-grinding, fist-thumping and motor-driven. I learned from the rock boys, and it was a boy's performance I gave, tinted by the pleasure I got from being unmitigatedly female. This stage image was fully developed on my first tour, backed by White Trash.

My tough delivery got me interned for two weeks in a countryside naturopathic clinic where I was ordered not to speak so that I could heal my ragged throat which I'd battered by singing with force instead of technique. Being there left me only ten days to put together and rehearse a new band before I had to climb the stage on 30 August at the Isle of Wight festival, where Bob Dylan made his first public appearance after a three-year absence.

I came on before the Who. I was the only girl rocker billed during that three-day outdoor extravaganza of hour after hour of music.

I looked out over the sea of people. The encampment of 250,000 music lovers made history by their sheer number and swarmed that tiny offshore island. One could have imagined that our revolutions in music, sex, fashion, drugs and alternative cults were all there was in the world – we were the ruling class. It was impossible to concentrate on one face or to see the audience in full because the expanse of bodies was too vast. The shockingly awesome sight of people the size of ants and dots crawling for nearly a mile back took me so off guard that when I stepped forward from behind a stack of speakers, I very nearly wet myself.

The tower that I had stood on at the Stones concert had let me look at the audience with aerial detachment and their mass was balanced against the background of trees and grass. But although the Isle of Wight stage was elevated, it wasn't so high up that it created an aerial view. Instead, I was looking just feet above the tops of heads and could see the crowd meet the horizon of blue-grey sky in a slow, pulsating wave of motion that almost made me seasick. I heard my bass player say 'Fuck me' as he looked out. There was nothing more you could say.

The press enclosure in the front of the stage was very broad and bounded an area larger than a big auditorium, set apart by white metal barricades. Even with this compound, it was impossible to see anybody specifically without taking a moment to focus, and it would have been ridiculous to suppose you could spot somebody you knew. Though it was full summer daylight, sometimes I pretended I was performing into dark stalls and that people could see me but I couldn't see them.

The festival stage was much larger than any that I had seen or been in, because it had as much depth as length and width. It was like a dance-hall floor stacked with huge speakers. I was accustomed to making eye contact with my musicians to give cues for the start and finish of a song, but I could hardly see them without turning around in full. There was such a distance between us, a glance wasn't enough. I was using the Who's equipment and their roadies, who were incredibly efficient and adept. I was indebted to them for their help, but we hadn't worked together before and they were one more unfamiliar quantity on the stage. The band had as difficult a time seeing me as I had seeing them, and this caused occasional problems, like the drummer thinking I'd announced a song that I hadn't. He drummed the one he thought I'd announced throughout the one that the band and I were actually doing. He was so carried away with his head down, totally into what he was playing, I just couldn't get his attention. It was wild.

I was wearing a torn black T-shirt and tight black leather gloves with my heavy rings worn outside them. I had had a pair of black leather short shorts made for me, like ones we used to wear in Philly in the fifties until the city officials banned them from being worn downtown. Because the press section was 10 feet below the stage and the cameras were shooting up, the shots of me featured in the international press reports of the concert were angled at my crotch. This was another occasion when I got more exposure than anticipated. The next fashion season, short shorts were featured and labelled hot pants.

This sounds corny, but performing that afternoon was like being in a dream. I was up there doing it, leaping about and making all the motions, wailing till I was hardly able to speak, and yet I wasn't. I don't know where I was, but I wasn't quite there somehow. It was like being stoned, but I was absolutely sober as always and hadn't touched anything. It wasn't a bad feeling at all, it was just different – out of the world. This wasn't the first time it happened, but it's the one I remember best, when I was bopping like a thing possessed and feeling at the end of it as if I'd been in a dream. Music could have a weird effect on me even when I was the one making it.

Mick was in Australia when the festival was on, understandably pining to be back in England at the biggest open-air concert in history (up to that point). As he promised in a letter, he was there in my head and heart.

During this summer, I spent most of my time gigging and when 'Walk On Gilded Splinters' was released in Europe, I was off to do television promotion. David Ruffell usually went with me. He shared a flat in Hammersmith with Tom McLean, an ex-dancer from Glasgow who took a personal interest in my work as he so often had to listen to David and me plotting my career. I was fronting a band which meant that my musicians expected me to define our musical direction, look after their interests when we were at a gig, pay their wages at the end of the week, and be responsible for the roadies, the gear and the vans that carried them. I was the boss and it was down to me. Aware of the strain, David and Tom tolerated my uprisings.

Rock fame for many wasn't just the promise of riches, it was also the right to act like the devil in front of the entourage of worshippers, flunkies and leeches. The high vibration of music added to the drug of applause made some musicians need to stay up there, hypnotized and reeling in the euphoria. I saw young gifted boys killing themselves with their determination to maintain or recapture the high by drink or drugs or whatever it took them not to come down. They didn't know when they'd had enough, and there was no ceiling to stop them. The pace of doing one-nighters – working through the night to prove you were an automaton of the thrill skill, wrapping an audience up into another sensory zone, and being treated like Jesus if you could – made a lot of people crazy. Drugs weren't necessarily the cause, they may only have been the effect.

It was hard not to get caught up in it, but I always knew that it was important to avoid it. Looking back, I guess my not getting stoned is what saved me. I'd probably be one of the dead ones otherwise, because my energy level was always over the top, hardly letting me sleep except when I was chauffeured around in my big white Citroën by my driver, Roger Searle, who with his long, dark tresses and goatee looked more like a musician than some of my musicians.

The travelling we did all around England and Europe from exquisite hotels to dives wasn't work, it was my education. I was less excited about the money I was supposedly making and the visibility I was establishing than the sense of freedom I got from being a person in my own right and making my own music.

Added to the pleasure of performing, I got satisfaction from the fraternity within the business. The relationship between musicians, technicians, roadies, and those on the periphery of management had more equality then, before the general stakes became so high. Musicians helped other musicians, road crews gave each other a hand, lead singers did backup on somebody else's session, and bands lent each other gear when equipment failed. This was never more apparent than at a gig I did at the Bilzen Jazz Festival in Belgium in August 1969. Steve Marriott, who had been the lead singer with the Small Faces, and Peter Frampton, formerly lead guitarist with the Herd, had put a band together, Humble Pie, which was on the Bilzen bill. They were managed by Andrew Oldham, who was also there, generously passing out pills and trying to keep spirits high for the long outdoor festival. I was in a bit of a state, because my conga drummer, Tex, had been busted at customs for an improper passport and I didn't find this out until my band arrived, an hour before we were due to go on.

Because of the rain, the festival carried on at a slowed pace. By the time I was announced, it wasn't only raining but it was getting dark and the audience was drenched. I'd never sung in the rain before and wasn't sure if we were all going to get electrocuted by our mikes and electric guitars, but I didn't have to worry long. One of the generators failed. My mike was dead and the lights went out.

We persevered for the audience's sake. The guitar and bass were powered separately, so my musicians kept playing. With the audience getting restless, suddenly Frampton and

Marriott and some of the other musicians bounded onto the stage and started banging on the absent Tex's drums, shaking his maracas and chiming in with my unmiked vocal to salvage what music we could out of air and rain and darkness. Our audience was spellbound by the sight of our joint effort more than by the sound of the music we made.

Not long after Mick came back from Australia in September, I landed my first film role in a picture that Walter Shenson was to direct, *Welcome to the Club*. Regularly, I had disagreements with either Kit or Chris at the Track office over my next single and who was to produce it, so I was relieved that I was going to be away for a couple of months. After Kit had partially recorded my second single and casually and irresponsibly passed it on to two other producers in succession to complete, I was angry with myself for having signed a contract that I couldn't get out of it. Kit and Chris had no interest in me, and David and Pete as my managers depended on them for their wages.

Welcome to the Club was a comedy about three Melangian USO performers who were sent to Hiroshima to entertain the troops, and the predicament they encountered stationed on a white base. I was excited about working with Walter, who had produced the Beatles' films *A Hard Day's Night* and *Help*. We were to shoot the entire film in Copenhagen and most of the cast, including Jack Warden, who was starring, were coming from the States.

In the late sixties films were often integrated on a small scale. The plot of this film managed to be controversial and funny. I was to play the frump of the trio and Walter agreed to let me play the character with my gap. It was the first time my gap was going to get an airing since *Hair*, because I'd continued after the test at Paramount to wear the piece that snapped over it.

Flying off to shoot the film that November, I was thrust into moviemaking on a major scale without any preparation, but none of the actors or crew behaved as though I didn't have a right to be there. I didn't take the opportunity lightly. I had to learn to act in front of the cameras. I was working with a company of experienced actors. I never saw any rushes, because I knew that if I saw myself acting, I'd be too self-conscious to carry on for the next day's shooting. When I could, I would be on the set to watch Jack Warden's work, because he was an education in nuance and comic timing.

I couldn't understand why so many opportunities came my way, but I didn't take them for granted. It still stunned me when my friend Pamela Colin tracked me down in Copenhagen to ask if I could fly back to do the cover of American *Vogue*. There had never been a Melangian on the cover and I imagine that Diana Vreeland considered it a progressive move. She wanted to have me photographed by Patrick Lichfield in London, and Walter kindly let me off for a weekend. I couldn't believe, sitting on that plane as it touched down in London, that it was happening.

Mick was touring in America while I was filming in Denmark, and I knew, with the number of girls that he had access to, he was very busy on stage and off. I was delighted that he was having a good time on the band's first tour of America since 1966.

Then came Altamont, California, on 6 December 1969, when a spectator was killed while the Stones were performing. This was the third tragedy that Mick had to confront in the time I'd known him. I stayed calm and was glad that he knew where to find me in my hotel in Lyngby, a Copenhagen suburb where the icy winter made the reality of violence and aggression at an open-air rock concert seem unthinkable. Mick and I stayed in touch by telephone. I only had a few days left of shooting and concentrated on the job. Getting my timing right in the shots was my minute-to-minute preoccupation.

Mick wanted to pick me up from Copenhagen on 10 December by private plane so that I could fly with him to the south of France to look at a house. I'd known that he and the band were leaving England for tax reasons and moving to France in the coming year. I wanted to see him, but I didn't want him to pick me up. Somehow, I always feared that my association with him would crowd out my own identity. I never wanted to be known as Mick Jagger's girlfriend. He and Marianne had split up, and I thought he needed time to readjust.

I knew Mick very well, because he had nothing to lose by showing himself to me not merely as he wanted to be but as he was. Our friendship relied on our being straight with each other. His traits were obvious and linked to his ambition: his goodness and badness, his obsequious interest in the upper class, his penchant for Melangian girls, his temptations, his strength and vulnerability. His interest in me was that I offered unconditional love . . . and why not? Why must we treat love as a form of barter?

I stayed with him for a couple of weeks after Marianne left, and tried to help him make the transition. She had a young son by her marriage who had also lived with them, and I got the feeling that he missed family life, the child and the dog more than the woman.

Mick was close to Keith Richards and Anita Pallenberg who lived on the same road. After one visit to their house, I decided to keep my distance. I didn't find their being into hard drugs cute or adventurous. (A couple of the people that I had met in Berkeley in the summer of 1964 were dead from overdoses.) Mick doted on Keith, and I didn't voice any opinion but I avoided contact.

I liked Charlie and Shirley Watts, Ian and Cynthia Stewart and Alan Dunn, Mick's all-seeing, soft-spoken driver. But on the whole I stayed away from the Stones and their entourage. I've always been wary of becoming one of a group and retained my sense of isolation while I appeared to be in the centre. It seemed the best way to hang on to myself and to be a valuable friend to Mick.

I bought Mick a puppy for Christmas. He spent it at Keith's house in the country, and I stayed in London puppy-sitting at David Ruffell and Tom McLean's flat. While I was in Copenhagen, Dave and Tom had made all the arrangements for me to take over the £14-per-week rental of Roger Daltrey's flat in St John's Wood a few blocks from the Abbey Road studios. However unbiased Londoners may have seemed on the surface, when it came to getting a flat in 1969, being Melangian meant extreme difficulties. So Dave and Tom arranged the lease, signing for a Mrs Ratledge who was abroad in Denmark. Surely I would never have got the flat otherwise. On the first day of the new decade, 1 January 1970, I was to take possession of my new home. Roger Daltrey had done some exceptionally fine carpentry work in it. It was a beautiful maisonette.

I couldn't have asked for more than I got in 1969. My artist/management relationship with David Ruffell as well as the friendship that we developed was one of the most important developments of that year, because David helped me stay grounded. He believed as I did that success was not the beginning and end of my world and that my notions about fairness and rights were still relevant to my life.

10

PRIORITIES

Sitting in Mr Chow's restaurant, I was more taken aback when Mick said I would be a good mother and we should have a baby than I had been when he stood in David Ruffell's kitchen after the Christmas holidays and told me that he loved me. On both occasions, I was deeply touched.

Mick was a notorious womanizer. Sometimes he would surprise me with a glorious gift or entrance me with his delicate kisses, and I would laugh at myself for being easy prey for cavalier charm. I would have died for him. But I was reluctant to think that I really mattered to Mick, although he shared his secrets and longings with me. I always assumed that I was just another of his fancies until that night we dined at Mr Chow's. Talking about having his child made me feel that I was special to him. Marianne had miscarried the baby that they would have had around the time that Keith Richard's son Marlon was born. It was understandable that he considered having a second try. Everything was going well in my life and moving into the big St John's Wood flat had given me a great feeling of stability and independence. It would be wonderful to have a baby.

It was modern to talk about a shared parenthood in a pragmatic way, which was how we went about it. He would live abroad as planned but be a good absent father. It was another indication of our being progressive as a new decade began.

The sun was shining and the air was crisp. We were walking through Hyde Park on the way to his meeting with Ahmet Ertegun of Atlantic Records when I told Mick that I'd got confirmation that morning that I was three weeks pregnant. We romped in the park and he was very happy. I wouldn't have been hurt if he had said that he'd changed his mind about wanting a baby. I told him so. I was prepared to have an abortion. He assured me he was pleased as long as I was, too. I was bursting with excitement, and while I believed at the time that I knew what having a baby meant, I didn't really expect it to change my life in any way. I was making money and had a lovely home. My prospects were excellent, and I was sure they'd continue to be so.

Going up to Ertegun's suite at the Dorchester, we bumped into Steven Stills in the elevator. I'd met him only a few nights before when he had joined Mick and me with Billy Preston and two of the Edwin Hawkins singers, whom I'd met in Berlin and who were in London to promote 'Oh Happy Day'. They had converged on my new flat to sing and bang their way through the night on the handsome old upright piano that Daltrey had left behind when he moved out. Billy did most of the piano playing and inspired the impromptu songwriting. A phrase of a few words became a song, a riff and, by four in the morning, merely a forgotten moment. The elderly Danish widow who lived in the flat below me was probably used to the racket, because no doubt Daltrey had made his share.

I didn't stay long at Mick's meeting with Ahmet. They had business to do, and I had a meeting at Track to discuss my next single. I was relieved to slip away from Ertegun's suite. I'd slung myself on an overstuffed floral sofa, which was uncomfortable because the custom-tailored green suede trouser suit I was wearing was so tight. I could hardly breathe while sitting down. It had nothing to do with my being pregnant. I always persuaded Keith and Connie Wyatt, the tailors who made all my leather clothes, to make everything as tight as they could. I assured them that I would lose inches by the final fitting. Of course, I rarely did.

A few of Mick's trustworthy employees like his secretary, Jo Bergman, receptionist Shirley Arnold, chauffeur Alan Dunn, and housekeeper Bruna Girardi were sworn to secrecy and told I was pregnant. I also shared the news with David and Tom, and Roger, my driver. Mick agreed that only a few people whom we trusted should know at that stage, to avoid unwanted press. I'd proved that it was possible to keep our relationship out of the newspapers although what Mick did otherwise was always bellowed by the press and turned into a circus. I certainly didn't want journalists to have a field day with my pregnancy. I had a good relationship with the press and tried to maintain it after I acknowledged how important my visibility was to my work, particularly with the music papers. But I still thought that I had a right to privacy in personal matters, which included my friendship with Mick.

Kit, unaware of my pregnancy, had taken a renewed interest in me. It probably had something to do with the Shenson film, the American *Vogue* cover (which was never used in the end) and the whiff of gossip that I was seeing Mick on the quiet. Kit booked an expensive session so that I could cut a Simon and Garfunkel song called 'Keep The Customer Satisfied'. We recorded it in the biggest studio in town, Olympic, and he'd hired a full orchestra, including Maynard Ferguson, who blew a howling solo across the end reprise of the final take. But the most important thing about the session for me was that Kit had me cowrite the B side. Ferguson put music to some of my lyrics and we also cut this song at that session. I'd been writing lyrics ever since I lived at Caroline Coon's but they stayed undisclosed in my exercise books. There was so much friction between Kit, Chris and me that I was reluctant to push my writing, because they would have wanted publishing rights. When my single was rush released, it went into the charts and nearly made the top 10 but not nearly enough for Kit. Again, he let the momentum slip and didn't take me back in the studio for a follow-up. So I trotted around Europe and England again, promoting the record through television spots and live gigs, carrying the baby.

The physical inconvenience and increasing discomfort of pregnancy reminded me that somebody else was dependent on my body. The right to consider myself first had ended. It wasn't a dramatic realization, it came to me gradually. I gave up cigarettes, though nobody had been able to convince me to stop smoking since I was thirteen. I could do without during the pregnancy. I was even willing to change my diet. I accepted that my passion for junk food wasn't nutritional. As my pregnancy advanced I got health-conscious and ate sensibly. I was adjusting to my imminent responsibility.

I gradually realized that I would have to relinquish my freedom once I became a mother. I hadn't really considered this when I had my coil removed. We both understood while making love that we might be creating something. But I was twenty-three and he was twenty-six, and the prosperity of the sixties had extended our adolescence, as it had done for most of our generation. The freewheeling, freethinking, free-spending movement and the rush of opportunity seemed boundless. No one predicted its decline. I took it for granted that it would continue during motherhood.

Mick wanted a boy, and I just wanted something healthy. When he proposed we call the baby Midnight Dream and send him to Eton, we had our first argument. Imagine sticking your head out of a window to call your child home and yelling, 'Midnight. Midnight! Time for tea.'

I was all for Mick 'doing his own thing', which was part of the liberating attitude of the sixties, but I had practical and definite ideas about bringing up the child I was carrying, and they didn't seem to tally with his. We had no course to follow, because we were doing something quite new. We were supposed to be the sophisticated embodiment of an alternative social ideal – parenthood shared between loving friends living separate lives. This was at a time when concepts like 'marriage', 'mistress' and 'illegitimate' were dismissed as part of a foreign body – the monolith of conservatism.

Mick slipped in and out of my life whenever he needed to, and I kept working. Flying was difficult after I started getting sick on planes, but I kept gigging and the bookings kept coming in. 'Keep The Customer Satisfied' was going strong in Europe. I did a cover for *Club International* magazine and as usual was expected to throw in a nude shot, nudity still being popular. I realized during that photo session, trying to hold my stomach in, that I'd have to make a gear change.

My tempestuous rock image was undermined by the femininity of pregnancy, so I hung up my leather gear and put hair rollers in my busby. I told my band that I was pregnant. When some girls rush to work and announce their pregnancy, they're congratulated. The long faces I got might have suited a mourning. I could understand the boys' misery and dread, because they knew it meant we'd soon be coming off the road.

On 28 June 1970 I modelled a Thea Porter maternity dress as the finale of a big charity benefit at the London Hilton, and that's when I told the press that I was pregnant but wasn't disclosing the name of the father. An article appeared on page three of the conservative major newspaper stating that I was single and pregnant, and there was no stigma attached to it. It was a salute to my pregnancy and a sign of the broadminded times. The media didn't use the old label 'unwed mother', but it was still very new then for a woman to have a child outside marriage when she had options to do otherwise. In the media, Vanessa Redgrave had broken the ground for pregnancy without marriage a year before when she gave birth to Franco Nero's son.

I managed to get through the pregnancy without any press association with Mick, although we stepped out together a few times. I felt it was important not to get involved with him and the press, although Mick was ready to have it reported. When some clever journalist guessed that the baby I was carrying was Mick's and threatened to print as much, I threatened to sue the paper. We got the Stones' publicist, Les Perrin, to quell the story by submitting a picture of another girl and saying that Mick was having an affair with her – which may have been true, too. He had an array of ladies and was still in and out of love with Marianne. It had always been that way, and it was something to cackle with him about.

Not touring left me with a bundle of untapped energy. One day it was music, musicians, planes, receptions, press, and the next I was sitting in my lovely large flat alone.

Aloneness is a self-imposed exile, a deliberate retreat, different from loneliness. I needed to take an accounting of my life, as you would a bank balance, to see what had gone in and come out.

It was a busy summer for Mick with *Ned Kelly* being released and the band preparing for a European tour. He didn't go to his film premier but his office arranged a ticket for me. I didn't like sitting so close to his parents in my long shimmering maternity dress, knowing that he hadn't yet told them that our baby was on the way.

I'd met Mr and Mrs Jagger when they had come to Mick's Cheyne Walk house for tea while I was staying there. It was soon after his younger brother, Chris, had returned from India with his American girlfriend, Vivienne Zarvis. I wanted to understand why Mick didn't want his parents to know that a grandchild was due. I felt they had a right to, whatever his feelings were about them. When Chris and his girlfriend had no work and no money after they came back from India, I gave them the job of painting my flat. While I'd been staying at Mick's, they'd been his houseguests for part of the time, and I'd got to know them and like them. Chris was my age. He hadn't firmly decided what to do with his life. He wanted to make music but first needed a London base and an income.

Mick went off on the Stones' first European tour since their Hyde Park launch. That tour was bound to be pandemonium, and although Mick invited me to go to Paris, he knew I'd refuse. That was all part of his other life which I had never wanted to get caught up in. While he was away, his telephone calls became less frequent but when he did call, he'd keep me laughing about the tour mishaps or whose girlfriend he'd had. He loved a bit of naughtiness. He told me that he was lonely and had met someone in Paris that he was taking to Italy. Her name was Bianca. She was Nicaraguan and spoke little English. Mick didn't mention her again, but after the tour I knew that she had travelled back to England with him and was staying at Stargroves, his house in the country.

I was in a very difficult position, because the notion of a baby became my total reality as it became Mick's passing fancy. After the fifth month he vacillated between approval and disapproval of the oncoming birth. It was too late for reconsideration, as I reminded him, but it alerted me for the first time that he was already forgetting that the baby was his idea. Boys will be boys. I decided to stay calm, avoid friction and wait for him to act like himself instead of Dr Jekyll and Mr Hyde. It's odd how men sometimes want to act as if *they're* pregnant. I didn't want to see him in less than the best light.

Mick knew that I was carrying his baby because I loved him and trusted him, and because it was something he said he wanted. I wanted to believe that if I was patient, he would come to terms with the new life that we'd created and for which we were both therefore responsible. So I left the door open, so to speak, trying not to force a confrontation that would build a wall between us. He'd phone as if nothing had ever happened. I was sure of one thing, whatever that ideal we'd had in mind at Mr Chow's, the baby kicking me in the stomach half the bloody night was real.

In the midst of all this, I had my work to think about. David Ruffell had gone into a sanatorium with tuberculosis and my relations with the Track office hit an all-time low. I'd always been on the puniest retainer while I was on the road, with the money I made going straight into my Track account for Roger, equipment, the car, the band and the percentage that Track took as part of my agency/management contract. People imagine you make so much money when you're visible, but visibility doesn't equate with income and, sadly, you don't get paid for getting your name in the paper. I'd have to go straight back on the road after the baby arrived, which meant I'd have to employ a live-in nanny. I could see the pounds-shillings-and-pence signs going up right before my eyes.

I finally convinced the Track office that I had money owed. I'd never seen any royalties or statements, and even the accounts for my expenditure on the road didn't seem to tally. Supposedly, my £40 per week while I was gigging left me nothing due. Going into the office and confronting the issue brought no results, just insults. Eventually Pete Rudge came with a month's wages.

During the latter half of my pregnancy, when I came off the road completely, I did voluntary work in a local mental-care day centre which had an autistic unit. I was assigned to work with a twelve-year-old boy named Adrian, who was nearly as tall as I was. He was beautiful, looked perfectly normal, but was unable to communicate or do any of the things that a child of five could do with full faculties. I worked with him a few mornings a week. I wanted to be useful, and my relationship with Adrian helped me to keep the rest of my life in rational perspective.

He was at an impasse when I began working with him. I imagined that life for Adrian was like an acid trip. He could see things that no one else saw because he would gaze for long periods at what appeared to be a blank space. He would repeat one word endlessly and roar with laughter at the sound of his voice, or sit evenly rocking, as though he was motorized. The challenge was to make contact, because for him to relate in any way to anyone was a steep mountain climbed. Adrian was one of a number of children in the autistic unit who had volunteers assigned to them in regular shifts. I went three mornings a week, less often towards the end of my pregnancy, because sometimes it demanded resilience to handle Adrian who was the size of a strapping teenage boy.

To attract his attention I wore bright make-up – eyelashes and colours on my face – and arrived smelling of delicious perfume. I'd poke my neck near his nose so that he could sniff as long as he wanted to and would put on my gaudiest Indian jewellery to attract his eye. The two female psychologists who ran the unit let us approach the child we attended in our own way, and I hoped it was obvious what I was doing.

To be occupied by his needs took me out of my world and made our encounter as therapeutic for me as it was for him. After several visits he looked at me. The first time he bellowed my name was more rewarding than thunderous applause. Some days he'd howl with laughter when he'd see me or run away from me giggling when I appeared, which was as good as his running into my arms. I loved him and when I had to admit it was time to sever our connection I can't tell you what I felt. There was no way to explain to him why I couldn't be there. He lived at home, but I knew that it was no good trying to keep in touch, because my own world was going to be complicated enough as soon as the baby arrived.

Mick's housekeeper, Bruna Girardi, who was a wonderfully effusive Italian, came to help me towards the end of my pregnancy. Mick was down at Stargroves when it was near time for me to give birth, and I was ashamed to ask him for a contribution but I had to because he hadn't offered. The £200 came with a sweet note saying, among other things, 'I know I haven't done right by you,' and the loan of a ring he always wore, which I thought would be nice to wear while I was in labour.

The baby didn't want to come out. I'd been feeding it watermelons and cucumbers, so it was no wonder. I did a pregnant session for *Vogue* and waited impatiently.

I'd planned a home delivery. It was a good way to keep the press at bay, left a way open for Mick to come to see the baby, and was part of the trend towards natural childbirth. A substitute for my National Health obstetrician told me at 9.30 one night that the baby was in danger and I should go into hospital the following morning. I didn't sleep.

It was funny to think, as I waddled down the three flights on 3 November, that when I went back up I'd be carrying a baby. I arrived at St Mary's Hospital, Paddington, to be told there wasn't a bed for me and could I please go home, because I was in no condition to be standing around the waiting room. I was using my married name when I tried to register and had disguised myself so nobody would recognize me. Standing there as Mrs Ratledge, I knew there was no chance of getting this brusque nursing sister to give me a bed. So I dragged my bags back out onto the street and hailed a taxi, hoping that I wouldn't be allowed to die quietly at home in unassisted childbirth.

I sat in my bedroom listening to the rain sprinkle on my skylight and waited for morning. I had to admit when I lugged my suitcase downstairs for the second time that a husband would have come in handy.

I was in a single-bedded room and took notes while I was working up to my induced labour. I was famished when lunch arrived. After I'd eaten it, a nurse rushed in to say that it had been left by mistake. On the National Health, I felt I shouldn't complain.

Hours of my grunting and yelling produced a bitty baby girl who was slightly green and still covered in yuck. Brand-new babies are a sight. I was being wheeled through the maternity ward when I heard a man's voice burst out, 'Marsher 'Unt! What are you doing here?'

Damn it, I thought, pulling the sheet up closer to my nose, you can't go anywhere without getting caught. It was a wonder anybody recognized me after the sweaty bout I'd just been though, wearing no make-up, with a scarf tied like a babushka around my head. I was supposed to look like Mrs Ratledge, housewife.

It was Richard Longcraine, a mad-hatter painter friend who had gone to Central Art School with Caroline Coon and stayed occasionally around the time when some people two floors up were into that crazy art movement called 'Destruction in Art'. (They held mini-explosions in their flat and Caroline was afraid they'd burn the whole house down, basement and all.)

I'd had nobody pacing in the waiting room or hovering at the end of my noisy labour to say well done. I was really happy to chat to him in the middle of the ward, but suddenly needed to bring up that lunch I wasn't supposed to have had. So he excused me from meeting his wife, who was parked a couple of beds away from me and had had a little girl too.

My baby was whisked off. I couldn't rest until I'd used the portable pay phone to call Mick at Stargroves and Ikey transfer-charge to California. I spoke in a whisper because there was only a floral curtain to close off my bed from the seven others.

I cheerfully told Mick that I'd given birth to a daughter, fully aware that he wanted a son. He would have to be content with a girl, and ours was lovely.

As soon as I held the baby, I could see that her hands, wrists, feet and knees were carbon miniature copies of Mick's. So were her lips a perfect replica. I couldn't wait for him to see her.

The baby was brought back to me first thing in the morning wearing a paper bracelet marked 'Ratledge'. When the nurse took her again, I didn't want to be treated like an invalid. Though my stitches were burning, I put on my high-heeled slippers and moseyed down the corridor. It felt good to be able to look down and see my own feet. I'd been impatient towards the end of my pregnancy not to have to walk like a penguin. I felt like a shopping bag after the seventh month.

The doctor recommended that the baby go on a formula, because I planned to go straight back to work. I fed her from the old-fashioned glass bottle they administered at the hospital. I didn't like being in that ward with seven women talking about babies and childbirth and families. I was a single girl, a bachelorette with a baby, not ready to be domesticated. Two women in the ward were in an emotionally low state they referred to as postnatal blues. They cried and fretted. I didn't doubt they felt the carry-on necessary, but depression can be more contagious than a cold. So I told the nurse I was leaving. The doctor insisted I stay in bed till the following midday.

I didn't like to be ordered to fold the nappy in a certain way and have the bottle held just so. I didn't for a minute think that I wouldn't know what to do with my own baby and wasn't vaguely insecure about the job. I just wanted to get on with the routine of it as soon as possible.

Thirty-eight hours after I gave birth, my red sling high heels were clicking down the side entrance steps of the hospital near the blue wall plaque that says that Sir Alexander Fleming discovered penicillin there. With Baby in my arms, I climbed into the limo that Mick's office had sent to glide us home. She was wearing a red and brown patterned sweater that Kaffe Fassett designed for her and looked like a papoose with her slick of brunette hair covering a skull so perfectly round that it looked like a manufactured baby doll's head. I'd tucked her long slim limbs in a white fringed shawl.

Bruna beamed as though I was carrying her first grandchild through the front door. Her Italian gusto for mothering made her seem mature, although there was only ten years' difference in our ages. She always spoiled me. Having her there to welcome me back to the flat, which she'd shined like mirrored glass, made Baby's homecoming feel like Christmas morning. Huge red roses arrived from Mick which Bruna arranged with the congratulations telegrams on the piano in the dark chocolate living room.

She fussed around the baby and me until the Pakistani nursing midwife made the first of her daily calls to check my stitches and the baby's umbilical cord. This was required as I'd checked out five days earlier than usual. She was putting her coat on to leave when the doorbell rang.

I could hear Bruna greeting Mick and Alan Dunn, his driver, as they came through the door. My eager hello brought Mick ducking into my bedroom but out again when he saw I had a visitor. You would have thought the little round nurse had seen an apparition when he came through. She didn't ask any questions, but I could see she wanted to.

Media magnetism has a strange effect on people, and the small round midwife looked decidedly giddy for an instant before she recollected herself. Patting down her coat and pushing back her glasses, she could hear Mick's voice in the adjoining nursery before she left. He'd brought champagne, and we stuck a two-and-sixpence piece in the cork and hung it on a nail protruding from the door. He said it was for good luck. He'd brought a miniature muse figurine for the baby and a silver spoon and some Indian earrings, the kind you'd find at a market stall. (I though the latter might have been some custom and didn't ask why.) I left him alone to look at his daughter for the first time. What we see in a human being so newly born is really in the eye of the beholder. She looked phenomenal to me, because I had felt her grow in me. A father is denied that luxury.

Something was missing when Mick dropped by that day and maybe that says it: he dropped by. He was cordial and charming and in a hurry to be somewhere else. I smiled when he rushed off. Shortly after, Bruna also left. I was suddenly alone with my newborn baby. There was an incredible silence that I had never heard before.

Visitors came for days after to peek and coo. The funniest was Mick Taylor, who looked decidedly uncomfortable holding Baby like a raw egg. I loved him for trying for those few minutes that must have seemed like an eternity to him. It was rather nice the way people who worked for Mick, like Jo Bergman, Shirley Arnold and Alan Dunn, rallied round after the baby arrived. It took the sting out of his noticeable absence.

He paid another rushed visit about ten days after his first. My first nanny had just moved in and I was trying to organize her. (I came to discover that a nanny can be more work than the baby if you make the wrong choice.) With our baby in my arms, I took Mick upstairs to talk, but I didn't know what to say. I didn't care if he'd been having a good time, I wanted him to ask if Baby had. I wasn't in the mood to entertain his detachment and had no compunction about it.

It doesn't take a lot to pick up a telephone and I said as much to him. I can be coarse and tried to be, because I was trying to provoke some genuine reaction instead of letting him hold me at bay with polite chitchat. I hadn't expected him to stab back. He said that he never loved me and I was mad to think he had. The pain in me burst forth in stupid girl-tears, but he saved me from a shamefaced emotional display by saying that he could take her away from me if he chose.

In a measured, sober tone I heard myself saying that I'd blow his brains out if he dared. At that moment all my loyalty which had been his became hers.

I didn't see him out but heard him close the door. What had begun as an ideal was a baby in my arms and for her sake, I pushed forward.

11

SAVE THE TEARS

If the Isle of Wight had made me think the alternative side was winning in 1969, the murder of four Kent students on their Ohio campus by National Guardsmen in 1970 showed that we were not. Nixon's 'law and order' was his alienating message for the new decade. The sense of it crawled over the front pages of our newspapers. America and my family seemed so far away.

At home, Baby whipped me into shape. She was fabulous, very no-nonsense. She knew what she wanted and wouldn't stand for less. Her first nanny slept late. I always got up with the baby at night, and when the nanny still couldn't raise herself in the morning, I knew I'd made a mistake.

I couldn't go out on the road yet, so I took the first job that was offered. I didn't have the time or money to consider what was a good career move because I was only concerned with what would buy nappies and formula.

I was asked to be in *Catch My Soul*, a rock version of *Othello*, conceived and directed by Jack Good, who was also acting in it. It had transferred to London's Roundhouse from Manchester. Originally Marianne Faithfull was to play Desdemona. 'Desdemona' was the name of the Marc Bolan song I had released in the autumn of 1969, and ironically, the name of the character I was to play was Bianca.

The producers were hoping that the play would transfer again to the West End. My salary would pay for my household and the nanny that I'd have to employ. The role of Bianca didn't suit my voice and the production left a lot to be desired. But the job would make it possible for me to be at home with the baby most of the day and have me singing regularly, which I needed after six months off the road.

I'd named the baby Karis, but nicknamed her anything that came to mind. That November Charis Horton, a friend from my student days at Berkeley, had written to me out of the blue. I hadn't heard from her since she visited me at Caroline Coon's in the summer of 1966. Her short letter said that she happened to be in a book store in Cambridge, Massachusetts, and saw my photograph on the cover of a book called *The History of Makeup*. Her letter was dated the same day that I decided to name the baby Charis and spell it with a K.

Karis was a thrill a minute, and the nanny had a battle getting hold of her if I was in the flat. I was there as much as possible, tending her till the very last minute before I rushed off to the theatre. Sometimes I took her with me and dragged the nanny with me.

I expected she'd be welcomed wherever I was and took her everywhere with me. After Pamela Colin, my editor friend at *Vogue*, married Lord Harlech and took on the title and social life that went with it, she and her husband, David, invited me one evening to a very small dinner party, and no doubt found me most odd turning up with Madame in her carrycot.

It was incredibly exciting to see her advancing. I doted on my daughter and she rewarded me with the purest baby love. She dragged me out of bed a few times every night but that never seemed like a great sacrifice, and my not having a lover made it easier. Had I resisted maternity, it could have made the experience a nightmare, but I jumped to it as to any other opportunity and took on motherhood with a sense of playfulness that I felt it deserved and warranted. In my childhood, I had observed mothering as automatic sacrifice. If I didn't resist that element of it, my new role was demanding but it was also bliss. I would fold baby clothes as if I'd been doing it all my life and pretended that I was Mother Efficiency as I stacked scrubbed Playtex bottles in the fridge. I must give the petite Spanish nanny some credit for my role-playing, because Maria was order itself, and I imitated her. Everything white that touched the baby's body was snow white, every undershirt was pressed.

With Aretha Franklin blaring on the stereo, we forged ahead. For me, Aretha's was the wail of a woman wronged, a demand for respect and the shout for freedom. I could put her music on and turn the nursery into a dance hall. I'd take the baby in my arms and we'd bop out. Baby would throw her head back, flash a toothless grin and we'd be off into a music high.

Maria was a qualified nanny who considered herself above house cleaning, so I had a Spanish cleaner in a few days a week. She and Maria had their private Spanish Civil War, determining who had the best job and came from the best part of Spain. The tension between them sparked our household atmosphere and added that little zing that I'd got used to with musicians bickering. I'd created my own little matriarchy.

I was cautious with journalists. They wanted to turn my profiles into a risqué discourse on love without marriage and brand the baby a 'love child', which I thought we could do without. I had to be very selective about my press, but my visibility wasn't stable enough for that. I refused to mention Mick in my interviews and avoided all questions about the baby's father. To keep something from the press is like waving a red flag at a bull.

Mick and the rest of the Stones were moving to France in April 1971. I'd known since 1969 that they had financial problems and tax exile was planned. It was one of those record business ironies that such a successful band had money problems. Before Mick left, he asked me to have Maria bring our baby, whom he hadn't seen since our argument in November 1970. I'd always made it clear through our musical contacts that Mick could see the baby whenever he wished or have her visit him with her nanny. I was relieved when he did. I imagined that the longer he avoided it, the harder it was going to be for him. His new Nicaraguan girlfriend, Bianca, became pregnant by him soon after Karis was born, and I hoped Mick's second baby would remind him of his first.

Several weeks after Maria had visited Mick with the baby, she sat watching a news report of his wedding. It showed the large jet chartered to take the revellers to the south of France where Mick was marrying Bianca. Maria started to cry and looked to me for a similar reaction. I wanted to tell her to save the tears because she might need them for something important, but I kept quiet.

When *Catch My Soul* ended its West End run at the Prince of Wales Theatre, I got a soft-drink commercial in Germany. I wouldn't have considered doing a commercial before, but having a baby was very expensive. As the bills piled up, I had to dismiss the cleaner and finally Maria too. I lived from day to day and tried not to think about the future. There was always a chance that some job would come up. I was hopeful, and Baby gave me a lot to be thankful for. I only had to think of Adrian and I'd remember how lucky I was that my baby was healthy. There's always a bright side and I was determined not to let my thoughts stray to any negatives. I talked to Baby in Melangian most of the time. She liked it, and it kept me spirited.

In June I had to go up to audition for a Sidney Poitier movie. After a month without work my purse was so empty that I couldn't afford a baby-sitter or the taxi fare to get to his suite at the Westbury Hotel. It was summertime and the weather was clear enough for me to walk the three miles. I was wearing a long white dress and Baby was impeccably behaved in her pushchair. I trusted her to put her best foot forward at my film audition. There was no breeze, and if I didn't walk too fast I knew we'd still look intact when we arrived.

I was only minutes late when I stepped out of the elevator and parked Baby next to a hotel service trolley laden with used breakfast trays while I had a last-minute shift of my dress and a pull at my hair. Too late I noticed that she'd taken a hard-crust breakfast roll from a basket and stuck it in her mouth. I paused for one minute to decide what to do: grab the roll and possibly upset her, or walk into this interview like a gypsy pushing a baby with a crusty roll that was bound to flake everywhere. There was no time for a scene. I had a go at cajoling her out of it, but she had that firm look a baby can give you that says 'I dare you'. So I rang and Poitier's wife, Joanna Shimkus, came to the door. I was relieved that she seemed informal. I'd taken Baby out of her chair to brush off some of the breadcrumbs when Sidney Poitier came out in his bathrobe, looking older and taller than I expected. I apologized for the crumbs on the carpet, took the script he gave me and tried to read it while I bounced the baby in my free arm. I didn't get the part, but I could have. I was comforted by a feeling I had that something could guide me to the right place and time, and change my luck. My optimism didn't dent my escalating money problems.

Mick invited me to bring the baby to see him in the south of France. We were met at Nice airport by his driver, Alan

Dunn, who was always very kind to me. The last time I'd been to Nice was after Copenhagen when I'd met Mick there. We'd been chased by reporters: I'd run in the opposite direction to avoid being snapped with him and nearly got lost. This time around I was coming to visit him and his new wife. At least I thought so until Alan explained that the baby and I would have to stay with Mick Taylor in Grasse, which was some distance from Mick's house. He didn't explain why.

I liked Mick Taylor and his girlfriend Rose and was pleased to see them, but I felt uncomfortable. I loathe anything that isn't straightforward, but I was too far from home and too broke to call my own shots. Mick and Rose had a lovely large house but I wasn't taking it in. It disturbed me to see that this young guitarist got more involved with drugs than he needed to be for playing or living. It was his life, so I didn't say what I wanted to, but sometimes I hate to have to keep my mouth out of somebody else's business.

Alan collected the baby and me that evening, to take us to see Mick and Bianca, who was very pregnant. She looked Melangian to me. The house with rolling lawns was palatial. The severity of Mick's financial problems was obviously over. He was living as if money was no object. My intention was to be friendly, meet his new wife and make it possible for Mick to spend a weekend with his precocious baby. By Dr Spock's reckoning she was very advanced, nearly walking at eight months and saying a few words way ahead of her time. I didn't want him to miss her babyhood. Neither did I want to put up with bad manners, which is what I was served at dinner along with the fish, as Mick and his wife sat through the meal nuzzling and speaking in French as though the baby and I sitting opposite had come to visit someone else. I was relieved when Baby and I were taken back to Mick Taylor's.

Jo Bergman came to Taylor's house and said she was delighted that Mick was making amends and coming to terms with having a child. I saw very little sign of it. The only effort he made while we were there was dinner, and that seemed no effort on anybody's part but his cook's, and mine to fly out with the baby to see him.

The following day the baby and I were dropped at Mick's house again for an hour before Alan whisked us to the airport. As we were leaving, Ossie Clark arrived with some other people. I hadn't seen Ossie since he visited me while I was staying with Mick in December 1969. I adored Ossie and was pleased that his hard work as a designer brought him success.

Before I left, I asked Mick to lend me £200. I'm proud and I found it hard to get the words out, but I knew he would never offer if I didn't ask.

He hadn't looked me in the eye during that visit. I guess he couldn't.

Back in London I'd been asked to do Marty Feldman's TV show and quickly put together some musicians, who rehearsed a couple of songs that I'd written. I considered the possibility of going back on the road, but with Baby so young it seemed impractical. I was behind with the rent and owed the rates, but I was covered in Baby's tactile affection from sunup to sundown. Then fortune smiled on me by way of a film offer: a minor part in a Hammer horror movie starring Christopher Lee and Peter Cushing.

I was able to hire a nanny while I was filming, a sweet well-spoken English girl who loved babies. Karis was learning to talk and needed a nanny who could speak English well. While I was filming, she had to depend on the nanny and the good will of my downstairs neighbour. *Dracula AD 72* had no aspirations to being anything but an entertaining horror movie. There were no delusions that we were making an important artistic statement. It was English film making at its formula best. Everyone just got on with the job.

Filming requires patience. The waiting between takes calls for a less racy energy level than mine was at twenty-five. Other people could sit down and knit between a take; I'd be pacing up and down like a jaguar trying to contain my energy. Live gigging was more appropriate for me. I could burn off my natural speed. But I enjoyed rushing off to the studio at dawn and contributing to the collective effort of the number of specialists that it takes to make a film. Women were involved and people of different ages, whereas the music business is mostly young and male. I met several people who became close friends: Edna Tromans, Rosemary Burrows and Stephanie Beacham. Edna was the publicist, Rosemary was in charge of wardrobe and Stephanie was an actress in the film. The work and the new friendships were a heavenly boost, and I earned enough money to put a bit aside and also arrange a trip to the States. My family still hadn't seen the baby, and I needed to go home.

Karis spent her first birthday on the set because I couldn't bear to think of her spending it at home with a nanny. I had the studio chef bake a big pink-and-white cake for her birthday party the following day. Mick had a handsome spotted rocking horse delivered to her.

I was so happy that Sunday when we took off for California with Stephanie Beacham in tow. She had never been to American and wanted to make the trip with me. I knew that for her to encounter my family, particularly my grandmother Edna, who had returned to Philadelphia with Thelma, would be a real experience. We flew to my mother's first. Ikey and her husband Allison were still living outside Berkeley, with my sister Pamala, a teacher, married and living next door. Dennis was working on his master's degree in criminology and lived near the Berkeley campus.

I wasn't the same person going back and expected that readjustment to being the girl my family knew would require effort on my part. As Ikey and Allison's wasn't the house that I grew up in, it held no memories of its own for me. Her walls wouldn't bring subtle comforts or discomforts. Instead, home was not a place, but people. As much as anything, I was going back to re-experience America. It had become a foreign country through my long absence.

Nixon's 'law and order' had taken its ugliest turn just before we went back. At Attica state prison in New York, inmates demanding better prison conditions had demonstrated for three days holding hostages, and the state police went in gunning down 39 people, including ten hostages. In London violent crime was still rare in 1971, and to read about this made me numb and horror-stricken.

I noticed a great change in America. My friends from Berkeley that I visited had a sense of resignation about the Nixon government which reflected a combination of things. They were older and the romantic ideals of their youth had been worn down by the realities of daily endurance. Having moved individually away from like minds to take on careers, it was hard for them to feel the power of their collective political voice. And they were each so caught up in the time-consuming mundanities of day-to- day life that there was hardly time and energy left to attack the system.

The Vietnam war raged on, and Nixon wore a hard hat. Although the Haight-Ashbury was still a hippie hideaway, the sense of hope and jubilation had totally disappeared. Having an English woman travelling with me meant that I was often seeing America from her fresh perspective. During our whirlwind visit from coast to coast, food made me feel that I was at home as much as family reunions and seeing Berkeley friends like Baby John and Andrea Luria. The smell of my grandmother's Thanksgiving turkey had a nostalgic impact. So did the taste of cornbread and Ikey's sweet potato pie. Food let me recapture my childhood. Though I came away happy and revitalized after seeing my family and friends, returning to England was for me a return home.

I was asked to do a *Harpers & Queen* cover when I got back from California and it seemed that I was on a roll again. But money was painfully low and that didn't change. Mick was regularly in the newspapers living a high life and I wondered if he'd lost his integrity or I'd lost my mind in thinking he had any in the first place. When I was unsure, I reread his old letters. They reassured me that he was capable of humanity and that our friendship wasn't a figment of my imagination.

Since I was released from my Track contract in late 1970, I'd been trying to sort out a new record deal. In 1972, after I joined forces with a Glaswegian band, I got us signed to Phonogram. The album we cut with Mike Hurst in Phonogram's Marble Arch in-house studio didn't capture the band's sound, which was strong on harmony. We tried to get it scrapped but it was released in Poland, of all places, and as recently as 1985 I was still getting royalty payments for the songs I wrote on it. With these four Scots, I was suddenly making music and cowriting with a group that I liked both as people and as musicians.

I called the group 22. Phonogram was unhappy that I intended to leave my name out. Yet I knew that it would just be a glorified backing band I was fronting if we called ourselves Marsha Hunt's 22. It also sounded odd. I was unwilling to accept that my name was a commercial commodity that we should trade on. The limelight was a discomfort and I kept trying to free myself from the transparency of it.

The Scots are a very down-home breed, very direct and

unsuperficial, and being with them was like being back on the reservation. I learned to speak with a Scots accent and used it whenever I was with them. It gave me great pleasure to joke and swear in the roughest Glaswegian. Communication was easier and I could be heard and listened to best when I spoke to them in their rhythm.

Karis, extremely clever and healthy, was thriving on my working environment as much as I was. She had a flock of replacement fathers in the four musicians and two roadies, who all adopted her. She was shy with most people but had an obvious passion for the bass player and the keyboard player, who went out of their way to give her attention. They called her Pocus and I trusted them with her as I trusted myself.

These musicians came from working-class Glaswegian families, and I thought they would be gritty, but they were mild-mannered and even-tempered. In spite of all their swearing and the pleasure they got from a good guffaw, they didn't talk a lot. I got the impression that Scotsmen aren't generally talkative, but whenever the baby was with us, they pushed that reserve to the background and indulged her. There was a strong family element about the band.

After 'Gilded Splinters', I had built up a solid following in Germany and had toured there on several occasions and done some of the more important television shows like *Beat Club*. This meant that when 22 was rehearsed to go on the road, by May 1972, we were able to get a solid tour booked there on the basis of my name, playing clubs and universities and a few big outdoor festivals.

I wasn't going to leave the baby behind while she was only a toddler. I hadn't been able to pay for a qualified nanny after the film and had to revert to employing live-in baby-sitters, glorified au pairs. Basically, I took care of the baby myself and used them as backup, which meant that she had the same person to deal with all the time – her mother. When 22 set off for Germany that May, I had an Australian nanny in tow. She had been a teacher. We flew with the baby to Hamburg to meet up with the rest of the band who drove across from England. Taking the baby and nanny meant we had to stay in better hotels than we would have done without them. While the baby wouldn't have minded, the nanny wouldn't have tolerated dives.

I'd tracked Mick down through his office and had asked him for £600, which was what it was going to cost me in hotels to take the baby with nanny on tour. He was getting ready to go out on the road himself, on an American tour that was expected to gross $4 million. On the two previous occasions I had asked him for money, I'd needed it urgently and had tried every other way of raising it, leaving him till last. I wanted to give him a chance to help out of his own accord, but he never offered. It should have seemed easy for him once an avenue of communication had been reopened by my trip to the south of France. The fact that he and his wife also had a young baby meant that he was aware that to maintain a child required money and time.

I'd been with Karis to visit him in London after his second daughter, Jade, arrived in October 1971. I sat with her in my arms in his Cheyne Walk garden. He took photographs of me holding his new baby, with our own toddling around us. A situation like this would suggest that he was nearly all right, and then a month's silence would follow.

It wasn't only pride that prevented me from asking for money. I still believed Mick's integrity would remind him of his responsibility for his child. To let him resolve this issue without my prodding him was more critical to our daughter's future than my immediate need for money to provide for her. So I stood back for as long as humanly possible.

The cost of calling him around the world added to my financial worries. I spent burdensome hours guessing when the time might be right. It took countless phone calls and messages asking him to return my calls. When the money eventually came, I was glad there wasn't an extra five pounds enclosed. I couldn't have coped with any last-minute surprises.

In Germany the band was playing well and the tour was a welcome change. It was wonderful to be gigging again. Our last date, in June, was at an open-air concert in Nuremberg. We arrived early in the afternoon and as the gates hadn't opened yet, the band went to a nearby café for something to drink. It was hot and I laughed about the boys wanting tea in such weather, but they could never get enough of it. German tea is usually served in a tall glass tumbler that sits in a metal holder with a handle. It comes as boiled water with a tea bag in it.

I only spoke enough German to order food and be polite, because most Germans spoke a bit of English. In this unimpressive little corner café, no one spoke English so I ordered for us in my bad German. We were all sitting together in a booth, and Baby was tucked next to me in a corner. She was precocious for nineteen months and liked to sit alone and drink out of a glass instead of a cup. When the tea was set down at our end of the booth, she reached for one of the tall glasses before I could stop her. It was so hot that she sharply pulled her hand away, which brought the glass down, spilling the near boiling water on her.

It must have hurt and startled her so much that at the very instant it happened she didn't yell. The pain took her breath away, and the sight of it took mine. She screamed out as I grabbed her and wrenched us from our corner. I pulled at her steaming long-sleeved dress, trying to get it off her, and the top layer of her skin, like soggy tissue paper, came with it. I think I was yelling for help and God at the same time, but the sluggish waitress attending another booth didn't know what was happening. The boys had leaped from the table in the panic, and one of them said 'put her under water'. '*Wasser. Wasser! Wasser! Bitte. Bitte*,' I was yelling. I don't know how I remembered the words. The waitress finally comprehended and rushed me with Baby to the kitchen, where a cold tap was turned on in a big sink.

We were trying to ask for an ambulance, but nobody understood us. I knew that I needed to stay calm, but I was frantic. We piled into the van and headed in the direction of the American hospital, which someone on the street corner told us about, not knowing the city or the signs or how far we were going to have to drive. The baby stopped screaming as we sped along. Her eyes were open and she must have been in terrible pain. I don't know if nature numbs babies in a situation like that, but it worried me that she had stopped making a noise. I just held her and kept talking to her, hoping it was some comfort and that she could hear that I was with her.

I don't know how Johnny, the piano player, who did all the driving, got us to the American hospital. It was an army hospital and the all-male staff had no emergency facility available because it was Sunday. They were smoking cigarettes and passing the buck as I stood there holding Baby with skin missing from her arm and leg and chest. It struck me that maybe they thought we had no money. I was in overalls and we looked scruffy as bands do on the road, but we were carrying all the cash with us that we'd been picking up from one gig stop to the next. I had Johnny produce a wad of it to prove that we could afford to buy their medical attention. It only made a slight dent and they took the baby to a cubicle and bathed her in water and Phisohex, and passed her back to me – no gown, no covering. It was like something out of *MASH*. The male nurse who had taken charge said that we should take her away and bring her back in the morning when the doctor came on duty. I couldn't believe what I was hearing. 'We'll pay you anything you want,' I kept begging, 'but please help her.'

The boys and I parlayed. I considered going to a German hospital, but I remembered a time in 1969 when I was working in Munich and one of the roadies got sick. He ended up in a German hospital, quarantined, and we weren't able to understand enough about his condition or the treatment prescribed, because we didn't speak the language. I didn't want that to be repeated, so I asked the boys to get us to an airport.

It seemed we were driving for hours but it was only two. The sky was falling. Buckets of rain came down, which slowed our journey, and I sat as silently as Baby. Perhaps both of us were in shock.

At Frankfurt airport I gave Mick's home number to one of the boys with instructions to ask Mick's wife to make arrangements for a hospital and someone to pick us up at Heathrow, because Mick was already on tour.

As I sat on the plane with the baby wrapped in an unworn red T-shirt of mine, because we hadn't been able to get a sterilized gown for her from the army hospital, someone came up and asked me to autograph a fashion picture of the baby and me in one of the Sunday papers that had been handed out. It was too unreal.

The hospital that Mick's wife had booked was in the country and there was no time to drive there. I couldn't believe that the burn was as trivial as diagnosed and it didn't seem right to me that Baby wasn't crying. I ended up with a friend driving me to a small hospital near my flat. The doctor on emergency admissions acted as if I was a criminal until I produced our passports and plane tickets to prove that we had travelled all the way from Germany. He could see that the burn hadn't just happened and wanted to know why I had waited to bring her in. He couldn't believe that any hospital would have released her. He bandaged her and admitted us. I was determined to stay there and asked to have a bed put in her room.

We were in hospital for ten days, and while she healed I had to confront the financial and other problems facing me. I had pulled out of that Nuremberg gig without notice and missed some gigs in England. One night I remember slipping off from hospital to a gig in Wales because we needed every penny. The band was off the road for two weeks. Mick phoned a couple of times from his tour, asking if he could help, and I asked him to get his office to send half the hospital bill, which was £75. It never arrived, and I had to flit the hospital with Baby without settling the account. They had been kind and it seemed ungrateful, but I didn't have the money for the bill. I kept leaving messages for Mick but didn't hear from him again until his tour ended.

I asked the band's lawyer how I should go about getting Mick to put an emergency fund aside for Karis. The lawyer explained that the only legal right our child had to contributions to her welfare by her father was through a paternity suit, because she wasn't conceived in marriage. Only children whose parents were married had rights and even theirs were limited.

I explained that Mick acknowledged that he was Karis's father. The issue was parental neglect. Surely a father has a binding moral responsibility when he created a human life, totally dependent on care to thrive. I tried to contain my fury.

A paterntity suit had sordid connotations and didn't approach our problem. I just wanted to be assured that our daughter would never be jeopardized again by lack of money.

Mick called to say that he was in London and invited me to lunch. He playfully dismissed not having his office send his share towards the hospital bill saying that I probably would have bought shoes with the money. This incensed me, because he'd never seen me be frivolous. To cry, to scream and shout abuse would have achieved nothing.

Instead I telephoned my lawyer, Michael Seifert, to say that

I'd spoken to Mick. Seifert reconfirmed that there was no legal alternative to my predicament but a paternity suit. I wanted to vomit. I asked him to follow the necessary procedure and to go about it in a way that would keep it confidential and out of the newspapers. To serve a writ did not mean that it had to be filed in court, if Mick was prepared to act reasonably. But to postpone service, Seifert said, meant that we would have to wait for Mick to come to England again. There was no way of knowing when that would be as he was based abroad. After two years, I had to stop pretending that he would assume his duty.

I met Mick on the steps of the Albert Memorial which overlooks the Royal Albert Hall. The towering monument is in Hyde Park near the spot where Mick and I romped after I told him I was pregnant. I sat near the top step and watched Mick climb the forty or so steps to reach me. The long black coat I wore didn't keep out the chill. Michael Seifert waited anxiously some feet away and looked as if he hated to be there as much as I did. I sat still and told myself to think with my head not my heart. I didn't want to hurt Mick and believed that in spite of his peculiar behaviour, somewhere within was a friend.

He didn't realize that the small, bespectacled young man in the suit and tie who served him with a writ was my lawyer. I explained as Mick and I descended the endless steps and took his arm to walk through the park to calm him. The issue of the baby and his responsibility to her was serious. She needed things. His pretence that he didn't have to help had to be confronted.

If his jet-set life made the situation seem remote, it was understandable. I suggested that he put aside a trust fund for the baby's future education and any emergencies. It could be administered by trustees and I could avoid asking him personally for help when it was needed. A £25,000 trust fund seemed adequate. He'd be free of further financial responsibility and have the satisfaction of knowing that he had made a provision.

We went for a drink at a dimly lit pub in Knightsbridge where Mick said that he'd put £20,000 in trust. I was relieved that we could find a solution without a lawsuit and unnecessary animosity. When I waved him goodbye, I reminded him that he was welcome to visit Baby whenever he wanted.

By the time our solicitors conferred in the early evening, Mick had reduced the trust investment to £17,000.

Baby turned two in November 1972, and I threw a party for her. Her half-sister, Jade, who was a year younger, came with her Indian nanny and Mick's trustworthy and dependable chauffeur, Alan Dunn. Jade was a pretty thing with fat dark blonde ringlets in her hair. She sat throughout the noisy children's party on her elderly nanny's lap. The fact that Bianca and Mick let her come suggested that things were all right.

During this time, a very simple and straightforward trust agreement was drawn up by my solicitor, but after many months of letters asking for signatures and funds, it still hadn't been signed and no money was made available. It never happened, and I can only now think that Mick and his solicitor wanted the lawsuit, which we finally had to proceed with. On 16 July 1973, the affiliation order was filed. The hearing was set for July.

When it hit the newspapers it stank. As no one had been privy to our friendship, the story was reported as though I suddenly appeared with a two-and-a-half-year-old to accuse a pop idol of paternity. A pack of photographers sat in my front garden like crows. The only way to avoid them was to slip out of my window across a roof and into the neighbour's house and sneak into a waiting car with Baby in my arms. The band were living in a house in Hornsey and we stayed there until the headlines faded. The headlines literally made me ill, but I knew that I had to push on.

Gigging was my livelihood and the band depended on me to get back to work. On my name, Phonogram made a large advance which financed our buying new equipment and kitting ourselves out to tour in a modicum of comfort. We bought a three-ton lorry to transport our equipment and a new VW bus for us to travel in with enough room for Baby and a nanny. I wanted to be less visible and more incorporated in the group's image, and in April 1972 I decided to crop my hair. *Vogue* wanted to cover the event and when I went along to Leonard's to get the busby taken down, Grace Coddington commissioned Norman Parkinson to photograph the hair-cutting. The final shot, done in a studio, included Karis, who had grown into a beautiful thing.

There was no doubt that the paternity suit affected how people perceived me. When the media asked Mick to make a statement, he snidely asked if I didn't have a new record released. I guessed he wanted to imply that the paternity suit was a publicity ploy. He knew that this wasn't the case. His wife Bianca was quoted as saying that she didn't give a damn. I said nothing. Only my closest friends understood the circumstances. Others questioned my motive. I avoided the press while 22's single, 'The Beast Day', was out.

The band and I split in 1973 on good terms. It's hard to keep a band going without a hit and with the kind of publicity that I had. We all had financial responsibilities and needed to make money as well as music. When the drummer joined another band we replaced him temporarily, but we'd been a tightly knit group and it didn't work when a link was broken.

Edna Tromans, whom I'd met on the Dracula movie, was the publicist for one of the two commercial radio concessions, Capital, due to start broadcasting in September 1973. She introduced me to the company as a likely candidate to cohost a nightly chat show with Ned Sherrin. I had never done anything vaguely related to presenting but this didn't put me off. The job had the added attraction of keeping me at home with a regular wage.

In their embryonic stages, Capital Radio and LBC were very competitive. No one knew originally which of the two stations would succeed to the throne of the independent radio hierarchy or whether local independent radio would survive. At the time I was employed, the station hadn't yet moved into the block it now occupies on the Euston Road. We worked from a faceless building at Piccadilly and it was a dream to walk out of the busy office into the calm of Green Park, leading to Buckingham Palace.

In spite of the DJs who were music buffs, the ambience of radio bore very little resemblance to the rock-and-roll business. I came straight off the raucous road to a sedate atmosphere. It wasn't as institutionalized as the BBC, and didn't have either the finance or the government association which gives the BBC its *1984* atmosphere. But it was a straight clock-in job, which I'd never had in England.

Perhaps because Richard Attenborough was our chairman, the making of Capital was like a large-scale filming production. He hadn't been knighted yet and although the possibility may have been in the back of his mind, it wasn't in the forefront of ours. He was just 'Dickie', our beguiling politician who mastered the art of combining the actor's charm with his tenacious ambition. Had he been American, he could have run for president. He had a bit of street in him and in a way he was more like the businessmen I'd met in the rock-and-roll business. Dickie rode his dream of Capital's success like a bronco buster and devised a scheme to make it a reality. His small stature was quadrupled by his energy, and for a while he invested all of it in Capital Radio. When it ran short of money it was whispered that he staked his personal collection of paintings. I found it intoxicating to work with a completely new organization with a sense of purpose.

Capital was going to be like an American FM station when it began, and decried all the ploys of Radio One's pop play list and personality DJs. We were going to be an alternative voice in the London community and having female disc jockeys and presenters was a part of this. The staff of variously talented people applied their undivided loyalty to make it work: DJs, secretaries, journalists, technicians, accountants, administrators, salesmen, publicists, canteen workers, music librarians, newsreaders, cleaning staff, telephonists, researchers, presenters and other artists, all pooling our wills to launch. It was like working at Cape Canaveral with a major satellite scheduled for takeoff. Since we were supposed to be part of a profit-sharing scheme, each of us felt committed to the project. Later, when the profit-sharing scheme was retracted, there was no way of recouping the energy we had expended at the beginning.

My job was initially defined as a copresenter. I was unqualified, but I was sure that I could learn to assist a main presenter. It was a bit of a shock when the show I was taken on to cohost with a media stalwart like Ned Sherrin ended up falling in my lap entirely. I didn't have enough time to comprehend fully what was expected of me. Thinking back, it was bizarre that anyone like Richard Attenborough or John Whitney, the managing director, anticipated I could do it. About four weeks before we were to go on air, I was informed that I'd be presenting the talk show on my own and that the format for my one-hour open-ended talk show was to be more specific than casual chat with celebrities. Instead, my show had to combine celebrity interest with topical issues:

education, strikes, legalizing cannabis, Watergate, apartheid, homosexuality – anything controversial. I had to generate a discussion that would provoke public opinion for the phone-ins in the music show that followed me. In addition the discussions were to be entertaining.

Considering that I hadn't cracked a textbook or read a serious journal since my Berkeley days, it was taking a whole lot for granted. The Capital administrators assumed that I could pit myself against specialists in the topics – politicians, media magnets and journalists – while steering an hour's discussion and preventing it from lulling into a yawn. I had not only to present the show, but also to do a lot of my own research and help my researcher and producer book the three or four nightly guests. (Try getting Frank Sinatra on a late-night radio talk show when he's in town for a few days.) Daytime reading was a big part of my job. I had to assimilate stacks of biographical material on the guests, as well as books they were promoting, and research the issues that I needed to be informed about to handle the conversation. I also had to attend functions to keep a visible profile, which was part of having a radio show.

Everybody was running around frantically to get ready for our 12 September launch. The programme controller told me I would also have to DJ a 'Black' music show on Saturday nights, reggae as well as what I was nursed on, and there was no music library yet. 'Black' music. I hadn't heard any for a long time. Marvin Gaye's album *What's Going On* had left its mark and I was a Gladys Knight and the Pips fan, but that hardly qualified me for the task of doing a four-hour Saturday-night music slot. Three weeks before our start date, I still hadn't been given any instruction or testing in how to modulate my voice on air or pick up commercial cues.

I was a token representative on two separate counts – Black and female. Both badly needed a foot in the door of the media in 1973 and not someone below par. There was no use quitting, so I thought I'd better put my shoulder to it. However much work it was, I needed the income. Baby had to come first, because the radio could get on without me, but she couldn't.

Nature compensated me for my trials by giving me the sweetest baby possible. She was divine to be with. I got indescribable pleasure from little things like singing her to sleep or watching her struggle to put her coat on alone and finally succeeding.

Gone and forgotten were the days of being chauffeur-driven. Gone the mature qualified household staff and the assumption that a boon was just over the horizon. I used to put Baby in her seat on the back of my bike, which didn't look unlike John Mayall's, and we'd be off on some zoo adventure or park exploit. I never had the feeling that time spent with her deprived me of anything, including freedom. I called her Pookie and she was my joy baby. The fact that she was terribly clever as well as pretty-pretty would probably have enthralled me even if she hadn't been mine. I adore little children and find their waking up to life fascinating.

Pookie was at a Montessori nursery a few blocks from the flat when my job at Capital started, and it was hard to find sleep time between mothering and radio work. Sometimes I'd drag myself home bleary eyed at three in the morning and fall into bed, knowing that I had to be up at seven to dish out her bacon and oatmeal. I wanted her to know I was there. I had a very reliable New Zealand girl living in at the time, but I knew she wouldn't stay long enough. A pattern had developed since my daughter's birth whereby we'd have somebody living in for six months and then we'd be six months on our own. I knew if she grew too dependent on any of her nannies she'd suffer at their departure.

When 22 broke up, I began an affair with the young guitar player in the band. He wasn't much younger than me, but he looked it. The band nicknamed him the Boy, but Hugh Burns was his name. He was a world-class guitar player whose talent was publicly unrecognized. He was a very gifted player and sought after for session work. His ability to sit down and practise for hours was alien to me, but it suited our relationship. He was so involved with his guitar that he didn't resent my being equally passionate about my daughter and never tried to encroach on the time I spent with her. Hugh loved my daughter. He was gentle and caring with her. I found it relatively easy to have him living with me. The fact that he was honest and trustworthy was what attracted me to him, that and my penchant for shy boys. He wasn't intensely emotional, which meant that I didn't have to try to be. With some people you share your bed but not your dreams. Hugh was my music connection and even while I was working at Capital, having a relationship with someone who was rushing off to recording sessions made me think that music was never too far away.

I stopped writing songs when I was working at Capital. There just wasn't time, and the inclination was dampened by motherhood and radio work.

Delirium, panic and emergency alert was the cocktail mix that we downed during our first day on air from our newly acquired (not quite ready) home on the Euston Road. It was like having first-night nerves throughout an entire 20-hour day, because every individual show that was counted down and every newscaster that stepped in a booth to broadcast marked a first. If anybody was casual, I didn't spot them.

The blood drained from my face when the programme controller informed me that the theme of my show that night was to change to the Arab–Israeli conflict that broke out that day.

There was no time to argue. I was caught up in Capital's overambitious endeavour to turn my show into a current-affairs programme. I would have to draw the actress Elaine Stritch into a discussion about the Arab–Israeli war. A news correspondent, John Carvel, was invited to join us, because he was versed in the topic. I assumed my main guest, David Frost, could talk about anything. I had been totally enveloped in rock and roll and wasn't foolish enough to think that I could brush up on the background of the Middle East conflict in a few frantic hours.

My guests were booked to arrive forty-five minutes before the programme went on air. There was an informal reception to introduce them and help them relax with a drink while they were being briefed about the show. Ten minutes before air time, David Frost hadn't turned up. There we were with the Arab–Israeli war to discuss and no headlining guest. He'd been stopped by police en route. We would have to start without him.

I was nervous and bogged down with information about the guests and the topic while I waited for the green light to indicate that we were on air. We sat in a brightly lit studio with ten people staring at us from the control room. Dickie

Attenborough was among them, smiling but anxious-looking. I'm surprised that nobody complained about my heart pounding when there was supposed to be silence. I had decided that I should bring out the human element of the issue rather than have a political discussion about it. When I asked Elaine Stritch how she would feel about the conflict if she had a son out there on the front, she saved the day with an emotional response. I didn't have any tissues and didn't know what to do when she started crying. Just as she was dabbing at her eyes, David Frost arrived fifteen minutes late. Whereas he may have otherwise been feisty with me in the interviewer's position, his lateness spurred an apologetic retreat into his most affable self. I can't remember what anybody said that night, but I managed to direct a discussion about the Arab–Israeli conflict with an actress, a media personality and a political correspondent. I'd pulled off my first show, exhibiting all the elements that its ambitious format aspired to. And better still, people liked it. Dickie was most complimentary.

Every night had the same intense degree of the unexpected and made me overstep the bounds of my knowledge. I grew to enjoy the adrenalin it produced and the feeling that my brain hadn't turned to pudding while I was on the road. After a couple of months, I felt more comfortable. There was a parade of people with my having at least three guests a night. Sometimes I had five and had to remember to identify them when I asked them a question so that the listening audience knew who was speaking. With the show airing five nights a week, that meant a lot of guests. A few people were totally different from what I expected, like Sarah Vaughan, who was incredibly shy.

The concept of commercial radio was new and people wanted to contribute to its survival as an alternative to the BBC. I got the full advantage of their good will which made it good listening, so the critics said. But I have no doubt that it was the three-day work week and the television curfew at 10.15 pm imposed by the government to deal with the energy crisis in 1973–74 which really made my late-night slot popular. People switched off their television and switched on to *Marsha and Friends*, which became *Sarah, Marsha and Friends*, when my programme was linked to the one that followed.

The Saturday-night music show was another story entirely. I had to be DJ, organize the music and feature a guest each week. Dionne Warwick, Barry White and Bill Withers were among the many that made appearances but it was my three-and-a-half-hour interview with Stevie Wonder that was considered a coup.

While Marc Bolan was at the height of his fame with T-Rex, I lost touch with him, but we were in contact again after I started working at Capital. He called to say he wanted me to meet Gloria Jones, who had done an album with Motown which Marc wanted me to hear. He and Gloria were obviously involved, but I pretended not to know as they were making huge efforts to conceal it at the time. Gloria had toured with Marc in the States as a backing singer. She was a good songwriter from an LA Melangian church background. Her father was a preacher. I hoped that she'd take Marc in hand. T-Rex had brought him great international acclaim as a rock performer and songwriter, but he looked lost and unwell. He was bloated to twice his size and although he was full of bravado, I was sad to see that his natural beauty and his elfin sparkle were merely memories I had of him. When he brought Gloria to meet me at the station, his satin jacked was pulling at the seams. I let the 12-foot blue-and-brown boa that he had draped around his neck divert my eye. When I mentioned how beautiful it was, he insisted that I have it.

(I was working in Portugal when I read that Gloria and Marc's son, Rolan, was born, and I was in LA in 1977 when I heard that Marc had been killed in a car crash in Barnes. He was only thirty. Gloria was driving, and the accident left her in a coma for days. Afterwards she was under a lot of pressure in England, and when she returned to Los Angeles with their son, I traced her and kept in touch. Marc wouldn't have wanted her ostracized.)

It was strange being on the other side of the microphone, trying to get people to divulge more than they planned to. I did it because it was my job. But I hated that part of it because I believed that they all had a right to their private lives.

The intense work load combined with mothering exhausted me and after a few months I was a zombie. I proposed doing a Sunday-night special instead of a nightly show. This was to be an in-depth interview with one guest about their life and work, and the format would allow me to do outside interviews. Gradually the idea developed so that I incorporated several contributors in an edited one-hour slot. Marianne Faithfull was one of the artists I did a Sunday-night programme with, when she was appearing in *The Collector* in the West End. I thought she'd had an interesting career, which at that time encompassed music, theatre and film. When I went to her theatre dressing room, her boyfriend, a young blond antique dealer introduced as Oliver, wanted to go to the cinema while we taped the interview. He didn't have any money, so I lent him four pounds, and he left. She looked healthy and I found her relaxed, and the interview, which went out with some of her early music, was successful. We didn't mention Mick before, after or during the chat, but he wrote to say that he liked it.

A few other interviews stick in my mind. The strangest was with Bob Marley. He was not a household name then but there was a buzz about him and Island Records was pushing hard for a hit. Bob was in London to promote the album *Burnin'*. As I had the Saturday-night Black-music/reggae spot, he was to be featured as a guest along with Del Richardson from Osibisa, a band that Tony Visconti produced.

It was obvious as soon as I met Bob that I was going to have trouble interviewing him, because his Jamaican accent was so pronounced that I couldn't understand a word he said. His smile was endearing, so I made the effort.

In addition to this little stumbling block, Bob insisted on feeling my leg under the table while I was interviewing Del or introducing a record. It was hardly what I'd expected, and was an added distraction in a particularly strange situation. I'd ask Bob a question and he'd respond but as I had no idea what he'd said, I'd say 'Thanks, Bob' and play another record. He might just as well have been answering in ancient Greek. But he understood perfectly well when I asked him to stop feeling my leg, not that it stopped him from doing it. He and Del laughed a lot and as we got no letters of complaint, I assume that the listening audience either didn't notice or didn't mind that the interview wasn't entirely coherent.

Bob's promotion man from Island called to say that Bob didn't know anyone in London and would like to visit me. I remembered that it wasn't going to be any easier to talk to him in my flat than it had been in the Capital studio, so I invited singer Doris Troy, who was a good friend of mine, to come and translate for me. Doris can turn any minor encounter into a party.

Bob never stopped smiling, nodded his head a lot and wasn't bothered that I didn't want any of his humungous joint, which he declared was part of his religious observance as a Rastafarian. Nor did he mind that I couldn't understand what he said, but he certainly made efforts to be understood on his following visit, when he insisted that I should return to Jamaica with him. I thought he was lovely, but to be his Rasta woman wasn't a notion that tempted me. He left his green wool Rasta cap with white and gold trim for me when he said goodbye.

When I next saw him, in LA eight years later, he had become an enormous star, having transformed reggae from a cult phenomenon to an international music force. I knew that he was ill but didn't realize that within eighteen months he would be dead.

However many times I thought that I had put Bob's Rasta cap away, it would appear as if by magic in a drawer or cupboard and have to be put away again.

I accepted that my listening audience liked big names, but I knew from my own experience how much celebrity was luck and hype. Yet when I got to sit alone and interview Tennessee Williams, I was ecstatic because I truly admired his work and looked forward to talking to a man of his generation who had no sexual interest in women and yet had a depth of perception about our psychology and pathos which was awe-inspiring. I did a Sunday-night special about him and his work and linked in interviews with actresses like Carroll Baker who had starred in *Baby Doll*, and Claire Bloom who was appearing in *A Streetcar Named Desire*. He talked with great candour and his Southernness made him seem Melangian. He'd laugh until he coughed or his eyes watered and had a contagious sense of humour. He mentioned that an actress who shall remain nameless spoke his prose with the accent of a 'Nigra', and the way he pronounced 'Nigra' was almost worrying. But he was generous and open in his revelations about himself and life and I felt very privileged to have an opportunity to talk to him.

Gore Vidal was equally interesting and initially razor-sharp in a different way. The first thing he said to me when I walked into his hotel suite lugging my heavy Sony recorder was:

'Oh. I know you. Bianca Jagger spoke of you.'

This was after Mick had denied paternity.

I turfed his slippery reference out of my way, defiant and determined to overcome the reactions that Mick's paternal denial had set off.

I was working at Capital when the lawsuit came up for the second time. Mick was not at the 6 November 1973 hearing, when the case drew sensational headlines. In spite of my work, I lived a normal life and even the mundanities of it were affected by this press. Shopkeepers were less cordial. The bank teller couldn't look me in the eye. Mothers at nursery school who had been friendly avoided me. Curious people who eyed my daughter too closely didn't know how close they were to a clout around the ear. People's reactions were as apparent as after the *Hair* opening. But these were negative.

When my solicitor took out the original write through court, Mick's name was on it, but we kept it from the press. I was horrified to see a journalist in the press box at the second hearing.

In spite of the news coverage, there was a conspicuous silence that was deafening. My telephone stopped ringing. I wasn't surprised, because being involved in that sort of lawsuit cast aspersions on me. A paternity suit is supposed to be a means to secure support for a child from its father. As it's issued as a civil charge against him, by law he is innocent until proven guilty. By denying paternity, he insinuates that the mother was sexually active with more than one man at the time of conception. Therefore, it's the mother who stands accused, and finally the child who is punished, because whatever the father's means, a child born to unmarried parents only has a right to five pounds a week maintenance from him. While modern society condones sex without marriage, the law condemns the children born of it.

My solicitor advised me to accept an out-of-court settlement. The best offer that Mick's side would make was £500 a year (about nine pounds a week) and a £10,000 trust fund that the baby would get after she finished school. This was offered only in exchange for my solicitor's signature on deeds stating that Mick wasn't the baby's father but that the settlement was made to avoid publicity.

I started proceedings in late 1972 and it was 21 January 1975 before I received the first monthly payment of £41.67. In 1975, that was a week's salary for an accredited nanny. The payment by standing order was a regular reminder that there was no justice in the world. That was an important thing for me to come to terms with.

Throughout my time working at Capital I managed to keep the issue under control. In interviews I would state categorically that Mick was not a subject to be broached. One of the things I learned from interviewing was never to be intimidated by somebody pointing a microphone at my mouth. It amazed me how many people succumbed to my impertinent questions because they thought it was their duty to give me answers. Anyway, I got very good at smiling but making it absolutely clear that I had no intention of discussing my private affairs and in particular anything to do with my daughter. After Mick's paternity denial I wouldn't allow any pictures of her. Karis wouldn't stand a chance, growing up with that kind of publicity marring her childhood. She had to be protected. As a result I became a no-no with the press.

I wish I were all hard shell, but there were moments when, instead of feeling angry about what had happened, I felt humiliated.

When facts are challenged again and again and fall under suspicion, you can come around to questioning them yourself. I realized that while Mick should have been a memory, the fact of our having a child together meant that it wasn't possible to shake him out of my life although I wanted to.

12
THE PLEASURE ZONE

When my six-month contract with Capital came up for renewal, I decided I wanted to step out of local radio. There were newspaper reports that a show I did about sex, in which the word 'fuck' was semantically discussed, had got me fired. Certainly Dickie and John Whitney called me into the front office about it, but as the prerecorded show had been submitted for approval as part of a standard policy and returned to me for airing as though it had been checked and approved, I refused to accept responsibility for the fact that it went out. In any case, I thought that my guests, who included Deirdre McSharry, the editor of English *Cosmopolitan*, had been cautious, not provocative, and remained within the bounds of a sensible discussion. In spite of the hoo-ha about it, I was asked to renew but didn't. Especially after my own bouts, I didn't like delving into people's lives and corralling them into self-exposure. While I appreciated the chance I'd been given to learn radio journalism, I didn't have the stomach for going at people tooth and nail. Life's too short.

The year that came and went after Capital was lean. Being in London without any opportunity for travel made me feel imprisoned. I wanted to be out there. My grandmother would have said I had ants in my pants and she would have been right.

I wanted Karis to have a seaside vacation, so I got my agent to book me into a singing stint in Portugal in July and August 1975 as a way of getting a long family holiday abroad, with Hugh booked to accompany us as my musical director and guitarist.

Trust us to land in Lisbon in the middle of a revolution. There were soldiers everywhere and a couple of times, when we looked from our hotel window, tanks moved slowly through the main street of Estoril. The resort atmosphere was nonexistent. There was no one at the fashionable Hotel Estoril, except us and the other acts booked at the Casino Estoril: tall topless Bluebell dancers from Paris and a German monocyclist and his acrobatic wife.

The Bluebell girls arrived with Miss Bluebell (Margaret Kelly) for the first rehearsal. This Englishwoman with cropped, tinted blonde hair was as stern as a drill sergeant watching the leggy girls, several of whom were in their teens, strut through their routine. She was gone when we put on the full-scale show, twice nightly and three times on Sunday with an orchestra and lights – the lot. Sometimes there'd only be a couple of little old ladies sitting out front.

We were booked to do a casino tour after Estoril. We went on to the Algarve and checked into a palatial golf hotel that catered for American golfing enthusiasts, now as empty as Estoril. Part of the government policy after the overthrow of the dictatorship was that no worker could be fired. So these hotels were fully staffed although the tourists stayed away that summer. When we ordered, the chefs were obviously so glad to prepare food that they served us three times more than a normal-sized human could eat.

While we were sitting in the grand restaurant at the Hotel Penina one lunchtime, some workers came into the kitchen with guns. We were asked to retreat to our rooms as there wasn't going to be any service during that mealtime.

I was pretending to be a cabaret singer, performing songs like 'The Shadow Of Your Smile' and 'What Kind Of Fool Am I'. I acted like Shirley Bassey, flouncing about the enormous chandeliered restaurant in long evening dresses. It was hardly my style, but I discovered I didn't have to scream my lungs out to think that I was singing.

My term in Portugal caused another break in my relationship with Hugh, which was always cracking, and he went back early.

Karis had a ball coming to the shows and sitting by the swimming pool with the Bluebell girls. She was getting swimming instruction from a 72-year-old Portuguese Olympic swimming master as well as learning her multiplication tables, but at four she still needed an afternoon nap. I got a young Portuguese nanny for her whom she adored, but she preferred coming to work with me when allowed, and lived by my schedule. I felt that Karis was better off living a nocturnal life and sleeping late, which meant she could be with me during her waking hours, than living the hours a child normally does and our paths rarely crossing.

She was always so well behaved that there was never a problem about taking her to work. Even at Capital I could trust her to keep quiet when the green light went on. Sometimes she'd sit drawing with her paper and coloured pens under the big round table where I gave interviews. I'd look under during the commercial breaks and make sure she was all right and didn't need her drink or anything. There was excitement wherever I was working and she was guaranteed some form of entertainment or experience.

She needed me at home for her sense of security and routine. To help her get ready for our daily walk to school was something I never missed. We were up at seven. Some mornings from a distance you could hear the click-clacking rhythm of iron horseshoes against the tarred street. The sound told us that the King's Troop of the Royal Horse Artillery was coming. We never got tired of rushing to see them from our third-floor window. The elegant 7.30 parade was their morning's exercise. The forty or so immaculately groomed horses, most of them chestnut, moved in a disciplined stream, two abreast between the parked cars on each side of our road. The pink-cheeked soldier boys astride them looked sharp in brownish-green uniforms, hats, and knee-high boots of the most durable leather, designed for horse riding but impractical for walking in the city. The ones of high rank were distinguished by white gloves. One carried a glistening bugle to be seen but not blown. Occasionally a soldier would look up and we'd smile at him, knowing he was not allowed to smile back.

We always watched until they were out of sight, with the riders at the rear pulling what looked like polished World War I artillery. Today, when *Time* magazine runs cover stories on Reagan's star-wars armoury, these soldiers with their sabres are like a vision. Watching them was worth the five minutes we'd lose from our morning schedule.

I had to take employment for us to survive. People who looked at my résumé wondered why my career leaped from theatre to music to film to radio. Nobody realized that I simply took what work was offered, because I couldn't afford not to. I wanted Karis to have the best schooling and that cost money.

In 1976, I returned to the West End in a musical called *Mardi Gras* written by Melvyn Bragg with music by Ken Howard and Alan Blaikley. My role as a New Orleans voodoo woman wasn't demanding. The six-month run at the Prince of Wales Theatre was memorable because of the friendships I made in the cast, and one renewed acquaintance.

I first met Eric Roberts when we worked together on a Roger Daltrey video session, directed by Richard Longcraine, who gave me a suspicious number of close-ups considering that I was on the shoot to sing backup and add colour. Eric is a Melangian, built like a quarterback with a chiselled, mahogany face. We quickly discovered that we laughed at the same things and shared a weakness for American junk food and ice cream. His father, a doctor, died when Eric was a boy in Rockford, Illinois. We had a lot of similar experiences in growing up in the States and to meet someone who could laugh with me about an obscure episode of *Amos 'n Andy* was a delicious treat in England. He had a master's degree from the University of Illinois but appreciated that I need to talk Melangian sometimes.

I helped Eric get a job in the chorus of *Mardi Gras*. After the show had been running for a month, I asked him to share my spacious dressing room at the Prince of Wales. I brought Karis to the theatre as much as possible and he brought his wild, furry terrier Tiger to keep her company.

Eric brought the best of the reservation to me.

One night when I was performing a strenuous five-minute song-and-dance number called 'The Calinda', my long heavy grass skirt fell off. I was downstage and only a few feet from the audience, because we had no orchestra pit. I kept dancing as if nothing had happened, but Eric and the other three chorus boys dancing with me could hardly contain themselves when they realized that not only had I lost my skirt, but I was wearing a pair of underpants which were very brief and had a large Indian's head with a tomahawk painted on the crotch. I didn't always wear knickers and was thankful that I had a pair on at all.

It was a major departure from musicals, in November 1976, when I was asked to do my first straight acting role, in

Thornton Wilder's *The Skin of Our Teeth* at the newly opened Royal Exchange Theatre within the old Corn Exchange in central Manchester. I played Sabina, a role originally played in the West End by Vivien Leigh.

Only now do I realize how cocky I must have sounded when interviewers asked me, 'How do you find acting?' and I said, 'A damn sight easier than singing.' It was true, though. I didn't feel that I had to blow every ounce of my energy and strain every muscle to make sense of a line in the same way as on a music stage when people expect to be transported to a high-energy zone. Acting seemed like such a calm, civilized team effort. Even though I was playing a principal role, it wasn't as taxing as being on tour.

Being in Manchester in the dead of winter made me homesick for a ray of California sunshine. The Mancunian sky was always grey and the people looked weatherbeaten, standing at the bus stop with their cheeks iced pink.

I had a small apartment in a building that catered for actors and actresses who came to Manchester for a limited stay. There was no central heating and no telephone in the room. The pay phone was one flight down in an unheated cubicle. Nothing should be unheated in Manchester during the winter and I found the cold unbearable. I used to phone Karis at home in London before she went to bed and my feet were so frozen by the time I walked back upstairs that I had to heat them in front of the tiny gas fire before I could think straight. The gas and electricity were on pay-as-you-go meters. However many 10-pence pieces I'd put in at night, there was never a fire when I woke in the morning. The room was so cold that the wall next to my bed always had condensation on it in the morning because of my body heat.

We played in repertory. On days off I rushed home by train to see Karis. She came to Manchester at the weekends. With the help of a nanny, good neighbours and a school one block from home which she loved, Karis thrived.

In the flat in Manchester I got word from home one day that my grandmother had died. Edna had been ill for some time, so it didn't come as a shock. I couldn't go back for her funeral and that seemed to hold her parting in check. I don't think she knew how much I admired her, and maybe I didn't know myself until she wasn't there to take for granted. In all the time I spent with Edna, I never saw her cry. I don't know whether she hid her tears or was saving them.

The news of her death came on a bitterly cold night and I sat on the floor in crosslegged Indian fashion as I always do when there is no one who expects me to sit in a chair. It didn't bring any comfort. Nor did the silly little gas fire, which burned me on one small area while the rest of me still froze. I'd turned off the lights, so I couldn't see the depressing dark-blue colour of the walls.

The gas fire cast enough light for me to write to Ikey and Thelma. I worried that not going home for Edna's funeral could have been taken to mean that I was too caught up in my own life to make the effort. They didn't know how much my grandmother meant to me. I had been disgracefully lax about writing to her or them but telephoned when I could. The right words wouldn't come and I realized that the English I was using would sound too formal when they read it 6000 miles away in California. But in the theatre you can't ask for time off even for the most important farewell.

While I was still at the Royal Exchange, a German record company offered to finance an independent production with me whereby I'd jointly own the distribution rights of the finished album rather than sign an artist's contract, which I was reluctant to do with a German-based company. I was still considered a music commodity in Germany where my rock reputation had had most impact. Pete Bellotte, an English producer based in Munich, was commissioned to produce my album. He was Giorgio Moroder's partner and together they produced and wrote a number of Donna Summer hits. They were one of the major writing and production teams responsible for the synthesized orchestrated disco sound that was to overtake rock in popularity by the end of the 1970s.

When I arrived in Munich with Karis during Easter, the backing tracks for my album had been totally written and recorded and produced by Pete in my absence. This was considered an acceptable process by 1977, but was completely different to the collaboration with a producer that I was accustomed to and needed. Producers were more influential with the big 24-track orchestral backings, and the singer became more incidental. It was a different recording experience to anything I'd been through, but I'd made a firm decision with myself to go along with the programme and not object to anything. I was tired of confrontations about music and the business of it. After Tony Visconti, I never had the opportunity to work with a producer who shared my musical taste.

To change record producers is like changing buses. Each wants to take you in his direction. I felt that there was no continuity of sound in the records I'd had out. Every record had a different producer. For the project with Pete, I adapted my voice to suit disco tracks. The music which was going to be marketed with my name was artistically more Pete's than mine, but I enjoyed working with him and had confidence in his sessions. He was very affable and the atmosphere of the small Musicland studio had a Germanic precision beneath its boys' clubs surface of dartboards and knotty pine.

Musicland was in the basement of an enormous block called Arabella Haus which contained a hotel, apartments, shops and offices. Karis and I stayed in one of the fully furnished apartments while I was recording. This meant that she didn't have to be in the studio but was on the doorstep if she wanted to skip in and out. Recording studios can get very tiring for a six-year-old. The first night of recording she begged not to get lumbered with a German-speaking baby-sitter, so we decided to try her sleeping in the room alone while I was five flights below. I'd never left her alone before and was loath to do it, but I thought I'd keep popping up during my session.

We'd do a few vocal takes and I willed the machine to fail or the tape to run out so that I'd have a momentary excuse to race up to the room to check that she was all right. I was wearing a pair of painter's overalls dyed sunburst yellow and three-inch high-heeled boots which were so tight that there wasn't time to pull them off every time I made one of the mad dashes. The hallways were a clinical modern maze and I was petrified that I'd get lost either trying to find our flat or making my way back to the studio. I tore along the hallways to our flat and back like a sprinter in stilettos. The mad dash took about five minutes. I'd stop to catch my breath outside the heavy soundproof door of the studio so that I wouldn't look too winded to jump straight into another take. Pete and the German engineer, Jürgen Koppers, were always raring to go when I got back. The singing took more energy than the sprints. When the session finished, I wanted to splay out on the floor and beg for a stretcher to take me upstairs. Of course Karis slept soundly throughout. We made other arrangements for the remaining sessions.

The album turned out well. This can't be said for the business arrangements. I thought that my tight co-ownership contract protected me. When it didn't, I was forced to get a German solicitor as well as an English one. I naively expected a fair deal and couldn't accept that the business of music had the artist at the losing end.

In the midst of resolving this problem, I arranged to exchange my London flat with an LA journalist who had a duplex apartment in Los Feliz, near Hollywood. My brother Dennis helped me find the swop. A month in Los Angeles would give me an opportunity to sniff around for a distribution deal for my album and reacquaint myself with the West Coast. I considered a move home, although I hadn't openly admitted it to myself yet. I saw no end to the problems that had been created in England through the paternity suit. I went from being tagged 'the girl from *Hair*' to 'the girl who sued Mick Jagger'. Under the circumstances, starting again in America, where I was unknown, seemed practical.

I also thought that my daughter could benefit from being nearer to our family.

Karis and I arrived in LA on the seventh day of the seventh month, 1977, with my new album, *Marsha Hunt '77*, tucked in my suitcase in the hope of finding a deal with an American distributor and introducing myself with a finished product to the West Coast music bosses and artists' managers. As Pete had a Donna Summer single in the charts, his name alone on my album would attract interest. A track called 'The Other Side Of Midnight' had been released as a single in Germany and was well received there, which made me optimistic.

In London I had been interviewed for a part in another film, which was to star Glenda Jackson. I had a meeting with the American coproducer in Hollywood the day after I got off the plane. She seemed 90 per cent sure that I had the part, and the promise of that swept me along for the first week. By the time the offer was withdrawn, I'd made a couple of important music-business introductions. I didn't know that I was one measly hunger in a citywide famine.

The high stakes in the music and movie industries let LA entice like a one-armed bandit. If you have anything of the gambler in you, which you must to be in the business in the first place, you can get trapped there believing that you can't leave because the next jackpot might be yours. The record deal. The script. The film role. Everybody seems to be waiting and hoping. Maybe the place is haunted by the spirit of those first gamblers, the gold diggers who rushed to California in 1849.

People who have regular jobs there may never get this feeling about it. My brother, for instance, writes for the *Los Angeles Times* as a music critic, and his stable employment lets him experience the city from a different perspective.

The moment we disembarked from the aircraft, I noticed that my visibility was gone and I was no longer perceived as an American or a foreigner. I was Black and female, which automatically provokes certain agitations, presumptions and assumptions in my country. Dealing with our luggage, getting money changed, buying gum for Karis at a newsstand – the quickest transactions had indirect undertones. Slightly patronizing, covertly antagonistic: after eleven years of being free of this, I couldn't pretend that I didn't notice people's attitudes.

What complicated this further was that to American ears, I spoke the English of England. I'd get one reaction before I opened my mouth, quite another after my accent spilled out, and another still when I was asked where I was from and I said Philadelphia.

I realized right away that I was going to have to keep juggling my head back and forth to accommodate the person I was speaking to and the situation I was in. I needed to readjust myself to be effective. I didn't feel completely myself speaking with an American accent, especially with Karis and the many English friends I had living in LA. The difference between American and English involves more than the accent. A culture, a whole manner and mentality accompany the separate languages and while I was versed in both, English had become more natural to me. It also allowed me to experience my own country with foreign detachment. So I spoke English sometimes and American at others.

My first month included mothering my English child, regular phone calls to England and Germany to speak to my lawyers, discussing record deals with Americans who saw me as only 'Black female', or meeting agents to talk about acting representation. I felt like bloody Joanne Woodward playing in *The Three Faces of Eve*. I wasn't about to get an Academy Award for my performances, though, more like a boot up the backside for refusing to play 'Black female' when that was the role called for.

By the time the month of the flat exchange neared its end, Pete Bellotte and his family had arrived from Germany and invited us to join them in an enormous house they'd taken for the summer in Beverly Hills. Street after street, there was no sign of activity or human life beyond an occasional gardener. Fred Astaire lived a couple of doors away, but he wasn't out tap-dancing on his sloping driveway. The big houses with landscaped gardens near Sunset Boulevard looked like film-set mock-ups; they were too extravagantly designed to look like homes and too self-consciously conceived to be as beautiful as they were meant to be. But living all together as we did turned our house into a retreat – we could have been in Switzerland.

During our first month I hadn't yet achieved what I'd set out to and needed more time to land a deal for my album. I considered that if one came through, we'd probably stay, but I was still in two minds. I wasn't sure if the move would be a good thing for Karis's education, which was the most important thing of all.

There was a summer school directly opposite the flat we were staying in when we first arrived, and I'd enrolled Karis in a morning group so that she could quickly make some local playmates. She usually resisted my playmate-finding schemes for two days – until they worked. During Karis's six-week summer-school adventure something important happened which changed everything for us.

I knew nothing about the LA school system and was relieved to learn from Karis's summer-school teacher how to go about finding a suitable school. On the basis of what she'd seen of Karis's classroom work, she told me to get in touch with the Gifted Children's Association. They in turn suggested that I should have her tested and gave me a number to call in September. It was August, but something told me to call that instant. The voice on the other end explained that the office and school were closed but that as we were from out of town, a special testing appointment would be made immediately.

I'd always noticed that Karis was extremely quick at grasping things. The three Rs came easily to her and very early. Her teachers in England had dismissed my queries about her cleverness and had given the impression that it didn't warrant concern. Yet it seemed to stand to reason that a bright child needed extra attention no less than a retarded one.

When I collected Karis after her examination by an educational psychologist, the doctor confirmed that nature had endowed her with a special facility for reasoning and retention. She said that Karis should be in a school where teachers were aware of her needs and where she could meet other children like herself. Finding a professional who understood this and knew how to help my daughter was like finding God. It lifted a great burden from me, because although I gave as much attention to her learning as I could, it seemed insufficient as she got older. It was one of the reasons I disliked leaving her with nannies, who were good at keeping her fed and clean but didn't have the inclination to teach her, which she seemed to need more than anything.

A place was offered at an expensive special school. I had Karis enrolled for the September term although I hardly had enough money in my purse to buy petrol to get us back to Pete's after the examination.

A small settlement payment came in August from the German label. Virtually all that money went against legal fees and on the substantial down payment for the school fees. Financially I was committed way over my head, but I was determined to continue to provide Karis with the education she needed. She'd had the best in London, and I saw no reason to give her less in LA. The label settlement also gave me the right to half of any money received for the sale of the album, which had cost $50,000 to make. So I believed I was in possession of a property worth $25,000 and trusted fate to help me get my hands on it.

Some television promotion dates came up in Germany. We

were able to return to Europe long enough to collect our things, do the shows, and make our way back to California.

On our return to LA after my German TV dates, I took advantage of a free flight detour so that we could visit my 90-year-old grandfather in Memphis. Karis was his only great-grandchild and he was her only great-grandparent, so I thought they should meet. Grandfather had had a series of major operations and our visit couldn't be postponed.

I'd promised Karis that if we returned to California, we'd take her budgerigar, Benjie, and her four-foot teddy bear, Big Ted, which had to be transported in her old pushchair. The Pan Am jumbo wasn't full, so Big Ted had a seat of his own. Karis shed three silent tears at the check-in desk when the stewardess said that she would have to put her caged yellow bird in the hold, and somehow the tears caused a change in flight policy and the budgie was allowed to board the flight with her. She wasn't a weepy child at the worst of times, so I knew that those three tears counted for a lot.

Benjie had banged into Karis's nursery window not long after his Christmas 1974 arrival and damaged a wing, which kept him from flying. He was always allowed to patter about in her room to get exercise and was trained to come when you called him. On board, he twittered around Karis's flight tray and ate the bread and cake we were served as part of our meal.

I knew that Karis didn't really want to leave England and those little things made the transition bearable for her.

Karis, myself and Benjie and Big Ted were a team and that's how we arrived for our overnight stay in Memphis. I'd never been to the Deep South and spending a night with my grandfather and his companion of forty years, Harry Mae Simmons, was quite an experience. I had to translate everything for Karis, who moved from lap to lap, smiling sweetly but unable to understand a word of what anyone said.

Grandfather was born in 1887 to two emancipated slaves, Emma Shouse and Blair T., his namesake. He went to Harvard, Morehouse and Roger Williams University where he got his master's degrees in education and theology, which was a great accomplishment at the time. He was a minister, and from 1932 he was principal at what was then the only 'Negro' high school in Memphis. He was a politician of sorts before we were allowed to be politicians, when 'yes suh' and Southern lynchings were par for the course. I didn't resent that he hadn't used his influence to help my mother after my father died, but he apologized for that, and it made me aware that he must have had his own misgivings. He sent me money when I asked for it, which was rare. It had been his purse that paid for my wig when my hair fell out.

I was glad we made the trip to see him because he died the following winter, and although he'd come to visit once in Philadelphia, I hadn't got a sense of him until I saw him in his Southern comfort.

America had been through major upheavals in the years I'd been away. Her self-image had been pummelled by race riots, Vietnam, Watergate and political assassinations. Although the Vietnam war had ended in 1973, there was a lot of residual bad feeling about it in 1977 because Americans generally had concluded that the war should never have been fought and therefore the death toll of 57,000 was unjustifiable. This made the emotional scars suffered by our generation of soldiers cut as deeply into the nation as the war itself; boys who grew up in the fifties with John Wayne and war movies came back from combat to a country that was ashamed of the conflict.

The fact that Melangians and whites remained separate but unequal was no longer discussed. In Los Angeles at least, racial politics were passé, as though it had only been coffee-table discussion. People reacted with fear and loathing to the riots although they had been provoked by poverty, suppression and the realization that things would never change if you were poor and Black.

Not only had talk of peace and love gone out of the window, but ex-hippies were buying hand guns.

I kept trying to get my bearings. Was LA a nation unto itself – another country that bore no resemblance to the rest of America? Or was America a continent of nations claiming to be one but merely bound by language and economic convenience and linked artificially by the press, television and radio?

I was preoccupied with petty cash problems. When your thoughts and time are consumed by the need for money, the broad issues slip into the background. From my new vantage point it was easier to understand how the poor were too caught up with the struggle to eat and survive to consider the issues that kept them that way.

John Mayall was living in Laurel Canyon and that's where we stayed on our return just as he headed off on a tour. He had a glorious three-storey canyon house with a swimming pool, sauna and a hilltop view of the city that brought calm and stillness by moonlight.

Karis's school, where she flourished, was 12 miles of winding canyon roads from John's house and taking her there in the morning and collecting her in the afternoon was an occupation in itself. Initially she had to eat soda crackers during the journey to keep from getting car-sick. My brother lent me a car that was economical on petrol. There's very limited public transport in LA, so Karis couldn't get to school by bus.

My relationship with John, when he came home, was purely platonic. Karis and I shared a frilly Laura Ashley-type room on a lower floor. To express my gratitude for his generosity, although he hadn't asked, I took over caring for the house and made myself indispensable. I can put a mean polish on a grand piano and gave 'good house guest' by being as unobtrusive as it's possible to be with a young child, and stocking our own food. John didn't want us to leave. We had a system that worked, largely because I worked hard at it. You have to when you're in someone else's house.

John was no less eccentric than he'd been in days of old, but he also reflected the influence of LA and a sturdy income. He'd practically built the house himself, and it was his baby as Karis was mine. He'd become quite gregarious, which made me laugh, because he'd been decidedly antisocial when we'd lived together before. An array of people cascaded through his life, within arm's length of mine. I was usually the only person up in the morning to empty their ashtrays and remove their glass marks from John's bar, which added a touch of English pub to his rustic living room with its enormous John-built fireplace. He refused to have a cleaner but he did indulge in a plant lady whose weekly task was to water the plants and pluck a few dead leaves – a typically LA service.

I don't think I ever saw John be as considerate to anyone as he was to Baby Sugar, which was Karis's latest nickname. It wasn't a spoiling kind of attention, but he always had time for her and a sweet delicate affection, and I did dearly love him for that. He ws terribly proud of her good behaviour and her work, which she did conscientiously on his eight-foot-long rustic oak dining-room table. They had an unusual friendship. Their obvious admiration for each other was moderated by a shade of English formality. He sometimes let her make his breakfast of vodka and orange juice with a ginger-beer chaser, which was a sign of trust.

John's passion for movies led to weekend video marathons and he would invite large numbers of people to a solid run of forty-eight hours of films. Somehow we lived through these weekends. The house also held a renowned collection of pornography, the detailed diaries that he'd kept since the fifties, his hand-carved guitars and his kneecap, pickled in a jar on the edge of the bar. (His kneecap had been removed after he tried to leap from the second-floor balcony into the swimming pool on the lower deck and missed.)

During our first eight months in California, I was relieved that Karis had John's household to shelter her from my money worries, which were becoming more prominent as another summer approached.

I'd been in touch with Mick through mutual friends that past September. My agent for the Shenson film had become a friend of Mick's and set up our contact. I still believed a child has a father and a father has a child, and that it was important that father and daughter saw each other. Mick was separated from his wife and living with a new girlfriend, the Texas model Jerry Hall. When they arrived in LA, arrangements were made for him to have Karis for an afternoon. I couldn't have been more pleased for her when she went off in a summery outfit for this special meeting. I was in touch with Mick afterwards and he realized how close to the edge I'd pushed myself by putting Karis into that school. But no help was forthcoming from him and no note of surprise that our daughter was more than all right. I had a number and a code name for contacting him, but it was back to the old routine – spending money I didn't have trying to telephone him.

We were offered a house-sit in May 1978 for three months by an ex-girlfriend of John's who was renting a cottage that he owned only a few minutes away in the steep drive below. The two-bedroom house was a bijou of lace, skylight and garden. It was nice that John didn't want us to go, but I needed relief from the responsibilities of being an attentive house guest with child.

Karis, Benjie, Big Ted and I re-nested, but when two more possible deals that I had been nursing fell through, I had to admit that I couldn't hold out any longer and went to sign on. I had a couple of small but encouraging territory deals clinched during that winter and through German imports my 12-inch single was getting popular in local gay discotheques, which that summer were a mainstay of disco music in general. Promising though all this was, it didn't cover the cost of survival. So I conceded that I was down to collecting social secrity as a temporary measure to relieve the worry that had developed into nightly anxiety, with me pacing the floor to burn up my banked-up adrenalin.

I was writing more songs than before and although I was frustrated that no record deal was panning out, musically I was feeling stronger and more sure of myself than ever. It was possible to work with musicians, which I couldn't expect to do at John's although I met a number of talented musicians. I had a couple of angels, solicitor Lee Phillips and art director Rod Dyer, both in the business, who were trying to get my record placed or help me get a management deal or a label deal.

California sunshine is positive and even the smog couldn't screen that off. Coasting along Mulholland Drive with the glaze burning through the windscreen and the radio thumping out disco beats lifted the pressure. Having old friends from *Hair* days in town, Tim Curry, Paul Nicholas and Sheila Scott Wilkinson, kept me in touch with myself. Karis and I were in a potentially productive situation and the advantages of her school alone made the money worries seem just an annoying side effect that sometimes comes with progress.

13
SMOKED OUT

I'd never been on the dole before, and my pride resisted it. The Department of Social Security should put out a pamphlet showing nothing but photographs of people a week after they can't find employment, and then a year and so on. Asking for a handout when you really want a job is demoralizing. I sat in a room, not as a singer, temporarily without a record deal or a starring musical role, nor as an English Equity member out of work, which is par for the course. I was Black-female-unemployed, another file number and statistic, and underneath my calm exterior was indignation at being in a social security office. When asked what my occupation was, I said singer and actress. I'm sure the clerk at the desk discounted it as my excuse for not taking a clerical job.

I filled out endless forms before I came to the snag. I couldn't get any government assistance without supplying the name of my child's father so that someone could contact him about support payments. Imagine a West LA social security employee trying to get Mick Jagger on the telephone. The government had to try with a mother's cooperation to get a father to provide maintenance through a paternity suit if necessary. This wasn't an irrational stipulation. But I knew that there was no way that I could put Mick's name on a social security aid form without fanfare.

A second case against Mick would affect our daughter, who was older and couldn't be shielded this time. Only she would be able to tell me if she could cope with it. Although she was only seven, she was astute enough to understand the examples I presented to her of what might happen if I had to take her father to court and how it could affect her, particularly at school. I wanted her to have a few days to think it over and talk about it. If she thought that she was strong enough to handle it, I would have to be, despite knowing how ugly the situation would become for me as the woman. I knew that the problem couldn't be dealt with by the district attorney's office, which had no jurisdiction outside California, but I had no money for a good solicitor. I also discussed the possibility of a lawsuit with my family, as they might be dragged across the coals with me. Among other things, I didn't want my brother's job as a rock critic jeopardized. I had to try to imagine every repercussion and the worst of what might happen.

Money buys laws and the lawyers who translate it. Justice is not fairness – it's only a legal proceeding. The nine pounds a week that I was still receiving for Karis from Mick drove that lesson home. No matter how much I wanted to avoid another paternity suit, it was my duty as a mother to acquire whatever security I could for my daughter so that if something happened to me, she would be provided for.

It took a lot of deliberation and my nerves were worn thin by it. Eventually, my grandmother came to mind with Fannie Graham and Grandma Mary. I stopped weighing up the problems and put the facts and principles back into perspective. I had to find a lawyer. My experience at Capital, booking my guests, taught me how to pick up the phone and call the best. I got legal advice from two lawyers before I approached a third.

Marvin M. Mitchelson sat across from me behind his neatly ordered desk, which was big enough for six place settings at a four-course meal. The panoramic view of Los Angeles from the wall of window behind him may have included half the San Fernando Valley. I had lost my bearings in his office, nineteen storeys above Century City. I swallowed a sip of the milky tea brought by a secretary and took my deepest breath before starting my story. He needed to hear it all to determine whether I had a case and decide if he would represent me.

I don't know who or what he thought I was. I tried to put myself in his shoes. How I appear to other people varies radically, depending on the territory and my work. Los Angeles, London, Munich, Memphis – a few hours on a plane could change my aura. I could have been a woman on the game, for all he really knew, a coke freak or an acid casualty. I made sure that he knew I was there for Karis and that I didn't want blood from Mick, I wanted adequate provision for our daughter.

Of course I didn't take her to his office. There was nothing that I had to disclose that she could gain from hearing. I always gave her a good impression of her father and wanted her to be proud of him. Mick had made great contributions to rock music, and I explained that his absence had something to do with his feelings about me, not her. It benefited her to know that. She was in a delicate situation. Mick was everybody's hero. He was pasted on people's walls, sang out from the radio and peered at her from magazine covers. People would talk about him while she sat in the room as if he had nothing to do with her. It was very important that I didn't. When his songs came on the radio, I turned them up and would smile and say, 'That's your daddy.' When we saw his picture, I'd make some reference to it so that she could relate to him.

Mr Mitchelson wasn't in the least forbidding, though he easily could have been if he had wanted. Some people can't resist the temptation when you're at their mercy. I was certainly that, using up his $2-a-minute office time after announcing that I couldn't afford to pay for it. He didn't waste it, but neither was he looking at his watch. I'd met lawyers in the music business who used words as if they were stalling for time. But Mr Mitchelson, who wanted to be called Marvin, was straightforward.

I told my story as succinctly as I could, and he asked fewer questions than I expected. He wanted to know where the documents were from the settlement deeds of 9 December 1974. I told him that my file and documents were in London and he did something startling. He called his secretary into his office and asked her to make sure his passport was in order, because he was going to London the following afternoon or the morning after. I wanted to jump up and down and yell, but I held it in and got goose bumps instead. Then we discussed what rights my daughter had that were worth fighting for.

Marvin's speed and tenacity were unbelievable. He took instructions to represent me on 14 July and by 22 July he had already been to England and back, served Mick with papers and had the courts withhold Mick's share of the gate receipts for the two Stones concerts in Anaheim, California, which reputedly grossed $4 million. Marvin said that he was taking the latter step to assure that we had leverage. He knew that Mick's lawyers could avoid the issue again if we weren't in a dominant position.

As if I didn't have enough to think about, I decided to give up smoking. I'd smoked since I was thirteen apart from the break from cigarettes during my pregnancy. My petty preoccupation with not smoking took my mind off any real problems. I was already good at pacing up and down. When I stopped smoking, I paced a double shift. To resist the temptation of a cigarette gave me a daily sense of achievement and took my mind off the major crisis.

The case carried on for months and I was advised to settle out of court. I told Marvin that I couldn't accept another settlement because Mick's contribution towards our child's wellbeing wasn't the only issue any longer. I wanted his paternity legally confirmed. However long it took, Karis had a right to know that Mick was indeed her father.

When I discovered that Marvin had also taken on Mick's wife's divorce, I did wonder if he planned to drop my case, but he said he was able to represent both of us. I felt uncomfortable about this, but wasn't in a position to quibble.

At the end of January 1979, the case was heard in court, paternity was declared and maintenance ordered which, it was stated, may not be disclosed. It was enough to keep Karis in school at the time. There was no lump sum and it wasn't retroactive, as most people imagined. I knew that if I didn't get work, we'd be in financial trouble again.

A few times I was asked to sell my story to newspapers for quite a lot of money. I wasn't even tempted. I wanted Karis to think well of her father and wanted Mick to feel that the settlement served him as much as it served her. He needn't have any secret pangs of guilt now that he was contributing towards her education and upkeep. I wrote to let him know what had happened was past and he was welcome to see her. I put the issue behind me so that I could carry on.

During the six months that the case ran, I continued writing songs and had gone to Canada for a few days, when my Peter Bellotte album was released there, to do TV promotion. *Record World*, a major American music-trade paper, had voted me one of the most promising new disco singers of 1978, but the accolade didn't get me a deal. Quite honestly, after the renewed paternity-suit headlines, I was expecting an uphill slog.

In spite of the lawsuit, I was able to keep Karis's picture out of the newspaper and protect her right to a normal childhood. The school was a blessing. The teachers and Dr and Mrs Mirman, who ran it, were very supportive throughout and put Karis on a part-scholarship when they realized that I was still having financial difficulties after the second settlement.

I needed a job badly to meet the $600-a-month rent on the two-bedroomed flat with garden that I'd taken in West Hollywood. It was the going rate for a flat in a safe area. The district was better known as Boys' Town, because it was primarily gay residential. From our new home, it was a long drive to Karis's school, but I wanted to live where I had easy access to appointments for work, and had opted for getting up early for the school run. To get Karis there and back was two hours' driving a day, so I'd returned my brother's car and bought a second-hand lemon. Karis would be sitting in the back seat cool as a cucumber listening to me sweet-talk the car or curse it out. Those daily jaunts to school became a wonderfully uninterrupted private time when we could have a good howl together or practise her spelling or discuss things that were easier to discuss in the car with the music thumping than in the house.

Five mornings a week, we had to endure the winding tree-strewn 12-mile stretch of Mulholland Drive between Laurel Canyon and Encino. Any distraction along the roadside was a relief in the monotony of this regular school run, which began at 7.45 am. We were grateful for signs of human life, whether it was Jerry Brown, then governor, jogging in his pale-blue tracksuit, or Tina Turner standing alone staring pensively at a cliff edge with her dogs on leads at her heel, or some unknown fitness freak sprinting along the roadside. We saw one jogger so regularly, usually between Coldwater Canyon and the San Diego freeway, that we were bothered when he wasn't there. He was blond, of medium height, probably in his midthirties, and had a lean, sinewy body like an Olympic distance walker. We speculated about who he was, made jokes about him, and came to feel that the journey was not quite complete if we didn't drive past him in the morning.

A dear English friend of mine named Hercules Bellville invited me to a party at Jack Nicholson's and among the dozen guests was the blond jogger. I was excited at the prospect of hearing him speak, being able to put a name to him, and astonishing Karis with the news. No doubt he thought I was very odd, interrupting his conversation with Joni Mitchell to tell him that I had been watching him jog for a year and that my daughter and I considered him an important element of our morning journey. His name was Harry Gittes, and he produced the film that Nicholson made with John Belushi in 1979 called *Goin' South*. Harry promised that the next morning he'd do something to surprise Karis.

I tried to hide my excitement when we saw him running in the distance the following day. I expected our mystery man to smile and wave when I honked, but I wasn't prepared for what he had in store. As we approached him from behind, we could see that he had spray-painted big black letters across the back of his white T-shirt: HELLO KARIS.

The three of us became friends. A Sunday afternoon visit to see Harry and his cat, and meet one of his various girlfriends, was among our little pleasures. Needless to say, we got a regular wave from him in the mornings, and he often wore his spray-painted T-shirt.

One day during the first summer after we moved to the flat, we'd been visiting with some friends in Hollywood and noticed as we were leaving that there was black smoke rising against the northern skyline. It was impossible to determine which hillside was burning. There had been a long dry spell and brush fires weren't uncommon. We rushed back into the house to tune into the news and were horrified to hear that the fire was raging out of control in Laurel Canyon. By the time we got home the news mentioned that some houses on John's road were involved. There was no way to find out if John was safe, because the reports weren't specific enough. It wasn't until the following day that cars were given access to his hilltop drive.

Many of the houses on John's road were unscathed. I wished that his had been one of those. It was daunting to see him standing shirtless in a pair of old shorts, picking through the ashes of his home. All that remained was the chimney stack. The complete contents of his life, his work and passion, stored in the house, were gone. My mind couldn't take that in. It was harder for me to comprehend than death, which at least I'd grown to tolerate as part of the human process.

There are times when you see someone confront tragedy and you feel that sympathetic words are out of place and observing their grief is a deplorable intrusion, yet you want to be within reach in case they need you. I wanted John to see me without feeling that I was seeing him.

He was the sort of man who revelled in a good boohoo at a sentimental movie, like *The Goodbye Girl*, but he was dry-eyed as he sifted through the disintegrating blackish ash that could have been his books or guitars, his diaries or piano. The house had gone up like a matchbox, but those on either side of his weren't even singed. John, his mother who was visiting from England, and his girlfriend were lucky to be alive. When they were alerted that the hillside was blazing they were in a small viewing room that John had built on the pool deck. They hadn't managed to grab anything, not even John's wallet, as they rushed from the house. They had only the scant clothes on their backs. The three of them came home with me.

The first thing John wanted to buy with the money I'd collected for him from his accountant in the Valley was a video machine. We barely managed to get it in its cardboard box into my two-door coupé. John sat with it on his lap in the front passenger seat and cradled it like a baby. That was the way he chose to start again, which he did with heroic bravery. John is a one-off.

Most of my male friends in LA were gay. I didn't consciously seek them out, but there was a large gay community and they gave me interesting male companionship without complications. I didn't have time for a relationship. My life was divided between Karis and seeking work. It was also my small rebellion against all the bed-hopping that went on. I wasn't the least bit excited by the notion of casual sex and would have had little respect for myself had I slept around for work. I lost a few deals and at least four jobs by not being more compliant, but I decided I'd rather scrub floors.

I did make the mistake of losing my heart once and wanted

to kick myself when I realized that I had but it was too late. It all began one afternoon on Easter Sunday. I'd gone to the Chateau Marmont to collect a TV producer friend in town from London whom I'd invited to a garden party that Karis and I were headed for. From the reception, I let him know that I was waiting in the lobby. I'd only been waiting for a few minutes when the receptionist requested that I please pick up the telephone. I was surprised to hear a strange man's voice ask if I was the person that had got out of my car (which he described) and had just walked into the hotel. I was astounded and irate that a peeper had seen me coming into the hotel and had the audacity to phone me. I jumped straight on my high horse, which drew his apology before I hung up on him. When he had the nerve to call back, I let rip and hung up again.

As the hotel entrance faces a narrow residential road, this bizarre caller might have been phoning from one of the houses opposite. It never dawned on me that he was phoning from within the hotel. Making my way from the lobby to the car, I was halted by the absurd vision of a man's arm extended from one of the upper-floor windows. I could hear 'Psssst. Psssst.' The drapes were closed and the hand and arm were waving about. It looked like something Salvador Dali would paint: rows of oblong lifeless windows on a stucco hotel building with one human arm beckoning from one of them.

It made me laugh, but it was no doubt the telephone crawly and I yelled, 'Oh, do fuck off!' in the best Queen's English, the way Princess Anne might shout it to the press, wanting to be effective but not sound like a hooker. When he pulled back one drape to expose a squint-eyed grin, I was caught momentarily in thinking that I knew him from somewhere. Often in LA you see a face that you think is familiar and initially you fail to associate it with films or TV where you've seen it.

It clicked. I didn't know this man, I'd seen him acting in *The Godfather II* during one of John's video marathons. His was one of my favourite film performances. This made the whole thing doubly funny. He joined in when I broke into another laugh. I yelled that if he wanted to meet me he should do something chivalrous and gallant like a leap down from his third-floor hotel-room window. From that moment, his effrontery became a cheeky exchange across a fenced courtyard on a summery afternoon.

He couldn't join us at the garden party and I couldn't have dinner, but that's how we met. He was anti-showbiz, anti-Hollywood and not the vain type who preened on the cover of movie magazines. He was right up my alley, and I proceeded with extreme caution to try to get to know him. Quiet, streetwise and considerate about his estranged wife and their two children, he was extremely sensitive about any public exposure and mistrusted people to the point of alienating himself. I'm a sucker for anybody who seems lonely.

I was pursued until I couldn't resist him and tried to hold onto my heart, but it wanted to participate fully in our affair and I couldn't stop it. It's terribly disrupting when your heart won't do what your head wants it to. I knew that falling in love with Bob De Niro was impractical. The night I realized that the sound of his noisy snoring was music to my ears, I knew I was in trouble.

I left without saying goodbye because I didn't want to get involved in an explanation. He thought I was playing games and I suspected that he was. Sometimes it seems that men don't want to be loved, they only want to be had.

If only closing the door on a passion were as easy as closing a door. Getting over Bob I decided that I'd expended too much energy on relationships with men over the years and that I should hang up my spurs. What began as an exercise in emotional discipline developed into a way of life. Celibacy is underrated. Nobody could quite believe that I gave up men in the same way I gave up cigarettes and drink. I consider them acceptable social indulgences – but not for gullible, romantic me.

It was very liberating to remove myself totally from the male/female foray. As soon as I made it clear that I had eliminated myself from those games, I had a growing assortment of straight male friends who, I believe, sought my company because they knew I was a safe date.

I didn't need to seek out love, I got more than my share of that from my daughter. She and I were a solid unit, and I had a lot to learn from her, but I had to set a good example. As a single parent with a young child, I was on 24-hour call, seven days a week. Being on hand to rush out in the nick of time to see her roller-skate down the sidewalk for the first time was just as crucial to her as my being there to nurse a fever at four in the morning.

Karis took priority, but she accepted that I had to work. We needed money, and the challenge and occupation of working were as essential to my life as she was. My career was an important part of my self-esteem.

Singing took me back to Europe for three short jaunts between 1979 and 1980, while we were living in West Hollywood. The value of the jobs was in the sense of accomplishment in addition to the incidental fees that I got.

The album I had recorded with Pete in Munich was never placed in the US or Britain. He put my voice on four more tracks in LA, but I didn't get a recording contract. I hid my frustration going to meetings and nursing one form of music-business deal or another that would nearly happen but not quite. At least I had the meetings to go to. Some people didn't even have that.

A lot of my energy went into songwriting and I collaborated with musicians as much as I could while Karis was at school. When another decade rolled in and there was still no record deal, I decided that it was time to stop chasing one and start gigging again, but I couldn't afford to put a band together. While I continued to write, I started looking around for musicians who were prepared to work for the love of it. My natural inclination was still rock and that was the basis of my songwriting, although managers and record-company people that I spoke to weren't at all prepared in 1980 to accept that a Melangian woman could find a market doing rock, which was considered white music. I was regularly appalled by the colour boundaries in music marketing in America.

I'd been given the phone number of a musician by an elderly Mexican clairvoyant. She told me to call a Mark Brunello and said he would help me. Mark and I didn't consider the introduction at all strange and immediately after we met, we worked together almost every day. I was also writing occasionally with other musicians, some of whom I'd worked with in England, like Canadian Steve Hammond, who played guitar for two of my *Hair* auditions, and David Dundas, whom I had also known during the *Hair* period.

I was collaborating with a Scottish guitar player, Ian

'Count' Blair, who was based in LA after working in London as a musician for *The Rocky Horror Show*, when I finally determined to make an all-out effort to form a band. There were enough clubs in the LA area to showcase an unknown group and build up local interest, which sometimes attracted a deal. Mark helped me find a drummer and a bass player and with Count on guitar, we were off. Later Mark joined us to play lead, with Count playing rhythm. I named the band Marsha and the Vendettas as a spoof on the name Martha and the Vandellas, one of my favourite Motown groups. Our first gig was at a club in Chinatown called the Hong Kong Café. We made eight dollars. Four dollars and 50 cents of it had to go to the bass player for parking his car. Well, it wasn't the Isle of Wight, but I was totally in my element on that puny stage. My brother Dennis came. He had never seen me perform before and he laughed at me, which I took as a compliment.

More gigs followed and by doing songs that I'd written the lyrics and melodies for, I discovered that I had developed a style that was a combination of American, English and Melangian influences. I didn't have to imitate anyone or adapt my voice to suit somebody else's song. With the players driving behind me, getting on stage and performing with the band took me out of the world. Our bass player, George Murphy, used to play for David Bowie. To find a Melangian musician who was totally into rock was uncommon and George tinged his rock feel with funk. I always sang to his bobbing bass riffs unless there was a tomtom rhythm which would carry me away. The satisfaction I got from working with that band more than compensated for the fact that I earned no money from it. The little we did make went to the musicians and I didn't mind a bit. After driving Karis to school, I used to sneak off and do housekeeping jobs for friends. I believed this had a certain dignity, because it kept me from borrowing money. 'Better women than me' have cleaned somebody else's house, and if that was what it took to get back to my music, it wasn't beneath me. Other people disagreed.

The reward for the band's efforts came in better bookings and a few packed houses at known venues like the Whisky A-Go-Go or the Starwood or the Bla Bla Café. It wasn't rare for me to look from the stage and see that Bette Midler or Christopher Isherwood or someone equally unexpected was in the audience. My friends, old and new, were very supportive and I could not have done it without their help and loyalty.

In spite of their help I decided that LA was not for me, because if colour was supposed to define music, it wasn't only my music that I needed to hawk, it was an anti-apartheid philosophy. I was too close to the breadline. People seemed indifferent to change anyway; an element of segregation is endemic to the American way of life.

During the autumn of 1980, Karis and I were asked to baby-sit for a baby boa constrictor named Lumpy who belonged to Richard Dashut, Fleetwood Mac's producer, who had gone on tour with the band. As Benjie had died in 1978, I was delighted for Karis to have the responsibility of a pet again, even if it meant fostering a snake that ate white mice whole. I never believed that snakes had a personality and was surprised to discover that Lumpy did. He'd sit watching television with Karis, wrapped around her forearm, and would respond with a flashing dash of his forked tongue when the spirit hit him. Lumpy was no trouble except that he used to escape from his glass aquarium by knocking the screen lid off it. We'd have to comb the house looking for him and it sometimes took two days to find him. My brother, among others, was not happy about visiting when Lumpy was on the loose. Considering that Dennis is six foot two, this seemed a little bizarre; Lumpy was at that time only a couple of feet long and an inch and a half in diameter around his midriff.

When Richard came home after the tour, he decided to let Karis keep Lumpy. I was nearly as happy about it as she was, although going to the local aquarium to buy a live mouse and carrying it home in a small brown paper bag to a certain death was not my idea of a good time.

Lumpy must have sensed that a change was in the air before we prepared to move at the end of March 1981. He suddenly disappeared and was not to be found. I thought he was probably hiding in one of the heating vents, either cooked to a frazzle or waiting to emerge when he figured that the time was right. In fact Lumpy had cunningly slipped his way into my small metal filing cabinet and we discovered him there two weeks after we moved out. He was a little weak from want of food and water, but alive all the same. We donated him to Karis's school when we finally left and last saw him during the summer of 1985. He'd grown to nearly five feet long and two and a half inches in diameter, and it was hard to imagine that he was once Karis's TV companion.

Ronald Reagan was elected president on 4 November 1980. It was also Karis's tenth birthday and we found out the news in the middle of her birthday party. The following days people walked around stunned, and there was a pervasive sense of doom. The media didn't report that. Nobody gave much attention to the despondency of the millions upon millions who didn't want him in the White House.

I'd been back in England the summer before the election as I'd had gigs booked in London and a recording session with Colin Thurston (who produced Duran Duran) to do a song I wrote with David Dundas called 'The Pleasure Zone'. When work permits for my rehearsed American musicians fell through, it was too late to cancel the bookings and I tried to do the gigs anyway with some players in London put together at the last minute. They did their best but had too little time to learn the material. It was a shambles and it pained me to be on stage presenting music that was underrehearsed. Added to this, the *Daily Mail* ran a third-page article about me which read as if I'd been interviewed. It headlined an accusation about Mick as a quote from me. I'd never spoken to them and the article was a total fabrication. I went to a solicitor to see if I could force a retraction. It costs a lot in time and money for an individual to sue a newspaper for libel. Newspapers protect themselves with legal departments. I got absolutely nowhere.

Next, a tax inspector was waiting for me backstage at one of the venues.

Fortunately, Karis was having a break with friends at the seaside during this three-week period in London. I was freaked and frayed by the time we got back to Los Angeles. For her sake I bustled about full of laughs and good cheer but internally I was bleeding.

Just before the trip to London, a film producer had come to one of my Starwood gigs. He had me sing the theme song for a movie, *Fade to Black*, which he was completing, and also contribute some songs for an album to be released from it. Problems which arose about film performance rights were waiting to be resolved when we arrived home. To determine when the doorbell rang whether it was a friend or a debt-collector became an intriguing game. I had to roll with the punches and went in for another bout with my head down.

Gigging in LA brought an introduction to George Miller, an Australian director whose first film, *Mad Max*, hadn't yet been released in the US. I had several Australian friends and no doubt he'd heard about my songwriting from one of them, as I'd heard about him. He was looking for music ideas for a film, *Roxanne*, he was planning with his Australian partner, Byron Kennedy. George arranged for me to bring some of my demos so that he and his partner could have a listen in their small West Los Angeles flat, and I could pick up a script.

Byron Kennedy came out to be introduced. I had to look away from him as soon as our eyes met. Sometimes, a glance that lasts for a split second carries a charge that blocks out everything around you. Eyes can communicate something beyond word explanations. This happened when I looked at this almost burly man of a boy whose brownish hair wanted to be red but wasn't. He was nearly handsome but hardly my physical type. I was afraid to look at him again because I didn't want what happened at the first glance to repeat itself. He was gentlemanly enough not to pursue it. I was hellbent on work. I did my looking at George.

I was sitting at the dining-room table reading *Roxanne* on 8 December 1980 when a newsflash interrupted Karis's TV programme. John Lennon had been shot outside his New York apartment. I telephoned Byron and George to relate the tragedy.

There was a silent vigil in Los Feliz Park to commemorate Lennon. Looking around at the people who gathered there, I felt that the loud voices of a generation that once demanded to be heard had become a silent minority.

14
WORDS WITHOUT MUSIC

Despite the swell of interest in Marsha and the Vendettas, in LA in 1981 there was still resistance to the idea of a Melangian female doing straight rock without R & B or disco leanings. Four labels liked the band but none of them felt that we had a ready market. Often the businessmen that I talked to could have been selling soap powder.

When I was offered a deal with Mushroom, a small but strong independent Australian label, I wanted to take it. Coincidentally, it came at a time when my good friends Penelope Tree and her husband, Ricky Fataar, planned a move to Sydney and suggested that Karis and I join them. I couldn't have afforded it without a gift of money that came inexplicably from an English music-business acquaintance who'd popped into LA from Switzerland, where he was living. After our casual dinner in a restaurant, when I told him about my label offer, he asked how much it would cost me to move to Australia. He said he could afford to be philanthropic and would arrange for the money to be in my bank account the following afternoon.

Karis agreed that we could move during her Easter break and the record label, which was also going to manage me, said they'd deal with the work permit. I wrote to Byron Kennedy to see if *Roxanne* had progressed. His friendly reply was that he and George were busy setting up *Max Max II*. At that stage, *Max Max* was a low-budget Australian movie not on major distribution in the States.

By April 1981 we were on a plane headed for Down Under. Big Ted went to my mother's. I'd got the name of a good school for Karis from Helen Reddy, an Australian singer whose son attended Karis's school. We couldn't stay in LA if I couldn't earn enough to keep the household going and ensure that she had what she needed to adjust socially as well as academically at a school full of gifted children from well-to-do families. She always supported my decisions. Although leaving LA was as hard for her as leaving London, she didn't let me see that.

Initially, we planned to share a penthouse with Ricky Fataar and Penelope Tree, their baby and nanny, with me paying a third of the rent. It was arranged through a mutual friend of ours, Ben Gannon, who'd been my agent in London for a time before he returned to Sydney to help run a film-production company financed by Robert Stigwood and Rupert Murdoch. Ricky had been the drummer on my first Track single and had made his way to America to play for the Beach Boys. When I first worked with him, he was a teenager fresh from South Africa but had developed in various directions musically and was hoping to produce in Australia. Both the music and the film industry were booming there. I'd met Penelope, a statuesque New Yorker, during her sixties modelling days when she lived with David Bailey and I worked with him.

Sydney was more beautiful than we expected, and our enormous penthouse in Woollahra had a large terrace overlooking the harbour. From my bed opposite a picture window I could see the ocean by moonlight and the red pulsating flash of a safety light.

We arrived in a city that we'd planned to make our home and didn't waste any time getting settled. My new record company was to release my first single within six weeks of my arrival. I'd done a video for the single with a laser company in LA, to be used for TV promotion, and a small tour was being booked. My record company assured me that my work permit would be sorted out and I was rushing around putting a band together. I was lucky to find three first-class musicians who were ready to rehearse and as good as any that I'd ever worked with. The music scene there was very like that in England in the midsixties, when it was possible for bands to make a living doing small gigs and the frequency of working enhanced their playing. I had that to anticipate even if my record didn't chart.

Being signed to the Mushroom label, which had a few successful bands, got me straight into the heart of the industry in Australia. I'd promised myself that this would have to be my last attempt with a band and record company since music was only acceptable as a career if it could provide us with an income.

I made a few new friends and saw a lot of Byron. He tolerated my determination to keep our relationship platonic while I put my life in order. I couldn't afford the distraction of falling in love, but I could sit writing and feel at peace in his tiny sparse apartment in Balmain while he studied for a helicopter-piloting examination, or we could take an afternoon drive and conversation was unnecessary. I never told him that I was afraid of entrusting my heart again, but he knew. I was grateful that he was happy to spend time with me, never confusing my fondness for him with passion. We were good, good friends. I had my daughter and music. He had his film projects and his black helicopter. Byron wasn't intimidated by my independence and I didn't have to play any games with him. We often disagreed, because he believed that idealism was bad for my constitution and I thought he didn't appreciate mankind enough. I refused to ride in his helicopter but liked him for carrying a photograph of it. He wanted Karis and me to join him in Broken Hill where he was going to set up production for *Mad Max II*, but I had my own work to do and wasn't sure that I wanted our relationship to take that turn. We were in touch by telephone and he was full of advice.

He warned me to stay away from the Australian press and not socialize because, he said, Sydney was a village. I couldn't take his advice because our household was socially active, and to promote my record I had to deal with the press. I'd had enough encounters with journalists to assume that I could handle them. But whoever set up my interviews didn't screen out the trashy pulp papers in spite of my warnings. It only takes one front-page headline to get the rest started and they were off with a wallop about the paternity suit as though it hadn't happened three years before.

The attention it brought set us off on the wrong foot with the government and I was asked to remove Karis from school while our immigration status was being considered. I hadn't realized that she wasn't supposed to be enrolled until my residency papers were in order, and as Mushroom hadn't started the immigration procedure, I had to keep her at home until it was sorted out. She took it in her stride and I helped her to keep up her work by collecting her lessons from school, teaching her at home and dropping it off to be graded. The family rhythm of our household helped make this situation more tolerable than it would have been if Karis hadn't the year-old baby, Paloma, and other diversions in the house to interest her, including everybody's affection. Obviously, I was very concerned that she wasn't at school and didn't think that my ropy tutoring was beneficial. It didn't last long, because the immigration problems swiftly escalated.

One minute Karis was pulled out of school, the next I couldn't do the scheduled tour because I wasn't given a work permit. The band would have to split up if I couldn't work. Our guitarist had been asked to join the Little River Band, and I couldn't ask him to pass up that opportunity when I hardly knew whether I was going to be able to stay in the country. All this happened within a few weeks of the press dragging up the paternity suit.

Suddenly, a call came from Ben Gannon's associate in London to say that I had a firm offer of a good part in a film directed by Lindsay Anderson. That kind of coincidence makes me think I'm being looked after.

We arrived in London on the day of Prince Charles's wedding. The streets were deserted and I climbed the stairs to our third-floor flat without the sense of being home. I felt like a fugitive and was too exhausted fully to appreciate our rescue from Sydney. What was also bothering me was that I had told myself that Mushroom Records had to be my last attempt at a music career. I knew that I had to stick by that resolution and it was as though the fates were helping me to make the transition with a film offer in England. I couldn't be so selfish as not to be happy for Karis, who had been around the world and was back again surrounded by memories and old friends.

Lindsay Anderson made my step back into acting as easy as it could possibly be. He was tolerant, patient, and knew exactly what he wanted from me as the English, tight-lipped, swivel-hipped Nurse Peril in *Britannia Hospital*. The experience of filming with him was a totally happy one, because he was generous with his direction and with his time on and off the set. When filming was extended, I had to consider what to do about placing Karis in a school when I wasn't sure what country we were going to be in. I decided that to put her in an environment where she could make friends easily and be happy was temporarily more important than her gaining a place at a school that was competitive. She showed no emotional scars from our globe-trotting or the problems with the lawsuit or the press. I was lucky to be able to enrol her in a girls' school not far from where we lived, but oddly, in my head, I hadn't committed us to remaining in London.

Some people strive for an acting career in the same torturous way I strived for my music. I was accustomed to thinking that I had to bleed for the privilege of working, and because I hadn't that devotion to acting, I couldn't be convinced that I had a right to act. Making music was my passion, the one thing that linked my various selves and provided an outlet for the wild thing in me that was contained through mothering but not tamed by it.

On the home front, I had to consider Karis's readjustment to what was at once home and yet also another beginning. The school friends that she'd once made had moved away while we were in LA. I considered it my responsibility to help her find new friends with each resettlement. I remembered that Richard Longcraine would have a daughter exactly her age and thought I'd try to contact them. I'd last been in touch with him in 1976 when he was directing the Roger Daltrey video. Finally, I traced him accidentally while having a conversation with Joan Plowright, a friend of mine who was also acting in *Britannia Hospital*. We were discussing her next film project and it turned out to be Richard who was directing it. Joan arranged for me to meet the two of them for lunch in Shepperton Studios after the filming began on *Brimstone and Treacle*.

Sting, who was starring in the movie, joined us in the studio restaurant. He sat down with his tray of food, dressed in character: loose brown corduroy trousers and pullover. His nose was red from a cold. I wasn't familiar with his music although I knew that the hits he had written, such as 'Roxanne', had firmly established his group, the Police, internationally. For someone who was having pop-chart successes, he seemed quiet and humble. There was no sign of an entourage. He was proud that he had made his way to the studios in the morning on his motorcycle.

I was excited to see Richard and hear about his filming and catch up on Joan's news. Joan and I met through director Tony

Richardson when I was living in LA. I immediately took a liking to her when she bounded down to the tennis court after lunch to play in a large-brimmed sun hat and ankle-length dress.

Joan is an exceptional mother and her three now grown-up children are evidence of it. I had never seen her work, but her reputation as an actress was not an element of our friendship. I'm drawn to women who really care about their kids. She's very genuine and doesn't play upon her role as Lady Olivier.

After lunch, as I was leaving the studio lot, I bumped into my old driver, Roger Searle, whom I'd also not seen since work on the Daltrey video. He was working from one of the Shepperton sound stages running the Who's equipment-hire company.

Towards the end of filming *Britannia Hospital*, Channel 4, which hadn't begun broadcasting, suggested that I come up with an idea for a television series built around me. I presumed they wanted a talk show and was surprised when they accepted my suggestion of a sitcom. I was more excited by the idea of writing the proposal than I was about the acting. I had to be realistic about what practical future work there would be for me as an actress. I'd seen enough Melangian actresses in LA, hankering after too few jobs and some brilliant ones not working at all. I couldn't believe London would be different, but it didn't stop me from approaching Jill Bennett with a sitcom idea. (Jill Bennet was also in *Britannia Hospital*. We got on very well during filming, and I was looking forward to working with her again.) She elaborated on it and I set about writing a treatment for us for *Emily*.

David Dundas and I wrote a theme song which we demoed. Pleased with my treatment, Channel 4 paid to have a first script written. I found a writer who drafted a half-hour pilot which was not accepted. While he was working on the first draft for *Emily*, I was rewriting a musical that I had begun in 1975, called *Man to Woman*. I incorporated new songs, some of which I'd written in LA, and developed the musical so that it could be produced on a very low budget like a fringe theatre production but presented with lasers, lights and rock sound equipment. It seemed as straightforward as putting a band together and going on the road. CBS, my music publisher, provided studio time so that I could organize the music. I had no intention of performing in it but was determined to have it put on.

The best thing about working on these two ideas was that I was able to arrange my work schedules so that my writing didn't interfere with mothering and the time I needed to spend with Karis. She obviously enjoyed being back in London and was basking in the familiarity of the neighbourhood where she'd spent most of her early childhood. Actually, she adjusted to it better than I did. Sometimes I felt as if I was backtracking and LA and Sydney were distant figments of my imagination.

I devoted most of my writing time to *Man to Woman* and an Australian producer I knew agreed to back it. I arranged to have it performed at the Roundhouse, which was the most suitable place to stage a large low-budget production. I found a choreographer, Bruno Tonioli, and an assistant to work with, and the project gained momentum. Even after the Roundhouse pulled out my proposed booking, as venues tend to do when a better offer is made, we continued preproduction and I looked for another venue that could house us. It was hardly different from setting up a gig. I went to an English producer, Michael White, a friend of long standing whose work in the theatre I greatly respected. His firm professional advice was that I shouldn't make any production commitments until I had firm financial backing. I thought that I was following his instructions when I set out to raise the financing and find the specialists – a director, designers, an associate producer etc. Roger Searle agreed to do sound and lights and I knew that with the Who's hire equipment, we could achieve a high standard.

In the midst of all this, I was asked by my director and friend, Tony Garnett, if I would like to submit some music for consideration for a movie he was finishing in Hollywood called *Hand Gun*. I had thought about going to LA to look for our production money, as I'd found none locally, and Tony's proposal was the extra impetus I needed to go. Jenny, the nanny from Australia, was in town, so I employed her to stay with Karis while I made a trip to the West Coast.

While the chorus and dancers for *Man to Woman* were being cast in London by Bruno Tonioli and assembling to begin rehearsals, I was racing around LA looking for money to stage the show, which was to involve a company of twenty-four. I introduced the project to Tony de Fries, at one time the manager of David Bowie, and he became a main financier after I returned to London.

I arranged a rehearsal space and tackled the mammoth task of whipping a show together. What was an idea on paper became a reality so fast, it made my head swim. I amalgamated the talents of various people I knew including Sonja Kristina, a friend from *Hair* days who had success in the seventies as lead singer of the band Curved Air. Even after our Australian investor pulled out, we continued working to get the show staged. It was no less frantic than the launch of Capital Radio. The full company, with technicians, included some thirty people.

Man to Woman was about four women and their relationships with men. Their separate frustrations unfold in a London nightclub where they celebrate the owner's birthday. There were sixteen kids playing the slightly punky chorus. To see them invest all their energy in getting the music tight and Bruno's choreography right was thrilling. Michael Ratledge (still my friend and husband; we never divorced) coproduced the cast album with the engineer, Chris Stowe, and me. Michael was no longer in a band but had become a wizard at the synthesizer. When the keyboard player Thomas Dolby bumped into me in Soho and heard that I was working in the studio with Michael, Dolby insisted on popping in to meet him. Dolby wasn't yet having his own international hits.

I'd written a track in *Man to Woman* called 'All She Wanted Was Marlon Brando' which I knew suited Robert Wyatt's voice. Michael and I were happy when he agreed to record it.

When I met Robert in 1966, he was not only a good drummer in the Soft Machine, he was also the lead singer. In some bleak and, I guess, desperate frame of mind, he had jumped out of a window in 1974. He had been a small wiry boy and the fall left him paralysed from the waist down. It stopped him drumming, but it didn't affect his voice.

Recording for us in the studio in 1982 Robert looked young and vulnerable though his face was lined and his blond hair thinning. For all his reticence, he turned out a heart-rending vocal from his wheelchair, where he sat with the cans over his

Fair Isle knitted skullcap which he kept on throughout the session.

On the basis of the recording and a rehearsal which he came to, Richard Branson proposed that Virgin coproduce the show with de Fries. I'd done some free modelling in 1969 for a student magazine he ran and he was living with a Scots girl I knew from the same period. It felt right, and Branson didn't waste any time making a decision. He immediately took me to see his club in Victoria, the Venue, which he thought would be a more suitable place to produce the show. We had a lengthy meeting which ended at a fish-and-chip shop a couple of doors from the Venue. It made me laugh when he asked if I would pay because he didn't have any money on him. These men must see me coming.

As on any project that has a low budget, the entire company worked out of their personal commitment to the show. Although everyone was on wages apart from me, nobody was committed because of the money. There was very little. Some of the dancers were extremely talented, and it was exciting to watch them developing through the rehearsals. We arranged to stage the production in a now defunct club in London, the Zig Zag, that had a 1500 audience capacity. Virgin pressed EPs with four tracks off the album, and printed the programmes. Both were to be sold at the door when the show opened for a three-week engagement.

The schedule was strenuous. I worked day or night, sleeping no more than two or three hours as I headed off the collisions that you'd expect with any show. On April 15, 1982 we staged a full dress rehearsal, including lasers, for family and friends. I didn't know that the owner of the club had invited hundreds of other people and the press. He kept the bars open throughout the performance. As they were located inside the auditorium where the show was performed, it was impossible to hear the production. What should have been a private party for a few hundred became a chaotic free-for-all. The hard graft of our enthusiastic company was destroyed by one person's greed.

I spotted Chris Stamp in the audience. I hadn't seen him in years, and I didn't think about how difficult and obtrusive he had been during my days at Track. Amidst the chaos, it was like seeing a long-lost friend, and when I invited him to come visit, I meant it. He had been handsome with prematurely grey hair when I first met him, but now his hair was snow white although he could only have been in his early forties. When he came to the flat a few days later, we discussed Kit Lambert's untimely and peculiar death on 27 April 1981, which was caused either by a fall down some stairs at his mother's house or by injuries he received at a gay dancing club in Kensington. Either way, Chris was left alone to sort out the problems of their joint music-business ventures. I felt sorry for him, even though he said he was happy living in New York.

The press were not complimentary the next day and yet couldn't be held to blame because they didn't know they weren't supposed to be there. Richard Branson was in the Caribbean when this occurred and when he heard of it he pulled out the company's investment. The problems were complex. The 3000 EPs that Virgin had pressed got shifted from pillar to post while I continued to attempt to relaunch the show, but eventually most of them were thrown out. Three thousand records in sleeves takes up a lot of space.

I felt wiped out. It appeared that I was carrying on, but I'd coiled inside in a way I hadn't imagined I ever would. I was used to bouncing back. On the surface, I was coping, but when I was alone I was still and quiet, which I took as a sign that all wasn't well.

I was invited to the Cannes Film Festival because *Britannia Hospital* was a 1982 festival entry. When I returned I accepted a small film role playing a psychiatric nurse in a mental ward. I would have been perfectly cast as a patient. During this summer, Rosemary Burrows, who had been a friend since the Dracula film in 1971, had invited Karis to Spain for a month, and while she was away I tried to unknot myself but wasn't able to. It scared me badly to feel that tightness. I would run three miles a day, not as a physical exercise, but just to ease my tension. Then I'd stagger upstairs to sit with a book in my hands, unable to read because I was too wound up to let the word images in. I couldn't even laugh at the absurdity of it all.

When I was asked by a producer at Granada TV to present a series of jazz shows, I wanted to refuse but knew that I had to force myself to keep moving. If I stopped long enough to consider what was happening to me, I'd be forced to confront something that I wasn't capable of dealing with alone. I told a couple of friends that I was in trouble and was lucky enough, through a recommendation, to find the right therapist, Ben Churchill, to talk to. I loved sitting in the cool calm of his green room. Its stillness suited my state of mind.

15
CHANGING FACES

In the autumn of 1982 I was offered an acting job at the National Theatre, playing Hippolyta in *A Midsummer Night's Dream*, directed by Bill Bryden. It was a perfect role and environment for my uncoiling: not too much responsibility and no one knew me well enough to see that I wasn't myself. It was like an institutional compound, unrelated to the real world. In spite of all the theatre activity that was going on, it had a gentle pace and was a retreat. The hospital food in the canteen was just what the doctor ordered. The wages were paid on time and there was no hassle. After the years in the music business, it was a relief to know that I could work and give a performance without worrying about deals and money and the fine print on contracts. In addition, I was working with people who wanted little fanfare. I didn't feel out of place but, as usual, not fully a part. Most of the actors and actresses won a place there after drama school and years of repertory work.

As part of my repairing process, I decided to redecorate the entire flat so that I wouldn't feel that I was in a time warp, looking at walls which hadn't changed colour since I'd moved in originally. Not capable of doing anything by halves, coiled or not, I had the entire flat done at once. It was an unbelievable sight. I guess I did to the flat what I was unable to do to myself. I turned everything out, emptied every drawer, shelf and cupboard until the past spilled out. I had an enormous collection of withdrawal of supply notices for my utilities from every year I lived in the flat. Some for the gas, regulars for the electricity, and one to accompany nearly every telephone bill that ever came. They were all over the house in the strangest places. I spotted one at the bottom of my underwear drawer. It was ten years old. I don't know why I had saved them. They had a strange power over me even though they didn't apply any more. I was afraid to throw them out, until I went on my purge.

During the time that I was producing *Man to Woman*, I saw Sting several times as an actor friend of his had a principal role in the show. Sting was recording tracks for the *Brimstone and Treacle* film at EMI while we were rehearsing in a Scout hall a block from the studios. He also knew Sonja Kristina, who was living with the Police drummer, Stewart Copeland. Copeland's brother Miles, who manages the Police, was one of the people I approached to finance the musical. He happens to live on my road.

Sting lived in neighbouring Hampstead, where he had moved after separating from his wife, the Irish actress Frances Tomelty. I loved to go to his house and find that he was playing Erik Satie or challenging himself to paint a picture, which he laboured at and showed off proudly. He knew he wasn't good but he tried. Money was still new to him and he didn't let it interfere with the quality of his life. He could go out and buy a new shiny black Bechstein piano. He practised on it regularly, which made it a worthwhile acquisition. He didn't just buy fine books, he read them. While I was finishing off my second treatment for the story I was developing from a French novelette, Sting was working on a script he'd written from a Mervyn Peake novel. As with Michael Ratledge, I found a friend in music who had other interests. I liked him and his work, particularly his lyrics, which were intelligent and committed while his music was commercial.

It was to Sting's house that I rushed for shelter when I redid the flat. Builders banged and the smell of paint everywhere was nearly asphyxiating. He hadn't been living in the house long and he had an actor friend living in the flat on the top floor. It was a bachelor household with a family atmosphere. Sting was very good with Karis and there was no better place for her during those days than sitting in his living room by the fire.

Having Sting as a little brother was infinitely satisfactory. It did not mean that I didn't notice that he looked sinfully good first thing in the morning when the sleep was still in his eyes and his hair was standing on end. My numerous friendships with beautiful gay men had let me develop an appreciation for a man's good looks without wanting to do more than look.

Having been in bands and fronted my own for so many years,

I am most comfortable with musicians. Whether it's the vernacular, the pace, or the way the music world functions outside the normal rhythm of society, it was a help to me to be close to it again.

The most important thing was that I had my daughter in a good environment and that if my spirits were lower than usual, it was less noticeable in Sting's busy household.

Demure is the word that best described Karis at eleven, stretching into adolescence, beyond childhood. I knew that she would soon declare herself and wanted to help her to do that. The years of holding her hand were soon to be memories pasted in our photograph albums. I had to prepare for the letting-go so that she could soar, and while I was sure that she was nearly ready for it, I didn't pretend to myself that I was.

My work always extended itself into her life, and at the National Theatre both of us were enveloped by theatre not as I'd known it in West End musicals but in traditional plays. It came at a good time, not only for me but also for Karis, who was old enough to enjoy sitting in an audience for three hours of Shakespeare.

We were back in our own flat in time for previews to begin of *A Midsummer Night's Dream*. Being home had a good feeling.

Paul Scofield played Oberon in our promenade production. Every move he made was graceful. His thick mass of grey and white hair was a crown that made him regal as the fairy king. Paul carried an unassuming elegance with him everywhere, but it was most apparent when he was acting. During out first read-through of the play something about him seemed totally different from the other actors in the company. He was contained without seeming restrained. Often when I wasn't on, I would slip down from my dressing room to the side of the stage and listen to the way he could ride the rhythm of the words, making the streams of Elizabethan prose sound as good as a cappella singing. It could have been 23rd Street but it was the South Bank, and on that stage and in that audience another Melangian face was hard to find.

We played in rep with two other plays and luckily I wasn't working on Karis's birthday. It was her twelfth. When we left Sting's house, her arms were full of the presents she received after she blew out the candles on the unexpected birthday cake. Our early evening visit had turned into a little party, because Sting's mother and baby daughter Kate were also there.

I knew there was another cake and more surprises to come. Three large boxes wrapped in gleaming china-red paper waited for her at home. It looked as if Santa had made a November drop. They were sent by Mick, and whatever was inside them wouldn't be as special as his phone call to her from New York. When that came, I wanted to jump up and down and cheer. Instead, I went and lit a coal fire in her room. It cast an amber glow over the newly decorated walls.

I knew that Mick would come through whatever had held him back for all those years. My intention was to smile and make him feel welcome.

I gained a lot in 1982, but the failure of *Man to Woman* and the money problems that it created for me arrested my dare-devil spirit which my confidence relied upon. While no one could see the change in me, I could feel it. I was in the *Dream* in the spring of 1983 when I saw on the company notice board that the American songwriter Marvin Hamlisch was coming to the National to develop a musical with Sir Peter Hall, the company's director. I signed up for their six-week workshop. After the stalwart casting director, Gillian Diamond, fore-warned me that there was no principal role, I asked to be in the chorus. The daily workshops with Hall and Hamlisch were sure to be an education. Two other Americans also headed our workshop. A screenwriter, Julian Barry, wrote the text based on the life of the actress Jean Seberg, and a 24-year-old lyricist, Christopher Adler, collaborated with Marvin Hamlisch on the songs. The original idea was Adler's. His father, Richard Adler, wrote *The Pajama Game*.

I had been living in LA when Jean Seberg was found dead in her car in a Paris suburb in 1978. Seberg's ex-husband, Dennis Berry – a young American director who spent most of his life in Paris – visited me frequently around the time of Seberg's death. I wasn't aware then of her extraordinary life which involved victimization by the CIA, FBI and J. Edgar Hoover and intrigues with the Black Panther Party. Her film career began when she won director Otto Preminger's nationwide talent search for an unknown girl to play Joan of Arc. Seberg came from a happy Midwestern, all-American background, but it was difficult to translate her subsequently tragic life into song-and-dance routines. With the writers and director and stage management our workshop company of twenty actors attacked the problem in the National's largest rehearsal room, which is painted black and feels like an American high-school gymnasium without a basketball court.

Throughout the workshop, many people in the company were disgruntled that our subsidized English theatre company should finance and present such an American project, which was angling for Broadway. Christopher Adler was sensitive to the discord and didn't feel welcome. Marvin Hamlisch's nasal New York accent sounded distinctly foreign in the labyrinth of corridors.

Nevertheless it was fascinating to watch a team of New York writers work together. Julian Barry's credits as a screenwriter include *Lenny*, a serious film about the life of American comic Lenny Bruce starring Dustin Hoffman. Marvin Hamlisch wrote the music for *A Chorus Line* and *They're Playing Our Song* as well as movie scores which included hits such as 'The Way We Were'. None of them allowed their ego or personal taste to get in the way of their first priority, which was to score a massive hit. Every day Barry would arrive with new pages of lines, Hamlisch and Adler would change lyrics and music, scrap songs, and there was a constant exchange of ideas as we worked on the piece.

I played two characters; one the Melangian Elaine Brown, who was Jean's friend and involved with the Panthers, the other a fictitious gossip columnist who maligned Jean. As the Black Panthers had headquarters in Oakland, the city was mentioned in the piece. I was astounded that my elderly, innocuous principal at Oakland High School was in one scene of the musical, introducing Jean as a speaker at a high-school graduation ceremony.

When the piece dealt with racial issues, I was concerned. With the two other Melangians in the company, Clarke Peters and Larrington Walker, I took issue with how our race was projected. Minor points became major when presented on stage. We discussed how the word 'nigger' was used and how we as actors had to react. As it was a workshop, everyone had the privilege to air an opinion. I did often when I felt that our racial image was at risk. Sir Peter Hall listened, and a couple of times, to show that my ardent stance wasn't personal, I bought him his favourite at lunch, a Mars bar.

Marvin Hamlisch is a brilliant writer. Whether or not one likes his contribution to shows like *A Chorus Line*, his talent as a writer and musician is exceptional. He's secure about his work and is easy about adjusting keys, rhythms and even a melody line to suit a vocal and achieve the best overall effect. As the gossip columnist, I got a solo to sing called 'I Was In Paris'. Marvin and I went over it several times one evening at the piano installed for him in Peter Hall's office. Marvin was funny when I kept asking him to change the key. He liked to mock my midatlantic accent. He was also helpful and full of ideas when Peters, Larrington and I worked on the three-part harmony and featured spots in the Black Panther number, 'Gotta Get A Partner'.

We presented the workshop for three performances to invited audiences that included other directors at the National, big-time producers from New York, and people's friends and agents. Of course, Karis came. Peter Hall's agent, Laurence Evans, took me on as a client after seeing it. He also represented such notable actors as Laurence Olivier, John Gielgud and Ralph Richardson (who died the following year). I considered his taking me on his books to be an honour.

I was committed to doing *Cinderella* with Bill Bryden's company and was not in *Jean* when it was presented at the Olivier Theatre. In spite of the talent, money and preparation that went into the project, and the endorsement of the National Theatre, *Jean* was a flop when it was staged in the autumn.

I had a short break from the company during the summer of 1983 and Granada TV asked me to do a pilot talk show. *The Marsha Hunt Show* (which I wanted to call anything but *The Marsha Hunt Show*) was taped before a studio audience on 2 July 1983. My guests were Julie Walters, who was up for an Academy Award for her performance in *Educating Rita*, James Fox, who was about to appear in *A Passage to India*, and Ian LeFrenais, a friend from LA, creator of the hit TV series *Porridge* and *Auf Wiedersehen, Pet*. My producer, Simon Albury, and I had worked together on the jazz series the summer before and Simon was a presenter at Capital when I was there, so I assumed that he knew my interviewing style. He wanted me to appear fluffy and gregarious, and I wanted to be entertaining but formidable. Our friendship suffered and neither of us got the satisfaction of having my show turn out as we wanted.

I first met James Fox in 1968 when I was awarded the £250 for looking bizarre. Since then he'd joined a small Christian denomination called the Navigators and married a woman who was a Navigator, with whom he has four children. He had written a book about his experiences as an actor and a religious convert and was on the show to promote it. James's brother Edward Fox and Edward's girlfriend Joanna David are dear friends of mine and James did the show as a favour to Ed and Jo. Julie Walters is from a Catholic upbringing. We talked about religious extremes and I interviewed them individually.

Although the pilot was not developed, I learned a lot from it. With a pilot you establish the precedent for all the shows to follow. The design of the set, my theme song, the style of dress (whether I should look tailored, formal or casual) and the type of questions I would be asking my guests all had to be decided.

I was based in London during the weeks of preparation for the show. I invited Sting to go to the Oliviers' with me for Sunday lunch. He'd just got back from Mexico where he'd been filming *Dune*. When he came to pick me up, I was shocked to see that his hair had been dyed orange for the film. I didn't know how much I liked him as a blond until I saw the new colour. He looked very healthy after completing his first big-budget movie. I rushed to give him a hug. I'd missed him.

His son Joe was in the car, and we collected Karis from a school friend on the way. Our midday drive was heavenly in the summer sun with the top down. Sting played a home-made compilation tape (labelled 'Kill Whitey') with old Motown greats on it, 'I Heard It Through The Grapevine' and 'Dancing In The Street' among them. It was all we listened to on our two-hour journey to the Oliviers' secluded house in Sussex. Sting had never been there, and I consider directing any driver through the English countryside a perilous task. Although Joan originally introduced me to Sting, the two of them didn't see each other socially.

Lunch that day was a family affair, very casual with no one

standing on ceremony. Sting was watchful of his son. Joe was a shy, sensitive seven-year-old, and Sting was gentle with him and concerned about the effect the split marriage had on him. My respect for Sting was sealed by the way I saw him deal with his children. He adored them and often had them visiting him.

When we first became friends, Sting was enthralled by the tarot and astrology. In 1982 he was aware that he was poised on a precipice and he was hungry for anything that could guide him and forecast his direction. By the summer of 1983 he was assured and determined. He already talked of a solo career.

After my talk-show pilot was completed, Mick asked if I would be interviewed by John Ryle, who was helping Mick write his autobiography. I hadn't read the anthropological study which John had written, but I assumed that he was more than a hack writer. Mick and I were on decent terms and I agreed to the interview but didn't feel that I could be as honest as Mick said I should be. I'd seen Mick fluctuate before and didn't want to do anything to get him going again. I answered John's questions but refused to let him see my letters from Mick. The gentle boy who wrote them to me is preserved in those letters. Maybe they're the only thing to show that he ever existed.

John stayed to join me for lunch. He was gnawing on a sparerib bone when Sting phoned to say he would collect me on his way to rehearse in Brixton with the Police. They were getting ready for the Synchronicity tour starting in the US in July. Sting was suffering from a chronic sore throat and wanted to save his voice. When he had to replace the backup singers for the tour, he'd asked me to deal with it. He had needed vocalists who wouldn't need US work permits. It had made the job of finding them at short notice tricky. This gave me an opportunity to reciprocate for his hospitality when Karis and I were his house guests the year before. I was glad to help, in spite of the amount of work that was involved, with my phone ringing, singers coming and going, complaints, fittings, rehearsals. For five days my flat had been buzzing with it all, and now I wanted to go to the rehearsal to hear how the backing sounded.

John said he was a Police fan, so I suggested he wait and meet Sting. I knew that Sting would be happy to get Bob Marley's hat as a talisman to take on the tour, and I had raked it out of the hall cupboard and was hiding it behind my back when he came up the stairs. It was summer and I didn't expect him to wear the woollen cap, but he pulled it down over his straight, very orange hair before he shook John's hand. We didn't have time for them to have more than a short, affable exchange. Sting's sore throat gave him a raspy whisper that made him sound sexy and mysterious. I hoped that he lived up to John's expectations, although he looked more like a bad little boy in the Rasta cap and had a cheeky glint in his eye while he made the effort to be charming.

A couple of weeks later something nudged me to go to the States, although I could hardly afford to. I knew that I had a job to come back to at the National when the *Dream* re-opened in the autumn. Sometimes I feel I need to go home, even if I know that it may not feel like home when I get there.

Eric Roberts lent me his sumptuous Manhattan apartment while he was staying in LA. I was thankful that it had a doorman with a walkie-talkie. It could have been a toy but it made him look as though he was ready for action. There was plenty of that out on the street with a parking lot next door and shops on either side. The Chelsea Hotel was a couple of blocks away. It was steaming hot that summer and Eric laughed when he heard that I wanted to be in New York at a time when anybody who has a choice is gone. Men walked the streets in singlets and sweaty shirts, and flies were everywhere except in Eric's cool sterile apartment block.

Mick and Jerry were at their house on the West Side and I was happy for Karis when they wanted her to come and stay after our arrival. I had my typewriter and a few friends in from out of town. I wanted to socialize as little as possible. I needed to practise being alone.

The Police were on the first leg of the Synchronicity tour and were giving a concert in Hartford, Connecticut. Karis had never seen Sting on stage, and I thought she would enjoy it. Mick agreed to take her, and I arranged tickets through one of the Police roadies. Sting wasn't returning my calls. I think it had something to do with an impersonal bouquet of flowers which arrived at my London flat with an equally impersonal thank-you message for organizing the three backing vocalists. When I realized that his signature was signed by his secretary, I was hurt. I would have been satisfied with a couple of daffodils or a phone call from him personally. I stuffed the flowers back in the cellophane they arrived in and had a taxi deliver them to him in Hampstead.

None of it had anything to do with Karis.

The weekend that Mick drove Karis and Jerry to Hartford, I went to stay with friends in Pennsylvania. Their house was hidden in a cluster of tall trees which blocked the intense heat of the sun. I took long walks through the surrounding woods. Two Doberman puppies insisted on coming with me. There was a brook, and I stood there thinking about my girl and if I could teach her to adjust to being a rich girl some of the time. The green growing things in Pennsylvania are bright.

When we flew back to London, I was ready for a second season at the National. There were loads of opportunities there with three theatres in the complex. I accepted every free ticket offered for every play and had Karis see as many as she could. I'd slip into other people's rehearsals when I was permitted. I snuck into the dress rehearsal of Athol Fugard's poignant South African play, *Master Harold and the Boys*. I was grateful when Fugard, who was directing it, spotted me sitting at the back of the dark, empty Cottesloe Theatre and didn't ask me to leave. At the invitation of director Peter Gill, I took part in the first reading of *Tales from Hollywood*, a play which he later presented in the Olivier Theatre.

When I heard that Karl Johnson, one of my favourite actors in the company, was doing a one-man show, I asked to help. The piece he was doing was a monologue about Vietnam adapted from Tim Page's book *Nam*. I was overjoyed to be given the job of directing Karl. It was exciting to work with an actor of his high standard and have him take direction from me as though I was a seasoned professional.

I doubt that my transition from music would have been easy without the National. That steadying factor also made Karis's going off to boarding school less traumatic. Joan Plowright arranged our introduction to the school that her three children had attended and Karis cleverly won herself a place there during a trial weekend, when her reservations about leaving home dissolved. A coeducational school close enough to home for her to pop back at weekends promised excitement. Although the school fees were almost as much as the annual settlement awarded in 1979, I could manage. With Joan's youngest daughter still there as a welcoming committee of one, Karis slipped into the most favourable form of English boarding-school life.

It was hard to let go when the time came, and I wasn't prepared for the quietness of our flat when she wasn't in it. I couldn't look at Karis's stuffed animals. They still lived in her room and always appeared to be waiting for her to come home. They reminded me that she was gone and that her glorious childhood, which had bathed them and me in her innocence and unconditional adoration, was also gone. When could I admit it was for good?

I packed these furry old friends in two tea chests and arranged them in sympathetic groups. Seymour, the huge floppy white polar bear who had travelled with Karis from LA to Sydney, went with some of her smaller ones who made the same journey. I swore that they could come out as soon as we were living somewhere that wasn't one big minefield of memories, a new place that wouldn't hold me to a deserted past. They could come out when their presence was less painful.

All the things that I had grown to do quite naturally to create and maintain a home for a child, were no longer necessary. Laying the table for breakfast seemed ridiculous when there was only me. I'd forget and rush home from the theatre, used to bolting home from work to see her or relieve a baby-sitter, and as soon as I turned the key in the lock I'd remember that there'd been no need. Why bother to shop for food when I wasn't buying her favourites? My life style had been built around music but my life itself had gradually been built around mothering and at first I couldn't remember how to be single. I didn't know what food I liked, because I ate what she liked. To be honest, I hadn't noticed until she went away to school that as much as she had been an extension of me, I had become an extension of her. I decided not to panic about it. Suddenly I had all the time in the world. More than I needed.

Norma Moriceau is Australian. She has a spike-tipped mane of short, jet-black hair. She always seems to have a cigarette in her hand which she sucks, swallowing great gulps of smoke that never get exhaled. We share the same birthday, which is not the only thing we have in common, but discovering this coincidence made us fast friends when we were introduced in LA in 1978. Norma's had various careers and was once the fashion editor of *Honey* magazine. When we first met, she was dabbling in photography and was commissioned by the *Sunday Times* fashion editor, Michael Roberts, to do some pictures of me. Since her costume designs for *Mad Max II* brought her deserved acclaim, work has kept her busy in Australia. I was still living in LA when she began preproduction work on *Mad Max II*, but I was resident in Sydney by the time filming started. Byron Kennedy was Norma's boss, but my friendship with the two of them remained separate even when they were both on location in Broken Hill. When I left Australia in July 1981, they were still hard at work on the film without any certainty of its success.

Passing through London, Norma stopped by to have breakfast with me on the first morning of the new year, 1984. I was excited to see her and hungry for news of my Sydney friends, whom I'd shamefully neglected after leaving Australia, apart from a couple of telephone calls to Byron in 1982. With some people, I expect to pick up where we left off when we meet again. In the meantime, I have the comfort of knowing they're on the planet doing whatever they do with their lives to get by.

As Byron was my closest friend in Sydney, he was the first person I asked about. When Norma paused incredulously to say hadn't I heard, I was prepared for a wild bit of news, because Byron wasn't predictable and since I left, he and his partner George Miller had international success with the Mad Max movies, and were making money and involved in new projects.

I wasn't expecting her to tell met that Byron was killed piloting his helicopter in the summer of 1983.

A piece of me broke off.

From the moment we met, I had refused to acknowledge any special feeling I had for Byron beyond a platonic relationship. The fact that he tolerated it made him an irreplaceable friend.

Two mornings later, when I read that Alexis Korner had died of cancer, I was still too stunned by the news of Byron's death to take in a second unexpected obituary. I hadn't seen Alexis for years but had been happy that he had some success after Free At Last.

16
BEYOND THE BRIDGE

I was visiting friends in Norfolk. We were watching the Michael Jackson video, 'Thriller'. Just as Michael turned into a werewolf, my agent, Laurence Evans, phoned from London to confirm that I'd been given a supporting role in a horror movie, *The Howling II. The Howling* had been a box-office success in the States, and the sequel was to be shot that summer in Czechoslovakia. The opportunity to play my first villain as a werewolf was exciting. Getting bitten by Christopher Lee as Dracula in 1971 had come full circle. He was to play the good guy in *The Howling II* and I'd be pursuing him.

Filming began in August 1984 in Prague. I had never been to a communist country and was looking forward to the experience. I knew that it would be an education for Karis, who was to come with me. In America in the fifties, communist countries were always referred to as behind the Iron Curtain. I imagined at that time that they were surrounded by a huge dark-grey metal curtain with the folds moulded into it. It was always cold behind it and the people who lived there were depressed and didn't wear bright clothes.

Prague's airport was dismal, but the city was stunningly beautiful. Remembering it, I think of soft pinks and ochre, the colour of many of the buildings in the Old Town. The Gothic buildings on both banks of the Vltava River and the Charles Bridge dating back to the fourteenth century gave the centre of the city a fairy-tale aura. It was hard to imagine that in 1976 Russian tanks had rolled into the well-tended square with grass and flowers half a block from our hotel.

The producers, the director Phillippe Mora and the rest of the cast flew in from LA. The camera crew was English but the technical unit was Czech and most of them spoke no English. The most mundane problem becomes an issue when there's a language barrier. To explain to the wardrobe mistress that there was a pin sticking into me or to indicate that my make-up needed adjustment required a translator. We only had three and they were run off their feet. I discovered that each of them was carefully screened by the government before they got their jobs translating for a film unit and actors from the West. Many of the Czech crew had also worked on *Amadeus*, so the experience of an American movie was not new to them.

After Karis returned to London, where she was to stay with Mick, Jerry and their new baby, Elizabeth, I spent a lot of hours just walking through the various towns we worked in after shooting in Prague was completed. Once, when we were driving back from a location, the car was flagged down by two uniformed policemen. One young Czech chauffeur, who spoke a bit of English, reminded us how serious even a routine check was. I could see that he was nervous when he got out of the car to show his papers. We were riding in a medium-sized, plain-looking black vehicle normally reserved for diplomats. The police may have been suspicious about the chauffeur's passengers. It was a tense situation, because we could have all ended up at the police station if the driver's papers hadn't been in order.

It was the only experience I had to indicate that the police and the government were not to be challenged and that underneath the exterior of Czechoslovakia, seeming as European as France, order was maintained by an element of fear.

Playing a werewolf was not as demanding as being made up as one. The make-up men who specialized in prosthetics came from the States. To rebuild my face with small plastic applications and paint it and cover it with fine individual pieces of wool glued to the finished paintwork took their time and artistry and my patience. One day it took five hours to get the make-up on and two to take it off. Just a close-up of my hand with the werewolf effect took an hour and a half for the make-up application. The finished hand was a work of art.

I don't like to recall the night we shot in a cellar full of real skeletons. Skulls and bones were stacked neatly on top of each other to form walls. It seemed too much like an art director's dream for a horror-film setting, and I kept hoping that those skulls hadn't belonged to living people, but

Phillippe Mora assured me that they had. They had been dug up from a cemetery which the government wanted to use for another purpose, and the bones were temporarily stored in the cellar opposite a church. No one had ever found another place to put them, so after nearly half a century, they were still there as a perfect setting for my death scene. Every time I had to brush against the walls of skeleton to do the scene, dust from the skulls and bones would drift down onto my black sleeveless minidress.

In spite of all the film lighting in the small place, it remained cold. By the time I'd been thrown several times on the floor and rolled around in the skeleton dust as part of my death scene, I well and truly felt that I had earned my day's wages.

When filming was finished, I didn't want to leave Prague. I loved the aloof temperament of the people and it was a relief to the eye not to be in a place that was plastered with billboards and signs and advertising.

I travelled a lot in 1984 and managed a trip to California to see my family before I went to Paris in mid-December to model for Kaffe Fassett's book *Glorious Knitting*. Steven Lovi was the photographer. From my hotel room window, I had a clear view of the boulevard St Germain. The only sign of Christmas was the presents stacked near the pile of paperbacks on the desk. The slanted, beamed ceiling gave the white room a rustic feel and the peonies I bought made it nearly pretty. Each morning my continental breakfast was brought in by a short, muscular Vietnamese woman in a starched pink uniform. To see her grinning at me first thing in the morning made a good start to my day.

After we got the shot Steven wanted of me wearing some of Kaffe's knitted capes on the Alexandre Bridge, there was no need to rush back to London, since Karis was in Rio with Mick for half of her Christmas holiday. I had waved her goodbye at the airport before coming to Paris.

I needed to practise being alone; I wanted to master it and being in Paris over Christmas gave me a perfect opportunity. I burned a trail around every museum and gallery that didn't have a queue. As in my first two weeks in London, I wandered the streets and inspected every cranny that caught my eye.

I was determined to go back, if only to share the city with

Karis during her Easter break. I booked our rooms before I checked out.

When I returned to London on the first of January 1985, I rushed to visit a friend, Peter, who had AIDS (acquired immune deficiency syndrome) and had been in and out of Middlesex Hospital. He was a vibrant, gregarious young English journalist whom I met in LA. His loyalty to me during my California lawsuit with Mick made me dedicated to him. To watch him deteriorate slowly and painfully in a quarantined hospital room was as hard for his family and friends emotionally as it was for Peter physically. I gave myself pep talks before I went to his room to look cheerful and talk positively and remember that the person in bed was Peter although it didn't look like him. I didn't realize that my first-of-the-year visit was my last. He died the following day. I was afraid to think that, with the number of gay male friends that I had, he would not be the only one to suffer from the disease, our modern plague.

Two weeks later I turned on my television set and Roger Daltrey came on the screen. He was not singing the Who classic, 'My Generation'. He was in a commercial and said not to leave home without your American Express card. It was a sign of the times. So was the miners' strike, which had raged on for nearly a year when the miners and their families challenged the government's decision to close pits and thereby destroy mining communities.

I was in danger of feeling morose after Peter's death, and after a trip with Karis to Norfolk on her return from South America, I decided to flat-sit for a friend as a means to forcing a change. With Karis back at school, I didn't need to be at home. June Roberts's flat is near the bottom of Ladbroke Grove. She was in LA to write a screenplay and needed a baby-sitter for her axolotl, Mona.

One night I couldn't sleep. It was pitch-dark outside at 5 am and freezing. London was suffering the usual February weather and I couldn't get warm. I'd gone to bed in my robe as well as my nightgown and fleece-lined bootees with padded bottoms that made my feet look the size of the abominable snowman's.

I went into the kitchen to take a Beecham's. June has no curtain at the window, which overlooks St Michael's church opposite. There's a street light below and as I swallowed the cough medicine, I thought I saw and heard my white MG go by like a bronco pony. It chugged, stalled, bucked and started off again. I freaked to think that it was in the hands of another thief. It had been stolen only three months before.

My brain did somersaults. When I remembered that I needed the downstairs communal front-door key to let myself out, I nearly panicked not knowing where they were. My heart was thumping. I spotted the keys and bounded down the stairs, sure that I was fighting a losing battle and that my car was halfway up Ladbroke Grove. Something said persevere. From the doorway, I could see my car had stopped again. I rushed into the road, screeching like a banshee, with the volume appropriate for open-air concerts. 'Hey, asshole! This is my car. Hey, you son of a bitch.' I was back on 23rd Street.

The car started moving as I ran towards it to bang on the right fender. I was running alongside it, slapping at the window on the driver's side. I couldn't see into the car because it was too low to the ground.

Suddenly the car stopped and the driver's door opened. The thief stepped out boldly. I was face to face with a tall West Indian who had a black woollen scarf tied around his face. With only his eyes showing, he looked menacing. I instantly sensed the danger I had put myself in by challenging a car thief on a dark and deserted street. I hardly came up to his shoulder and for all I knew, he had an accomplice sitting in the passenger seat. I could feel the freezing cold on my ears. I was panting from all the shouting and running. I must have looked wild, standing there in my bright green knee-length towelling robe, long nightie and big floral bootees. My hair was in two spiral buns pinned above my ears.

He flew off, and his cowardice gave me a second bolt of confidence. I watched him tear along the road and turn into Ladbroke Grove, and I jumped into my car. The windscreen wipers were going and he'd pulled out the wires from the space where the stereo should have been. It had been stolen by the first thief. Having seen too much television, I decided to cruise Ladbroke Grove looking for him. I figured he might duck into a doorway. After five minutes the cold and a flicker of common sense forced me to give up my pursuit and go home.

I parked the car in the same space that it had been stolen from and went upstairs to make a cup of jasmine tea. I don't know what got into me, but as I sat up in bed thinking about the episode, I realized that I'd saved my car and maybe staked my life. I wasn't sure whether it was an indication that I'd lost my street instinct or that I'd refound it.

In spite of that isolated incident, I liked living in Notting Hill Gate. The stolid respectability of my St John's Wood neighbourhood made me feel that I was sleepwalking when I went out. Notting Hill has an urban rhythm, an edge.

I was alone and comfortable with myself. To read instead of joining a friend for dinner was important. The purpose became apparent when my agent confirmed that I was commissioned to write this book. I could work in Paris. The Easter holiday I planned for Karis there would be a perfect time also to find a base for us.

It was a coincidence that Mick intended to be there too. I suggested that he spend Easter with Karis. I didn't expect to be invited to join them. It was a special afternoon. I saved the chocolate egg they gave us at the Tour d'Argent.

I tried to decline Mick's second invitation to dinner two days later. I suspected that he was being polite, but he insisted.

Mick was staying in a small exclusive hotel in a side street off the Champs Elysées. Karis and I arrived there ten minutes late and took the tiny oak-panelled elevator to Mick's floor. I felt uncomfortable, not sure what to expect when we met. I gauged his mood by the tone of his voice when he yelled 'Come in' to the ring of his doorbell.

When we walked into his living room, I was glad to see the six amaryllis blooms that I had sent to thank him for a lovely Easter Sunday. The blood-red flowers brightened his pale-green suite, which had satin-upholstered Louis XIV furniture and gilt-framed, sombre paintings. The setting was odd for the music that played. Mick knelt on the floor with his feet tucked under him. He wore his faithful running shoes and a T-shirt which made no statement tucked in his dark-grey Issey Miyake trousers. He wanted us to hear the disco mix of the track 'Just Another Night' that had arrived from his New York-based record producer, Nile Rogers. I hoped that whoever was paying an arm and a leg for the suite below Mick's liked the track as much as I did. It was loud and the rhythm rocked and throbbed along. Mick sat completely still as he listened. His first solo album meant a lot to him. He was in Paris to cut the *Dirty Work* album with the Stones, who were staying in the large modern hotel next door that catered for American tourists.

We ordered tea. Jerry phoned twice and when the second call came I had a friendly exchange with her before I went to the bathroom in case he wanted privacy. She was having a difficult pregnancy and her doctor had ordered her not to travel. She and Mick were expecting their second child. It would be his fourth.

There were several dark-brown pill bottles in the bathroom with typed prescription labels on them. Mick looked exceptionally thin. I hoped he wasn't ill and sprayed some of his cologne on me to avoid the temptation of reading the labels.

Karis read and Mick poured tea. Before he made a long-distance call and dinner reservations I skimmed the day-old English newspaper lying on the sofa. It was our third meal together in five days. I teased Mick that he invited me because he knew I was writing my autobiography. His solicitor had asked me about the contents, but Mick didn't broach the subject. There were certain things that we never talked about, such as money and the past and things related to either. I hate to mistrust his motive when he is friendly.

Mick took us to a Russian restaurant. We walked. I lagged behind and it made me smile to hear Mick and our daughter chatter away. The hefty young doorman in Russian costume guarded the entrance like a bouncer. He blocked our entry when he saw that Mick wore no tie. When we finally got in I thought they were lucky to have us. The restaurant was empty apart from one couple. We slid into the long red velvet seat and giggled when the cabaret began. We had no idea that they would play so long and require our undivided attention when they came up to the table to serenade us while we discussed the expected baby.

I was about to put a forkful of blini, black caviar and sour cream in my mouth when Mick blushed and said that he and Jerry were having a son. I congratulated him and laughed when I pinched him hard on the leg, because five minutes earlier he had tried to entice me to lay a bet on the baby's sex.

Mostly, I was happy that Karis had a brother on the way. We drank a toast and joked in Melangian.

When the music got faster and the singer asked us to take part in the wild hand-clapping, I joined in. I loathe being expected to participate when I'm in an audience, but I thought Karis would enjoy seeing me act like a nurd. I got totally into it and even swayed back and forth. Karis and Mick wanted to crawl under the table which made me smile broader, sway wider, and clap with ungainly enthusiasm. Mick had to sign autographs for the buxom, middle-aged, bleached blonde waitresses on our way out and have his picture taken with them.

A few days later, an old friend from Berkeley, Charis Horton, came to visit us at our Left Bank hotel. She has lived in Paris for years and is married to a Frenchman. Her French is flawless, but being from Tennessee, she speaks English with a Southern accent. She and her husband, Antoine Compin, are both film producers and wanted to sublet their Paris flat while working on an assignment in LA. It was an ideal arrangement. A beautiful two-bedroom flat near the Opera. It was full of music and books.

The sun blasted though the living room window and the neighbours didn't want to say more than good day. Karis and I spent the last few days of the Easter holiday there. I stocked the refrigerator, bought some fresh flowers, sorted out the front-door keys and put my name on the mail box. It was too good to be true. As soon as I returned with Karis to England and found someone to sit with June's axolotl, I packed my bags and was Paris bound.

Paris in the spring is a drug. I couldn't get enough of it. It kept me high all the time. To be totally foreign, grappling with the language, oblivious to subtleties, gave me a sense of freedom and abandon when I was in the streets. A friend in London asked if I had a secret lover in Paris but, on the contrary, I had little contact with anyone until the third week in May when I had a house guest arrive and also got a call from a friend I rarely see, Nando Scarfiotti. He's a Hollywood-based Italian art director whose film work includes *American Gigolo* and *Cat People*. We are seldom in the same country at the same time. He was in Paris to design the set for Sting's solo debut at the small Mogador theatre three blocks from my flat. When Nando and I met opposite the theatre during his morning coffee break, I was reluctant to accept his invitation to see his set design, because Sting and I hadn't spoken since I returned the flowers in July 1983. Nando assured me that he wasn't due at the theatre until lunchtime.

From the dress circle, I admired Nando's tiered grey stage set when a sleek young Melangian drifted onto it and sat behind the drum kit. Others followed, including Sting, wearing a long stylish trench coat that made him look French with his cropped hair. It had receded slightly. He had a decidedly different image from the leather-clad, bleached blond rock champion.

Not to speak seemed petty and ridiculous, but I wondered what I was letting myself in for when I resolved to make my way onto the stage to say hello. He was looking over some sheet music when I stole up to him and tapped his shoulder. Instead of the cool reception I expected, he threw his arms around me. His cheek had the velvety feeling of a fresh shave. We kept hugging and smiling as if we were two long-lost friends meeting at an airport.

I was pleased that he invited me to hear his rehearsal. Sting had surrounded himself with three first-rate jazz-oriented Melangian players. When he shouted up to me in the dress circle to ask me if I liked his new band, I could honestly say that they sounded brilliant.

I ducked out before they were finished to do my own work and left him a good luck note. I walked home in the rain as if the sun was shining.

Sting arranged two tickets for me that evening. I took my friend, Baby John, who was visiting me from LA. We've remained close since the days at Berkeley when he was the first person that I told I planned to leave for Paris. He is now a baby-faced Californian judge who looks like a choir boy when he sits at a court bench in his black robe.

Sting's first public performance was a triumph. The studious French audience appreciated that he bothered to introduce his songs in French as much as they liked his new songs. They were on their feet before the end of the set. Sting's music remained lyrically committed although commercial, with songs like 'We Work The Black Seam', a haunting, poetic tribute to the plight of the English miners.

Baby John and I walked home. Being with him reminded me that when I left Berkeley, I didn't make it as far as Paris, but I wouldn't have missed the twenty-year detour for the world.

I hadn't been to Philadelphia since I took Stephanie Beacham there to meet my grandmother and Thelma in 1971. Stephanie had never seen an American soap opera or the impassioned reaction of a dedicated viewer. Edna was an addict for afternoon soaps like *Search for Tomorrow* and *The Guiding Light*, which in 1971 had been running on television for over twenty years. From her rocking chair Edna rooted and hooted at the goings-on like somebody ringside at a wrestling match. Stephanie couldn't believe it. If someone had told Stephanie that she would become an American soap-opera star, she probably wouldn't have believed that either. But in 1986 she plays Sable, the snarling English wife of Jason Colby played by Charlton Heston on *Dynasty II, The Colbys*; I'm sure that Edna would have been a *Dynasty* fan, and I regret that she didn't get to see Stephanie Beacham as a soap-opera queen.

After my aunt Thelma got married in Philadelphia in 1973, she and her husband, Ben Palena, moved to Oakland and took my grandmother, so I had no family in Philadelphia when I went there for a day trip on 5 August 1985. That summer, while Karis and I visited my family in California, Thelma forewarned me that the old neighbourhoods we lived in had deterioriated. I didn't care how they looked, I hadn't seen them in twenty-five years and wanted to see if I could spot a little girl who looked as if she thought she was Doris Day.

Twice in 1985 Philadelphia had been in the international headlines. Six adults and five children had been killed there on 13 May when the Melangian mayor, Wilson Goode, authorized the aerial bombing of a house in a residential neighbourhood where a sect that called themselves survivalists were harbouring explosives and causing trouble. The bombing caused a fire which destroyed 61 homes and left 250 people homeless.

Two months later, the city was in the world spotlight for more humane reasons. The American link of the Live Aid concert to raise money for Ethiopia's famine was staged at Philly's JFK stadium. I was pleased that Mick was among the marathon of rock performers who contributed their talent.

When I arrived in Philadelphia, I was on West Coast time and my watch said 4.30 am. I picked up a rented car and telephoned Mrs Bivins from the airport to say that I was on my way to Musgrave Street. Her telephone number hadn't changed. She sounded the same and I tried to. My accent shifts between English and American when I'm tired. I didn't want to seem affected and make her uncomfortable. I would make an effort to be as she remembered me, which was how I hoped to find her.

I was glad that my daughter had been invited to New York to be with her father and await the arrival of her baby brother, due that month. I was meeting her in New York later that night.

The big corner house where the Holy Roller meetings were held looked as if it had been boarded up for years. The front yard was overgrown and badly burnt by the sun. The apartment block, which in the fifties had a tended lawn, looked equally sad. I was afraid to look at my old house and went straight to the Bivinses'.

I begged my eyes not to be cruel and worldly and to give my memory a chance to indulge in my reunion with my past.

I was a head taller than Mrs Bivins who was sure that she hadn't shrunk. It was impossible to tell that she was seventy. Her short grey hair was styled as I remembered it and her pale skin was hardly lined. She had a young smile.

I put my arms around her and realized as I did it that I had never touched her before. I stopped myself from kissing her on each cheek when it crossed my mind that it might seem a little theatrical.

Her daughter Lynn, who had once been my best friend, was upstairs getting ready for work. She had moved back home to her mother's after a divorce. The tall seventeen-year-old boy who said hello was hers. I wanted to rush upstairs to Lynn's bedroom, where I had smoked my first cigarette, but when I did, it actually frightened me to be there sitting on her bed and watching her comb her prematurely silver-grey hair. For a moment it seemed as if I had never been away and my experiences beyond her room had only been a dream. I wanted to talk about her and hoped that she'd ask little or nothing about me. My life had been extraordinary and in her room I knew that I was ordinary, hardly different from the girl she once knew. I remembered how I had resisted the move to California and knew it was lucky that I didn't get my way.

Lynn looked beautiful in her crisp, white nurse's uniform and she patiently answered my endless questions about our old friends, many of whom still lived locally.

I hurried to Chestnut Hill when she went to work. I was happy that she couldn't take the day off. I wanted to see my old school alone, and the surrounding neighbourhood. I was strangely reluctant to see my old house. It would have seemed ghostly without my family spilling out from it.

I followed the trolley tracks along Germantown Avenue. The street names were more familiar than the sights. The rickety old 23 trolley cars looked as if they'd been hand-painted with house paints. Their shabbiness grew more obvious as we passed through Mount Airy and into Chestnut Hill. It hadn't only been my childhood imagination that made me think the sun was brighter after the bend at Maiden Lane. The district became more affluent and the sun glistened on the trees and the clean, orderly sidewalks.

John Story Jenks school was still standing and looked more handsome than I remembered. Everything was familiar except a fire hydrant that had been installed in 1960. Once my life had been divided between this pristine WASPish neighbourhood and Musgrave Street. The disparity between the two hadn't been so great then. Chestnut Hill was still predominantly white and Musgrave Street was now in the heart of a reservation so large that it was a city unto itself.

Before I left Chestnut Hill, I popped into a baby boutique to buy a present for Karis's brother. The helpful saleslady was pleasant until I asked her about Jenks school and whether it might be open at any time during the afternoon. She said that the Melangian children bused to it from the neighbouring districts were ruining the neighbourhood. I was surprised that she had the nerve to say it to me.

Germantown was only a couple of miles away. I went there to find Grumblethorpe but wasn't prepared for the sight of the surrounding district. It was a concrete desert. The August heat made me feel as though I was tasting the dusty streets. People moved slowly, giving the streets an agrarian peace. I didn't imagine that it could have deteriorated so much. My old house at 234 Ashmead Street was gone, replaced by government housing. Little boys played stick ball in the middle of the street. When I stopped the car to ask them directions to Bringhurst Street, they swarmed around the car, pushing and giggling. I must have looked as if I didn't belong. I wanted to tell them that this had once been my neighbourhood. I also wanted to pile them into the car and rescue them from it.

Two blocks away on Germantown Avenue stood Grumblethorpe, its windows caked with dust. The door was locked and I banged on it like somebody who belonged inside and had forgotten her key. Across the street was the German Historical Society, proud of its oak floors, austere eighteenth-century portraits, grandfather clock and history. There was something sadly ironic about this building standing at the heart of a crumbling community to represent the aspirations of the original settlers. Several storefront churches with hand-painted signs, the work of devoted believers, remained on the site of Penn's holy experiment.

I didn't go to 23rd Street. If it had changed as much as Germantown, there could hardly be anything left of it. But I was thankful for the memory.

I wanted the sights to prompt heart-rending nostalgia. Instead, I felt like a tourist. Only the people mattered, because in the Melangian district, I was one of the tribe. I was glad that my midatlantic accent and French get-up didn't affect that. Whatever we are called, we are undeniably American. America is not just a place, it's a state of mind. This is why I turned my charmed life into a battlefield, continuing to believe that I have the right to defend myself, my child and our human rights.

EPILOGUE

18 February 1986
I bounced downstairs from my bedroom in time to see Mick sweep our daughter in his arms. He threatened to lift me off my feet, but I loudly protested and we settled for a rocking bear hug. I hadn't seen Mick in months, although Karis had. I missed the christening of his new son James in London in November 1985 because I was working in Manchester. Mick stood in our hallway and flashed a big toothy grin. I no longer mind the diamond in his front incisor. He looked relaxed and healthier than I've seen him in years. He beamed as if he were in love, proud that he had given up meat and alcohol for Lent again. I asked facetiously if he went to church on Ash Wednesday, 12 February, when he was in LA. He joked that he sorrowfully missed the service at Our Lady of the Cadillac.

He maintained good form while I made tea. Karis and I roared as he minced around our kitchen to imitate the two tawdry English girls he met the night before in a club. His comedy was interrupted for a serious moment when Karis's school progress was discussed.

I tried on his blue-and-brown Claude Montana leather jacket. Karis rolled her eyes to heaven. I didn't do haute couture justice with my hair in two braids and wearing a baggy black track suit. I looked as I had done when Mick phoned unexpectedly that morning to say he would collect Karis. He liked my braids if they were real and did a falsetto mimicry of a young Melangian girl showing off a new hair weave.

Karis packed while he thrashed out some chords on our jangly-old upright. He was taking her to a fancy Soho restaurant and on to a spy movie before she caught the 7 pm school train that ended her half-term break. The three of us paraded noisy and giggling down the three flights of stairs with Mick at the front carrying the suitcases.

Karis looked confident and radiant when she kissed me goodbye and climbed into her father's slick, chauffeur-driven car. With that same natural grace, she boards a Greyhound bus with me or disembarks from a Concorde flight with Mick. I didn't wait for them to drive off before I sprinted back upstairs, two stairs at a time. Sixteen years on, we were winning. What began as a worthy ideal was almost real.

INDEX